Jackie Clay's Pantry Cookbook

By Jackie Clay

www.backwoodshome.com

ISBN 978-0-9846222-1-4
Copyright 2011

Backwoods Home Magazaine
PO Box 712
Gold Beach, Oregon 97444
www.backwoodshome.com

Edited by Rhoda Denning, Lisa Nourse, Ilene Duffy, and Annie Tuttle

Jackie Clay's Pantry Cookbook

Contents

Cooking from a well-stocked pantry 9
   Stocking up your pantry 10
   Basic staples for a modest-sized pantry 11
   What if there's no room for a pantry? 14

Main course 16
   Red meat 16
   Pork 29
   Poultry 36
   Fish 46
   Casseroles 48

Soups and stews 59

Side dishes 67
   Vegetables 67
   Salads 91
   Rice 100
   Pasta 102

Breads 104
   Biscuits, rolls, and tortillas 104
   Quick breads 111

- *Yeast breads* 117
- *Sweet breads and coffee cakes* 132
- *Muffins and scones* 138
- *Pancakes, waffles, and donuts* 141

Eggs 150
Snacks 157
Desserts 162
- *Pies* 162
- *Cheesecakes* 182
- *Cakes* 184
- *Frostings and fillings* 199
- *Cobblers, crisps, and shortcakes* 206
- *Puddings* 212
- *Bars* 220
- *Cookies* 233
- *Candies* 249
- *Dipped candies* 253

Basic pantry mixes 263
Miscellaneous handy recipes 268
- *Salad dressings — ready made* 270
- *Salad dressing — dry mixes* 273
- *Sauces* 274

Cooking from a well-stocked pantry

One of the most satisfying things about having a pantry chock full of tasty foods is putting them together in a symphony of mouth-watering, wholesome meals. I'm so thankful to have so much good food stored for our family. It is free of chemicals, dyes, and additives, and it doesn't come from countries with questionable growing and processing methods. I know that no matter what the outlook for the economy is, no matter what the weather does, and no matter if we have long-term visitors, we'll still be able to sit down to delicious homemade meals.

I learned to keep a well-stocked pantry from my grandma and Mom, who had been through the Great Depression. In those days, food was as scarce as jobs unless you had a farm or large garden. Food was regarded in my family as a precious resource. It was gathered carefully and preserved well for future need and use.

With the "ease" of our fast-paced society, keeping a well-stocked pantry has fallen into disuse. People often shop daily for their meals, and the cupboard is full of junk food. The pantry became too "old-fashioned," and often if there was one in an old house it was cleaned out to make space for a hobby room or storage closet. Gardens were let go, too, and planted with unproductive grass. Soon people forgot even the basic skills of simple cooking with common and homegrown foods.

But now more and more families are waking to the provident thinking of stocking up a nice-sized pantry, planting a productive garden and a few fruit trees, canning and root cellaring their produce, and even raising some small livestock.

A few years ago, people asked why I "bothered" to have a big garden and can up all that food when I could "go to the store and just *buy* it." Now, with a lot of our food coming from China, Mexico, and other places with questionable growing practices, not to mention the increase in food prices, more people are asking me questions about how to garden, how to can their own food, what to stock in their pantry, and especially for recipes for home-cooked meals like Grandma used to serve.

Your pantry can be large or modest, but I feel that every family should have enough food to last a year or more, in case of emergency or hard times. At the very least, keep a stock of commonly-used foods on hand, so it is more convenient to whip up a quick meal. Keeping a well-stocked pantry has financial benefits, too. When you keep a wide variety of foods on your shelf, you'll only buy staple foods when they're on a really good sale. You won't be subject to the high prices of grocery stores, when you *must* buy a certain food because you need it right now. Cooking from your pantry does not mean you'll be eating endless meals of beans and rice — in fact, it's much more like having your own little grocery store, and the variety of meals you'll be able to make are nearly endless!

My book, *Growing and canning your own food*, has detailed information on gardening, raising livestock, and canning your own food. In this book you'll find tips on what to stock in your pantry as well as hundreds of recipes for everything from homemade mixes (they sure come in handy when you're in a hurry) to pot roasts (nothing like a good old hungryman's supper) to candies (who says you have to live without treats and comfort food?).

Don't look for fancy foods with exotic ingredients or recipes that take forever to make. I like delicious, wholesome foods that are quick and simple to put together. If you want to cook like Grandma did, using your own homegrown foods and those right out of your pantry, come along with me, and we'll get to cookin'!

Stocking up your pantry

There are a whole lot of foods that can be kept for long-term storage. By doing that, you free yourself from having to run to the store all the time (where you know you'll come away wondering how you bought so much other stuff). Your food can be bought on sale, a little at a time, and you'll be amazed at how convenient it is to have all those staple supplies on hand all the time. You'll also be worry free, because no matter if the power is off for a week or more, a blizzard hits, or a hurricane roars outside, your family will eat well from food you already have at home.

Although I feel strongly that every family should have a pantry stocked so well that they can eat from it for a year, you should at least keep the basic staples of cooking on hand. We'll start with these first. After you see how handy it is to live with a modest pantry, you may want to expand it so that your family can handle any situation that should pop up in the future. Many foods stay good for *years* with no special treatment, other than keeping them dry, insect and rodent-free, and relatively cool. The "freshness date" stamped on cans and boxes is primarily an advertising gimmick to get people to throw away perfectly good food and buy "fresh." If you buy 10 cans of tuna on sale today, it will still taste great 10 years from now, so stock up when you find a good deal!

Where to start

The first things that should go in your pantry are ingredients you use frequently. Equipping a pantry is best done in steps, not by going "whole hog" and buying thousands of dollars worth of "emergency" food. If you don't yet can your own foods, start picking up cans of vegetables and fruits as they come on sale at your local market. If you need one can of corn today, buy six — if you can't afford six, at least buy one more than you need today. Any extras go in your pantry. Remember, *always* buy on sale. Having a well-stocked pantry lets you wait until an item is on sale before you resupply, helping you save a bundle of money. Often stores will have "truckload" or "case" sales of canned goods in the late summer. Even when items are not on sale, sometimes buying by the case will get you a better deal; ask the manager at your local market.

One thing you'll notice is that I recommend very few store-bought mixes or premade foods for the pantry. There are two reasons for this. First of all, my recipes taste better. I use better quality ingredients than what you'll find in the premade version, and there are no preservatives or other weird ingredients. Second, those prepackaged mixes are almost always more expensive than made-from-scratch recipes. Remember, we are not only trying to have plenty of food on hand, but we're saving money, too.

If you have a garden or can purchase fresh, organic fruits and vegetables locally, such as from farmers' markets or a local grower, take advantage of the season's bounty by canning up all those delectable foods. Nothing beats peaches picked in the morning and canned in the afternoon — either for taste or nutrition.

Basic staples for a modest-sized pantry

Dry staples

Unbleached white flour	25 pounds	Store this in the original, unopened bags, inside a rodent- and insect-proof container. This should store for years when protected from dampness and vermin.
Whole wheat flour	10 pounds	Store this in the original, unopened bags in the freezer. Whole wheat flour is whole grain and tends to get rancid unless kept frozen. If you can't store it in the freezer, keep it in a rodent- and insect-proof container. When frozen, it will keep for a year or more; when not frozen its shelf-life is limited to a few months.
Cornmeal	5 pounds	Store-bought cornmeal can be stored in one-gallon glass jars, clean popcorn tins, or other rodent-, insect-, and moisture-proof container. It will store for years. Home-ground, whole-grain cornmeal turns rancid quicker, so it's best to either freeze this cornmeal or else grind just what you will be using within a few weeks for best taste.
Brown and white rice	10 pounds, in combination	Store in clean popcorn tins, glass jars, or other rodent-, insect-, and moisture-proof containers. Most rice will store indefinitely, but whole-grain brown rice will go rancid after about three months, so it should be stored in the freezer, if possible, for extended storage.
Rolled oats	10 pounds	Store in clean popcorn tins, glass jars, or other rodent-, insect-, and moisture-proof containers. It will store for at least several years.
Dry beans	10 pounds, in combination	I store my beans in both one-gallon glass jars and in sealed three-gallon plastic pails. Keep them in a rodent-, insect-, and moisture-proof container and they will last indefinitely.
Dried pasta	10 pounds in combination	Dried pasta can be transferred into glass jars, tins, or other rodent-, insect-, and moisture-proof containers or else stored in the original bag or box and placed inside a sealed plastic pail. Pasta will store nearly indefinitely.

Sugar	10 pounds	Always store sugar in an airtight glass jar, tin, or other rodent-, insect-, and moisture-proof container. If it gets the slightest bit damp it will become hard. You can save hardened sugar by breaking it into pieces, then running it through a sieve. If this doesn't work, try putting the large pieces in the microwave for a few seconds, or placing a slice of bread in the sugar jar overnight. In the morning your sugar will be workable again. Sugar stays edible indefinitely, even if it becomes hard.
Brown sugar (light or dark)	4 pounds	Store brown sugar as you do white sugar. If it gets hard, put a piece of damp paper towel in the jar overnight and the sugar will soften. Brown sugar will remain good indefinitely.
Confectioner's sugar (powdered sugar)	4 pounds	Store as you would white or brown sugar. If your powdered sugar should get lumpy, just run it through a sieve or flour sifter. It'll remain good indefinitely.
Dry yeast	1 pound	I keep a ½-pint jar of dry yeast on the shelf and store the rest of a one-pound bag in the freezer. Dry yeast should remain active for two years in the freezer, one year in the refrigerator, and several months on the shelf. Each year, I replace my 1-pound bag in the freezer with a fresh bag, so I will have a guaranteed supply for at least two years. Even after these "ideal" storage times, yeast will still work, it will just be weaker. If your yeast is getting a little old, just add sugar to the yeast as you proof it in a little warm water or add a little more yeast until it "perks up."
Baking soda	1 pound	Store baking soda in its original box on the shelf. Keep it dry, and it will remain good indefinitely.
Baking powder	1 pound	Store baking powder in its original can on the shelf. It will remain "lively" for several years.
Salt	1 pound	I store salt in its original box on the shelf, but if you have high humidity, I'd recommend storing it in jars with tight-fitting lids to keep moisture out. If your salt gets hard you can break it up with a tenderizing mallet, then run it through a sieve or flour sifter. By keeping a few grains of raw, long-grain rice in your salt shakers, you can prevent salt from caking up in the shakers. Salt remains good forever.
Dry milk	4 pounds	Store your dry milk in one-gallon glass jars for optimum shelf-life. It will remain good for several years at least.
Dry buttermilk	1 pound	Store dry buttermilk in its original container, in your kitchen cupboard. It remains good for years.
Cornstarch	1 pound	I store my cornstarch in its original container on a shelf in the kitchen. It remains good indefinitely.

Spices and herbs (pepper, garlic powder, onion powder, cinnamon, nutmeg, basil, thyme, oregano, cloves, allspice, mustard, and other favorites)		I store some spices in their original containers and others in half-pint canning jars. While it may be true that old spices lose their flavor, I've never found it much of a problem; I just use a bit more seasoning, if necessary. I store my home-raised dried herbs in sealed glass jars to keep them safe from moisture and insects. As long as they stay dry, herbs and spices store forever.
Cream of tartar	3 ounces	Cream of tartar will last forever in its original container on the shelf. If it gets lumpy, simply crush the lumps between your fingers before measuring.

Liquid and baking staples

All of these can be stored in their original containers. Unopened, they will last many years under normal storage conditions. After opening, some require special care, as noted below.

Honey	1 pint	Honey that has crystallized and turned white can be returned to normal by placing the container in a pan of hot water until it liquefies once again.
Molasses	1 pint	
Vanilla extract	8 ounces	
Shortening	1 3-pound can	
Vegetable oil	48 ounces	Peanut butter, olive oil, and vegetable oil will become rancid relatively soon after opening. So if you don't use much of them, buy more of the smaller bottles.
Olive oil	1 pint	
Peanut butter	2 36-ounce jars	
Vinegar	1 quart	
Corn syrup	1 quart	
Lemon juice	1 12-ounce bottle	Once opened, store lemon juice in your refrigerator.
Chocolate chips	2 12-ounce bags	
Chopped dates	1 pound	
Walnuts	1 pound	Walnuts and other nutmeats are high in oil, so they tend to get rancid after about a year. By freezing or canning them, they'll last at least 10 years. (Instructions for canning nutmeats are on page 76 in my book *Growing and Canning Your Own Food*.)
Pecan halves	1 pound	
Raisins	2 pounds	Raisins that are stored for a very long time may harden, but they are still usable in recipes.
Coconut	12 ounces	
Candied fruit peel	12-16 ounces	
Candied cherries	12 ounces	

Handy food to have on hand in addition to your staples

A good supply of jams and jellies are nice to have on hand, along with plenty of Jello. I use these in many of my baking recipes. Cake and brownie mixes are one of the few things I sometimes buy "pre-mixed," because they are often very cheap on sale and provide a quick dessert for a buck or less. They also keep very well on your pantry shelves.

"Cream of" soups, such as cream of celery, cream of mushroom, and cream of chicken are handy, not only as soups, but as casserole ingredients. Canned tuna, roast beef hash, salmon, and ham are economical sources of protein — especially important to have in your pantry if you don't raise your own meat animals. You'll also find plenty of uses for canned spaghetti sauce and tomato sauce. I use my own home-canned spaghetti sauce and tomato sauce in many recipes, including bread sticks with marinara sauce, chicken cacciatore, and pizza. Other canned goods you'll want to keep on hand include mushrooms, vegetables (corn, peas, green beans, etc.), fruit, pie fillings, barbecue sauce, catsup, prepared mustard, pickles, and pancake syrup.

Don't forget to add things such as bleach, laundry and dish detergent, toilet paper, and pet food to your pantry.

As you get more involved and enthusiastic about your pantry, it's time to consider buying a few long-term storage foods such as powdered eggs, cheese, shortening, buttermilk, sour cream, butter, and margarine. These foods come in a #10 can (about the size of a three-pound coffee can), and will last for decades when unopened. To use them, you can either reconstitute the powdered food with water or oil (the directions are on the can), or simply add the powder to a recipe along with a bit more liquid. These foods are also very handy in creating your own shelf-stable mixes, such as biscuit mix, casserole sauce mix, cake mix, and pancake mix.

These foods are available through many emergency preparedness companies such as Emergency Essentials (www.beprepared.com/store). I always keep some of these dehydrated foods in my pantry, and find that they come in handy in so many different recipes I use in daily living.

What if there's no room for a pantry?

Although I now have a nice, roomy basement, including a 7x12-foot walk-in pantry, I have lived in homes where I had to get a little creative in order to plan for a pantry. Our little cabin in Montana hardly had room for our wood kitchen range, let alone a pantry. We knew we would be snowed in for at least five months out of the year, so we needed a large pantry, both to store such things as flour, sugar, shortening, beans, rice, and cornmeal and also to hold my home-canned foods. The easiest remedy was to add on to the cabin. Using log rafters and other materials we scavenged from the local dump and bought cheap, we built a kitchen and pantry as a shed-type addition to the existing cabin. To keep the roof slope steep enough to shed snow, the outer wall ended up only five feet tall, but we *did* end up with a 10x10-foot kitchen and a 6x10-foot pantry.

In New Mexico, we lived in a small old house in the middle of the high plains. It did have a kitchen that my kitchen range fit into, but it did *not* have a pantry. In fact, there wasn't even a closet in the whole house. What we did have was a back porch that we didn't really need, except to go in and out of the house. It only held our water heater and assorted homestead junk, so we turned it into a 6x12-foot pantry. I blocked up the window to keep it cooler and darker, then built shelves on three sides. It worked great, and it was directly off the kitchen to boot.

I have several friends in southern states who have no basement or root cellar, but they have air conditioning or at least a swamp cooler, so they were able to turn a small, unused room into an effective pantry. Any time you turn an unused room into a pantry, it's a good idea to put heavy drapes over the window to keep out the sun and heat (and nosy passers-by).

While an apartment dweller can't have the ultimate pantry of a farm kitchen, with a little creative thinking, you should be able to add a pantry somewhere. You could even build a free-standing pantry with double doors that you can fit through the door and take with you when you move.

Think about wasted space when you are designing a pantry. When we were building our log home, we were getting ready to sheetrock the basement stairwell. I looked at the area at the head of the basement stairs and realized that instead of covering the wall with sheetrock, I could fill the area with small shelves between the wall studs. Now it is a handy "mini-pantry" right off the kitchen where I can keep cans, baking soda, baking powder, cornstarch, salt, yeast, dried herbs, spices, and a bunch of other often-used items. It's amazing how much I can house on those little shelves, and it sure cuts down on the trips down to the basement. Another often-overlooked possible pantry location is underneath a stairway. We recently built shelves under our basement stairway. The deep shelves make a handy place to store large containers of dry foods and other bulky items like toilet paper.

Main course

On our homestead, we are lucky to have not only a wide variety of home-raised meats available, but also plenty of wild game. A peek into my pantry or freezer will often reveal beef, pork, chevon, chicken, and turkey as well as elk, deer, and moose venison, fish from nearby lakes and streams, upland birds such as grouse and pheasant, and wild waterfowl. Of course, not all of these are always available, so my recipes are pretty interchangeable as far as the meat goes. If you don't have venison for a recipe, substitute beef or chevon. If you don't have salmon, substitute northern pike. If you don't have grouse, use chicken. Your results will still be delicious.

Because I can a lot of my meat, I've included directions for using canned meats in many of these recipes. As canned meat is precooked, the directions are often quite different, but the result is nearly the same.

Red meat

Old-fashioned pot roast

1 BONELESS BEEF CHUCK OR OTHER ROAST (ABOUT 3 LBS.)
    OR 1 QUART BONELESS ROAST CHUNKS (SEE VARIATION)
6 TBSP. FLOUR, DIVIDED
6 TBSP. BUTTER OR MARGARINE, DIVIDED
3 CUPS HOT WATER
3 MEDIUM ONIONS, HALVED
1 TSP. SALT
½ TSP. PEPPER
4 MEDIUM CARROTS, CUT INTO 2-INCH PIECES
4 POTATOES, CUT INTO LARGE CHUNKS

Sprinkle roast with 1 Tbsp. flour. In a Dutch oven, brown the roast on all sides in half of the butter. Add the water, onion, salt, and pepper; bring to a boil. Reduce heat; cover and simmer for 1 hour. Add carrots and potatoes. Simmer 45-60 minutes longer, or until meat is fork tender. Remove meat and vegetables onto a serving dish. Cover to keep warm. Strain cooking juices and set aside. In the same Dutch oven, melt remaining butter. Stir in remaining flour; cook and stir until well heated. Add 2 cups of reserved cooking juices and blend until smooth, making a nice gravy. Cook and stir until thickened, adding additional cooking juices until gravy is the right thickness. Season to taste with additional salt, pepper, and herbs of your choice.

Variation using boneless canned roast chunks:

In a Dutch oven, heat 4 Tbsp. shortening or oil on stovetop, then lightly sear all the vegetables. Add the broth the meat was canned in, salt, and pepper, then cover and simmer for 30 minutes or until fork tender. Add the large roast chunks and again cover and simmer for at least 15 minutes. Remove meat and vegetables to serving dish. Cover to keep warm and proceed with directions above for gravy.

Barbecue beef on a bun

This makes a big batch, so you'll have plenty of leftovers.

- 1 BONELESS 3-LB. CHUCK OR OTHER ROAST **OR** 2 PINTS CANNED STEWING MEAT OR ROAST CHUNKS, DRAINED WITH LIQUID RESERVED (SEE VARIATION)
- 1 MEDIUM ONION, CHOPPED **OR** 2 TBSP. DEHYDRATED CHOPPED ONION
- ½ CUP FRESH OR CANNED CELERY, CHOPPED (**OR** 2 TBSP. DEHYDRATED CELERY)
- WATER
- 1 PINT TOMATO SAUCE
- ¼ CUP FIRMLY PACKED BROWN SUGAR
- ¼ CUP VINEGAR
- 2 TBSP. DRY MUSTARD
- 2 TSP. SALT
- 1 TSP. LIQUID SMOKE (OPTIONAL) OR
- 2 TSP. WORCESTERSHIRE SAUCE (OPTIONAL)
- 1 TSP. GARLIC POWDER
- HAMBURGER BUNS (I USE THE HALF-TIME SPOON ROLL RECIPE, WITH A LITTLE MORE FLOUR)

Place beef, onion, and celery in an enameled Dutch oven (don't use cast iron here); add water to almost cover meat. Bring to a boil, then reduce heat and cover. Simmer for about 2½ hours or until meat is very tender. Remove meat; strain and reserve cooking broth. Trim and shred meat, returning to Dutch oven. Add 2 cups strained cooking broth (save remaining cooking broth) and chill. Skim and discard fat. Add tomato sauce, brown sugar, vinegar, and seasonings. Cover and simmer for 1 hour, stirring occasionally to prevent scorching. If mixture becomes too dry, add reserved cooking liquid. Serve on warmed hamburger buns.

Tip: To keep sauce from soaking into buns, lightly butter or toast buns before filling.

Variation for using canned ingredients:

With a fork, mash and shred canned meat into a large saucepan. Mix onion, celery, tomato sauce, spices, vinegar, and brown sugar with meat and heat slowly. If too dry, add broth from canned meat. Simmer, stirring frequently, until all are well heated and flavors blend (about 15 minutes).

German pot roast

- 1 boneless beef chuck or other roast (about 3 lbs.) **or** 1 quart boneless roast chunks (see variation)
- 2 Tbsp. oil
- 1¼ cups water
- ¾ cup beef broth
- ½-pint (8 oz.) tomato sauce
- ½ cup chopped onion
- 2 Tbsp. sugar
- 1 Tbsp. vinegar
- 2 tsp. salt
- 1 tsp. cinnamon
- 1 bay leaf
- ½ tsp. pepper
- ½ tsp. ground ginger
- cornstarch and water

In a Dutch oven, brown roast in hot oil. Mix water, broth, tomato sauce, onion, sugar, vinegar, salt, cinnamon, bay leaf, pepper, and ginger. Pour over meat and bring to a boil. Reduce heat; cover and simmer until meat is tender (about 2½-3 hours). Remove meat and keep warm. Discard bay leaf. If desired, thicken juices with a cornstarch and water paste to make a gravy. Serve with roasted vegetables or over hot, buttered noodles.

Variation using boneless canned roast chunks:

In a Dutch oven, lightly sear roast chunks in hot oil. Use reserved canning broth in place of the water and proceed with directions above, reducing cooking time to 30 minutes.

Peppered steaks

- 4 steaks **or** 1 quart boneless canned steaks
- 1 Tbsp. olive oil
- 1 Tbsp. garlic powder
- 1 Tbsp. paprika
- 2 tsp. ground thyme
- 1½ tsp. pepper
- 1 tsp. salt
- 1 tsp. lemon pepper

Brush fresh or canned steaks with olive oil. In a small bowl, mix all seasonings and sprinkle steaks on both sides, pressing to hold them onto the meat. Cover and chill for 1 hour. Grill steaks over medium hot coals until done, or fry them in olive oil or margarine on your stovetop. Thick steaks can be cut across the grain, while thinner steaks are served whole.

Pepper steak

1 lb. boneless round steak, cut into convenient serving-sized pieces
   or 1 quart boneless canned steak (see variation)
½ tsp. salt
⅛ tsp. pepper
2 Tbsp. flour
1 Tbsp. cooking oil
1 sweet green bell pepper, seeded and cut into slices (may use dehydrated dry peppers)
1 cup onion slices or rings
1 garlic clove, minced or ½ tsp. dehydrated garlic powder
1 can (16 oz.) chopped tomatoes with liquid
¼ cup beef broth

Lightly salt and pepper meat. With a meat-tenderizing mallet, pound all of the flour into both sides of the meat. Heat oil in a skillet and brown meat on both sides on medium-high heat. Arrange onion and pepper slices over the meat. Combine remaining ingredients and pour over onions and peppers. Cover and simmer until the meat is very tender. Remove meat and keep warm. Cook sauce, uncovered, until reduced and thickened, about 5 minutes, stirring frequently. Season to taste and serve immediately.

Variation using boneless canned steak:

Gently free steaks from jar so they don't break. Sprinkle with salt, pepper, and flour on both sides. Lightly brown each side in oil, then remove pan from heat and arrange onion and pepper slices over the meat. Combine remaining ingredients and pour over onions and peppers. Return to heat, cover, and simmer for about 20 minutes. Proceed as above to thicken sauce.

Jackie's baked beef stew

2 lbs. lean stewing meat, cubed or 2 pints lean stewing meat, undrained
6 carrots, cut into 1-inch pieces or 1 pint carrots, drained
4 medium potatoes, peeled and quartered or 1 quart potatoes, drained
½ cup celery sliced into 1-inch pieces
   or ½-pint celery sliced into 1-inch pieces, undrained
1 can (16 oz.) whole kernel corn or 2 large ears from the garden
   or 1 pint whole kernel sweet corn, drained
3 large onions, quartered
1 can (16 oz.) or 1 pint tomato sauce
1 cup water

Mix all ingredients (if using canned meat, reduce water slightly) and place in large, covered glass or enamel casserole (not cast iron). Bake at 325° F until meat and vegetables are tender. Remove lid and continue baking until sauce thickens and a "skin" forms on top of stew.

Beef stew

    2 Tbsp. cooking oil
    2 lbs. cubed stewing meat
        or 1 quart canned stewing meat, reserve liquid (see variation)
    3 large onions, cut into large pieces
    2 garlic cloves, peeled and crushed or 2 tsp. dehydrated garlic powder
    2 tsp. salt
    1 tsp. pepper
    7 medium potatoes, peeled and quartered or 1 quart canned potato chunks
    1 lb. carrots, cut into 1-inch pieces or 1 pint canned carrots
    1 cup cut celery or ½-pint canned celery slices
    ¼ cup flour
    ¼ cup cold water

Heat oil in a Dutch oven. Brown meat. Add onions, garlic, salt, and pepper. Cover and simmer until meat is tender. Add potatoes and carrots. Continue cooking until vegetables are tender. Mix flour and water, first a little water with flour, into a paste, then add the rest and add to the stew when smooth. Stir into stew until thickened.

Variation using canned stewing meat and vegetables:

Lightly sear drained meat in oil, then add onions, garlic, salt, and pepper. Pour liquid from canned stewing meat into Dutch oven. Add potatoes and carrots. Simmer for about 15 minutes. Proceed with directions above to thicken the stew.

Herbed beef stew

    2 lbs. stewing meat, cut into 1-inch cubes or 2 pints stewing meat, cut into 1-inch cubes, undrained (see variation)
    2 Tbsp. cooking oil
    3 cups water
    1 large onion, cut into medium pieces
    2 tsp. pepper
    1 tsp. salt
    1½ tsp. garlic powder
    1 tsp. rosemary, crushed
    1 tsp. oregano
    1 tsp. dried basil
    1 tsp. marjoram
    1 can (6 oz.) tomato paste or 1 pint tomato sauce
    2 cups cubed, peeled potatoes or 1 pint canned potatoes, drained
    2 cups sliced carrots or 1 pint canned sliced carrots, drained
    1 large green pepper, chopped or ½ cup dehydrated green pepper
    1 cup green beans cut into 1-inch pieces or 1 pint green beans cut into

- 1-INCH PIECES, DRAINED
- 1 CUP GARDEN PEAS OR ½-PINT GARDEN PEAS (YES, I KNOW THE OTHERS ARE PINTS, BUT THIS IS ½-PINT OF PEAS) DRAINED
- 1 CUP WHOLE KERNEL CORN OR 1 PINT DRAINED WHOLE KERNEL SWEET CORN, DRAINED
- ¼ LB. SLICED MUSHROOMS OR ½-PINT CANNED MUSHROOM SLICES OR 1 SMALL STORE-BOUGHT CAN SLICED MUSHROOMS, DRAINED
- 3 MEDIUM TOMATOES, PEELED AND CHOPPED OR 1 PINT OF CANNED TOMATOES

Brown meat in oil in an enamel Dutch oven (don't use cast iron for this one). Add water, onion, seasonings, and tomato paste. Cover and simmer until meat is tender. Stir in potatoes, carrots, and green pepper; simmer 30 minutes. Add more water if you need to. Stir in remaining ingredients. Cover and simmer 20 minutes.

Variation using canned stewing meat and vegetables:

Brown meat in oil then add all remaining ingredients and reduce overall simmering time to 30 minutes.

Beef stroganoff

Throughout all of our homesteading adventures, this beef stroganoff has always been a quick family favorite. I've used venison, elk, moose, chevon, and beef as the "beef" and it always disappears quickly. I like it because it cooks up quickly to serve homestead-sized appetites! And it stays with you for a long time, giving extra stamina for chopping wood, digging fence post holes, and harvesting the garden.

- 2 LBS. SIRLOIN (OR OTHER) STEAK, CUT INTO THIN STRIPS OR CUBES OR 2 PINTS CANNED SIRLOIN (OR OTHER) STEAK, CUT INTO THIN STRIPS OR CUBES, DRAINED WITH LIQUID RESERVED
- ¼ CUP FLOUR
- ½ CUP BUTTER OR MARGARINE, DIVIDED
- 2 LARGE ONIONS, CHOPPED
- 1½ CUPS WATER
- 1 TSP. DRIED BASIL
- SALT AND PEPPER TO TASTE
- 1½ CUPS CHOPPED FRESH MUSHROOMS OR 1 PINT CANNED MUSHROOMS, DRAINED
- 1 TBSP. WORCESTERSHIRE SAUCE
- EGG NOODLES
- 1 CUP SOUR CREAM

Dredge meat in flour. In skillet, melt ¼ cup butter over medium heat. Sauté onions until tender. Remove from pan and set aside. Melt remaining butter and brown meat on all sides. Add 1½ cups water (if using canned meat, use reserved canning broth in place of water), basil, salt, pepper, mushrooms, Worcestershire sauce, and onions. Cook until mixture thickens, about 5 minutes. Boil noodles in water until tender. Just before serving, add sour cream to skillet and stir in well. Heat well, but don't boil; it'll curdle. Serve immediately over hot buttered noodles.

Chicken fried steak

    4 cube steaks
    ½ cup flour
    ½ tsp. salt
    ½ tsp. pepper
    ¾ cup milk or buttermilk (may use reconstituted powdered milk or buttermilk)
    1 cup crushed Saltine crackers
    3 Tbsp. cooking oil or shortening
    3 Tbsp. flour
    1 can (16 oz.) chicken broth or 1 pint home-canned broth
    ½ cup milk (may use powdered, reconstituted milk)

In a bowl, combine ½ cup flour, salt, and pepper. Place ¾ cup milk or buttermilk in a shallow dish. Place Saltine crumbs in bowl. Coat steaks with flour mixture, then dip into milk or buttermilk and coat well with crumbs. In a large skillet over medium heat, cook steaks in hot oil for 3 minutes on each side or until golden brown and done. Remove and keep warm. Add flour to skillet drippings, stir well, then slowly stir in chicken broth and enough milk to make a nice thick gravy. Heat pan as you stir, mixing in pan browned bits for your gravy. Serve gravy over steaks.

Roast beef hash

    2 cups cooked roast beef or 1 pint canned beef chunks, drained
    2 cups cooked potatoes or 1 quart canned potatoes, drained well
    1 medium onion, chopped or ½ cup dehydrated onion rehydrated
    salt and pepper
    vegetable oil to fry

Grind meat, potatoes, and onion together with hand meat grinder set on coarse grind. Heat oil to medium heat in large frying pan. Put hash into pan, being careful not to spatter hot grease. Pat hash down into a thick layer, covering the bottom of the pan. Allow to cook until bottom is browned, then turn over and brown top. Stir to brown more, if you wish.

Oriental beef stir-fry

    1 lb. boneless sirloin (or other) steak cut into 1-inch cubes
    3 Tbsp. soy sauce
    3 garlic cloves, minced
    1 tsp. ground ginger
    1 tsp. Chinese Five Spice (optional)
    4 Tbsp. vegetable oil, divided
    1 large onion, cut into 1-inch pieces
    1 medium green pepper, cut into 1-inch pieces
    1 medium sweet red pepper, cut into 1-inch pieces
    1 large carrot, sliced on the diagonal into ½-inch slices

2 LARGE CELERY STALKS, SLICED INTO ½-INCH SLICES
1 CUP SNOW PEA PODS
5 TSP. CORNSTARCH
1 CUP COLD WATER

In a bowl, combine soy sauce, garlic, ginger, Five Spice (optional), and 2 Tbsp. oil. Add beef; toss to coat. Cover and refrigerate for half an hour. In a large skillet or wok, heat remaining oil. Stir-fry meat over medium high heat for 3 minutes. Remove meat and set aside. In the same skillet, stir-fry onion for 1 minute; add peppers, carrots, and celery. Stir-fry for 2 minutes. Return meat to skillet and add snow pea pods. Stir-fry for 1 minute. Mix cornstarch and water until smooth; add to skillet. Bring to a boil and boil for 1 minute to thicken. Stir constantly. Serve immediately over hot rice or noodles.

While you can substitute canned stewing meat for the fresh cubed meat in this stir fry, marinating the drained meat and adding it after the vegetables are cooked, this recipe really turns out better with fresh or frozen meat.

Swedish meatballs

1 LB. LEAN GROUND MEAT **OR** 2 PINTS CANNED LEAN GROUND MEAT, DRAINED AND LIQUID RESERVED
⅔ CUP MILK
1 EGG, BEATEN
⅔ CUP CHOPPED ONION **OR** 3 TBSP. DEHYDRATED CHOPPED ONIONS
¼ CUP FINE DRY CRACKER OR DRY BREAD CRUMBS
½ TSP. SALT
½ TSP. ALLSPICE
½ TSP. PEPPER
2 TSP. BUTTER
1 CUP BEEF BROTH
2 TBSP. FLOUR
½ CUP COLD WATER
1 CUP MILK
1 TBSP. LEMON JUICE

Combine milk, egg, onion, crumbs, salt, allspice, and pepper. Add meat and mix well. Chill. Shape meat mixture into walnut-sized balls. In large skillet, brown meatballs in butter. Pour beef broth over meatballs and bring to a boil over medium heat. Cover and simmer for 15 minutes, then remove meatballs from skillet. Skim off excess fat and reserve cooking juices. Blend together cold water and flour, then stir into cooking juices in skillet. Add milk and stir until thickened, making a gravy. Return meatballs to skillet and stir in lemon juice. Heat well over low heat, covered. Serve over hot cooked noodles which have been buttered and tossed with poppy seeds.

Note: Meatballs are harder to form when made from canned ground meat, so I often use my own home-canned meatballs for the base of this recipe, adding the gravy when I am preparing a meal.

Cousin Jack's pasties

Pasties (rhyme with nasties, but they're definitely not!) have always been a family favorite of ours. They are a meat and vegetable-filled pastry brought over by Cornish, Swedish, and Finnish miners. Wives would bake pasties for their husbands' lunches, carefully folding up the hot pastries inside many layers of paper. In this way, the miners could enjoy a hot meal right from their lunch pail.

When I was young, Dad and I often took long canoe trips through wild forests. Mom would bake pasties for us to take along so we would have a real stick-to-the-ribs meal on our first lunch stop. Now, every time I bake pasties, I remember those pristine little lakes, wild rushing water, the call of loons, and sight of moose in the shallows.

Pastry:

- 4 CUPS FLOUR
- 2 TSP. SALT
- 1½ CUPS LARD OR SHORTENING
- ICE WATER

Mix salt and flour in large bowl. With a pastry blender or fork, cut shortening into dry ingredients until the texture of coarse cornmeal. Add a little ice water at a time, tossing lightly to mix. Don't get the dough too wet. Use only enough water to hold the dough together well. Press into a ball, handling as little as possible. The more you handle the dough, the tougher the crust will be. Cover and refrigerate for at least 30 minutes. Chilling the dough sets up the shortening, making the crust flakier after baking.

Turn out chilled dough onto a lightly-floured surface. Roll out into large oblong, just a little thicker than for a pie. Using a dinner plate for a guide, cut the dough into rounds. Place each round on a lightly-greased cookie sheet and repeat. You can reuse the dough scraps for your last pastry circles.

Filling:

- 2 CUPS CUBED ROUND STEAK OR STEWING MEAT
  OR 1 PINT STEWING MEAT, DRAINED
- 1 CUP PEELED, DICED POTATOES OR ½-PINT HOME CANNED, DRAINED
- 1½ CUPS SLICED ONIONS
- ½ CUP SLICED OR DICED CARROTS OR ½-PINT SLICED OR DICED CARROTS, DRAINED
- ½ CUP DICED RUTABAGAS (FRESH OR CANNED)
- SALT AND PEPPER
- 3 TBSP. BUTTER
- 2 TBSP. CREAM OR MILK FOR EACH PASTIE

Mix meat, vegetables, and seasonings. Place on each pastry circle, to one side of center. Dot with butter. Moisten edges of circle with water, then fold dough over filling, making a filled half circle. Pinch edges together well to seal. Turn edges up slightly so pasty doesn't leak. Bake at 275° F for about 2 hours. About 15 minutes before they're done, make a slit in the top of each pastie and pour in 2 Tbsp. cream, then finish baking. If the crust edges are getting too brown, cover with tented aluminum foil. Serve hot with gravy, if desired.

Mom's glazed meatballs

1 lb. ground meat or 2 pints canned ground meat, drained
¾ cup chopped onion or 2 Tbsp. dehydrated onion
1 egg, beaten
¼ cup milk
¼ cup dry bread crumbs or cracker crumbs
1 tsp. salt, divided
¼ tsp. pepper
¾ cup catsup
⅓ cup water

Mix all except catsup, water, and ½ tsp. salt. Shape into walnut-sized balls. Brown in skillet with a little oil. Mix catsup, water, and ½ tsp. salt and pour over meatballs. Simmer on low heat and stir often. You can also bake uncovered in a casserole dish until a nice glaze forms. Baste if necessary.

Note: Meatballs are harder to form when made from canned ground meat, so I often use my own home-canned meatballs for the base of this recipe.

Porcupine meatballs

1 lb. ground meat
⅔ cup uncooked rice
¼ cup cream
½ medium onion, chopped
salt and pepper
1 can (16 oz.) tomato sauce
1 cup water

Mix ground meat, rice, cream, onion, salt, and pepper and make into meatballs. Place in a casserole dish. In a bowl, mix water with tomato sauce. Pour over meatballs. Bake at 325° F for 1½ hours. If getting too dry, add a little more water and cover.

Using canned ground meat:

2 pints ground meat, drained
⅔ cup uncooked rice
1 egg
¼ cup cream
½ medium onion, chopped or 1 Tbsp. dehydrated chopped onion
salt and pepper
1 pint tomato sauce
1 cup water

Note: As meatballs using canned ground meat are harder to form into balls and hold their shape, I often use my own home-canned porcupine meatballs as the base for this recipe.

Stuffed peppers

- 6 MEDIUM SWEET BELL PEPPERS (RED, YELLOW, AND GREEN MAKE A PRETTY DISH)
- 1 LB. LEAN GROUND MEAT **OR** 2 PINTS GROUND MEAT, DRAINED
- ½ CLOVE GARLIC, MINCED
- 1 MEDIUM ONION, CHOPPED
- ½ CUP CHOPPED CABBAGE
- 1 CAN (28 OZ.) TOMATOES WITH LIQUID, CHOPPED **OR** 1 PINT TOMATO SAUCE AND 1 PINT CHOPPED TOMATOES WITH LIQUID
- ½ CUP UNCOOKED LONG GRAIN RICE
- 1 TBSP. BROWN SUGAR
- ½ TSP. DRIED BASIL
- SALT AND PEPPER TO TASTE
- CHEDDAR CHEESE (OPTIONAL)

Cut the tops off each pepper and remove seeds. Remove stems from pepper tops, chop tops, and reserve. Put peppers in boiling water for 2-3 minutes until crisp-tender. Remove from water and rinse with cold water. In a large skillet, brown ground meat. Add garlic, onion, cabbage, and reserved chopped peppers. Sauté until vegetables are tender.

Add tomatoes, rice, sugar, basil, and salt and pepper. Cover and reduce heat to simmer. Cook until rice is tender. Stuff hot meat mixture into peppers. Put in oven and bake at 350° F until peppers are tender. Sprinkle shredded cheddar cheese over the tops (optional).

Popovers with cheese-topped Sloppy Joe mix

Tired of plain Sloppy Joes? Here's a different variation I discovered in Mom's kitchen years ago.
Popovers:

- 1 CUP FLOUR
- ½ TSP. SALT
- 2 EGGS
- 1 CUP MILK, DIVIDED
- 1 TBSP. MELTED SHORTENING

Mix flour and salt. Sift together. Beat eggs until light and thick. Add 1/3 cup of milk and continue beating. Add flour and beat slowly until all flour is moistened and gradually add remaining milk and melted shortening. Fill well-greased custard cups, popover pans, or muffin pans a little less than half full. Bake at 425° F for about 40 minutes or until done. About 10 minutes before finished baking, prick top with fork to release steam. This allows the popovers to dry out a little inside.

Filling:

- 1 LB. LEAN GROUND MEAT **OR** 2 PINTS CANNED GROUND MEAT, DRAINED
- ½ CUP CHOPPED ONION
- ¼ CUP CHOPPED GREEN PEPPER
- 1 PINT TOMATO SAUCE
- 1 TSP. CHILI POWDER
- ½ TSP. SALT

¼ CUP BROWN SUGAR

CHEDDAR CHEESE, SHREDDED (OPTIONAL)

Brown meat in large skillet. Drain off any excess grease. Add onion and pepper, sauté until tender. Add tomato sauce, chili powder, salt, and brown sugar. If using canned ground meat, simply mix ingredients well and heat through. Simmer until thickened.

Remove popovers from pans, cut tops open and stuff immediately with filling, adding shredded cheddar cheese to the tops. Serve when the cheese is melted.

Stuffed cabbage rolls

1 LARGE HEAD OF GREEN CABBAGE (I LIKE LATE FLAT DUTCH CABBAGE, IT HAS THICKER LEAVES)

1 TSP. SALT

Remove 12 outer large cabbage leaves. In a large pot, bring water to boil. Add cabbage leaves and simmer 3 minutes to make leaves limp. Drain, reserving 2 cups of liquid.

Stuffing:

½ CUP BUTTER OR MARGARINE, DIVIDED

1 CUP ONION, CHOPPED **OR** ¼ CUP DEHYDRATED CHOPPED ONION

1 CLOVE GARLIC, CRUSHED

½ LB. FRESH SLICED MUSHROOMS **OR** 1 SMALL CAN **OR** ¼ CUP DEHYDRATED MUSHROOMS

1 LB. GROUND MEAT **OR** 2 PINTS CANNED GROUND MEAT

1½ CUPS COOKED WHITE RICE

Melt ¼ cup butter in large skillet. Add onion and sauté until golden (if using dehydrated onion, omit this step). Add rest of butter along with garlic and mushrooms; sauté, stirring occasionally, about 4 minutes. (If using dehydrated mushrooms and onion, rehydrate mushrooms before this step and also add dehydrated onions to butter and rehydrated mushrooms.) Add remaining stuffing ingredients, cook uncovered about 5 minutes or until meat is done.

Tomato sauce:

¼ CUP BUTTER OR MARGARINE

¼ CUP FLOUR

2 CUPS LIQUID RESERVED FROM BOILING CABBAGE

1 PINT TOMATO SAUCE

½ TSP. SALT

DASH PEPPER

Melt butter in medium saucepan; remove from heat. Stir in flour until smooth then gradually stir in 2 cups reserved liquid from cabbage. Bring to a boiling point, stirring over medium heat. Remove from heat; stir in tomato sauce, salt, and pepper. Preheat oven to 350° F. Fill center of each cabbage leaf with ½ cup stuffing. Fold two sides over stuffing and roll up from the end. Arrange rolls, seam side down, in greased 3-quart casserole. Pour sauce over all of them. Bake uncovered at 350° F for 25 minutes.

Country meatloaf

- 2 lbs. lean ground meat
- 2 eggs, lightly beaten
- 1 cup Saltine cracker crumbs
- ½ cup chopped onion
- 1 cup catsup, divided
- 1 green pepper, seeded and sliced lengthwise

Mix meat, eggs, crumbs, onion, and ¾ cup catsup well. Shape into a loaf and place in a greased loaf pan. Arrange pepper slices over the top and drizzle ¼ cup catsup over the peppers and the top of the loaf. Bake at 350° F for 1¼ hours or until done.

Sloppy Joes

- 1 lb. lean ground meat **or** 2 pints lean canned ground meat, drained
- ½ medium onion, chopped (may use 1 Tbsp. dehydrated chopped onion)
- 1 clove garlic, minced (or 1 tsp. garlic powder)
- ½ sweet red or green pepper, chopped, finely (may use 1 Tbsp. dehydrated peppers)
- 1 can (16 oz.) tomato sauce
- ½ cup vinegar
- 3 Tbsp. brown sugar
- 1 tsp. Liquid Smoke or Worcestershire sauce (optional)

In large frying pan, fry ground meat, separating it into fine bits, until lightly brown. Drain off excess grease. Add chopped onion, garlic, and pepper, continuing frying all while stirring. When onion, garlic, and pepper are tender, add tomato sauce, vinegar, brown sugar, and Liquid Smoke or Worcestershire sauce. Continue cooking until as thick as you wish. Serve hot over hamburger buns. (I usually make my own, using the recipe for Half-Time Spoon Rolls, adding a bit more flour.)

Burritos

- 8 flour tortillas
- ½ lb. ground meat **or** 1 pint canned ground meat, drained
- 1 small onion, chopped (may use 1 tsp. dehydrated onion)
- 2 cloves garlic, minced
- 2 Tbsp. mild or hot powdered chile (this is pure powdered chile peppers, *not* store-bought chili powder, which is a blend of spices)
- 1 pint canned pinto beans **or** 1 can (16 oz.) refried beans
- 8 oz. shredded cheddar cheese
- salsa, fresh chopped onions, and sour cream for serving

In a large skillet, fry ground meat, separating the bits. Drain off excess grease. Add onion, garlic, and chili powder; continue frying until they are tender. Add refried beans. Mix well and cook until thickened.

On an ungreased griddle, heat tortillas, one at a time, on both sides, to soften. One at a time, fill warm tortilla with filling and add cheddar cheese. Roll the ends of the tortilla in over the filling, then roll up both sides, making a neat package. Keep warm on cookie sheet in warm oven until all burritos are filled. Serve with fresh or canned salsa, chopped fresh onion, and sour cream.

Chimichangas

Chimichangas are fried burritos. Any recipe you use for burritos can become chimichangas by frying them. In an effort to avoid as much deep fried food as possible, I usually only lightly pan fry them to "crisp up" the surfaces, then I lay them, seam side down, on a cookie sheet, and sprinkle with a little more cheese and bake for about 10 minutes in the oven at 300° F degrees. If you wish to deep fry the chimis, hold them with tongs when you first place them in the deep fryer to hold the tortilla closed until it begins to get crisp. (You don't want the filling to come out!) Serve chimichangas warm with salsa, sour cream, and hot sauce of your choice.

Tacos

TACO SHELLS
1 LB. LEAN GROUND MEAT **OR** 2 PINTS CANNED GROUND MEAT
8 OZ. TOMATO SAUCE **OR** ½-PINT CANNED TOMATO SAUCE
1 SMALL ONION, CHOPPED
1 TSP. GARLIC POWDER
1 TBSP. CHILE POWDER (HOT OR MILD)
CHEDDAR CHEESE, SHREDDED

In a frying pan, brown meat, separating into small pieces. Drain off excess grease. Add tomato sauce, onions, and spices. Place in taco shells (either homemade, heated individually in a lightly-greased, hot skillet to get limp enough to form or heated, then placed in a taco-holding tong and deep fried until crisp and formed). Top with cheese and either serve or put in an oven on a cookie sheet for 10 minutes at 300° F degrees to soften the shells a little and melt cheese. Top with chopped onion, fresh tomato, and lemon juice and serve with salsa and sour cream.

Pork

Sweet Italian roasted pork loin

1 WHOLE OR ½ OF A BONELESS, TRIMMED PORK LOIN
OR 2 QUARTS BONELESS PORK LOIN CHUNKS, DRAINED (RESERVE LIQUID)
1 CUP SWEET ITALIAN DRESSING

Rinse pork loin and pat dry. Place in large roasting pan and pour sweet Italian dressing over the top. Roast uncovered at 350° F until done (about 2½ to 3 hours for fresh pork, about 30 minutes for canned pork). The dressing not only marinates the pork as it cooks, but it forms a nice glaze over the top.

Scalloped potatoes and pork chops

6 PORK LOIN CHOPS (1-INCH THICK)
 OR 2 PINTS CANNED SLICED BONELESS PORK, DRAIN AND RESERVE LIQUID
5 CUPS THINLY SLICED, PEELED POTATOES
1 CUP CHOPPED ONION
SALT AND PEPPER
3 TBSP. BUTTER
3 TBSP. FLOUR
1 CUP MILK
½ CUP SOUR CREAM

In a greased 13x9x2-inch baking dish, layer half of the potatoes and onion; sprinkle with salt and pepper. Repeat layers. In a saucepan, melt butter and stir in flour. Gently, stir in milk, heating until thickened; add more milk if too thick. Cool to lukewarm and stir in sour cream. Pour over potato mixture. Cover and bake at 375° F for 30 minutes. Meanwhile, in a skillet, brown pork chops on both sides (omit this step if using canned chops). Place pork chops on top of casserole in a single layer and brush with butter. Cover and return to the oven for 45 minutes (30 minutes for canned chops) or until chops are tender, uncovering during the last 15 minutes of baking.

Mustard pork medallions

1½ LBS. PORK TENDERLOIN
½ CUP SEASONED DRY BREAD CRUMBS (MAKE YOUR OWN BY ADDING ¼ TSP. THYME,
 ¼ TSP. PEPPER, ¼ TSP. BASIL TO YOUR OWN DRY BREAD CRUMBS)
¼ TSP. GARLIC SALT
½ TSP. ONION POWDER
¼ CUP DIJON MUSTARD
1 TBSP. BUTTER OR MARGARINE, MELTED

In a bowl, combine crumbs, garlic salt, and onion powder; set aside. Cut tenderloin crosswise into 12 pieces and pound each one to ¼-inch thick. Mix mustard and butter; brush on each side of pork, then coat with crumb mixture. Place in a greased baking pan. Bake, uncovered, at 425° F for 10 minutes; turn and bake about 5 minutes more or until meat is done.

Pork ribs in plum sauce

5-6 LBS. PORK SPARERIBS OR 2 PINTS OF PORK SLICES OR CHUNKS (SEE VARIATION)
¾ CUP SOY SAUCE
¾ CUP PLUM JAM
¾ CUP HONEY
2-3 GARLIC CLOVES, MINCED

Cut ribs into serving-sized pieces; place bone side down on a rack in a shallow roasting pan. Cover and bake at 350° F for 1 hour or until meat is tender; drain. Combine remaining ingredients; brush some of the sauce over the ribs. Bake at 350° F uncovered for 30 minutes, brushing sauce over ribs occasionally.

Variation using canned pork:
You can create this same taste by placing pork slices or chunks in the bottom of a roasting pan and covering them with sauce. Bake at 350° F, uncovered for 30 minutes, basting meat occasionally with sauce.

Roast pork

    BONE-IN OR BONELESS PORK LOIN ROAST (3-4 LBS.)
    ½ CUP FLOUR
    1 TSP. PEPPER
    1 TSP. SALT

Rinse and pat pork roast dry. Mix flour, salt, and pepper in a bowl and coat top of roast as thickly as possible. Place roast on rack in baking pan. Bake uncovered at 350° F for about 1½ hours. Remove roast when done. To pan drippings, add ½ cup water and stir to loosen crusts. Mix 1 cup water with 2 Tbsp. cornstarch well. Stir into hot pan drippings, heating while you stir on stovetop. Serve when thickened.

Baked pork chops or steak

This is a very versatile dish, consisting of pan-fried pork chops or steaks, which are put into a casserole dish and smothered with a variety of sauces, giving them a very different taste.

    2 LBS. PORK CHOPS OR PORK STEAK
    DASH OF PEPPER AND SALT
    3 TBSP. VEGETABLE OIL

Fry pork chops or steaks over medium-high heat. When first side is golden, turn over and fry other side. Remove from heat. Stir ½ cup of water into pan drippings and stir well to loosen crusted drippings, then make sauce (see ideas below). Arrange pork chops/steaks in casserole and pour sauce over meat. Bake at 325° F for 30 minutes. Serve over rice or noodles, or with potatoes.

Mix one of the following sauces, then add to the drippings, mixing well:

Tomato: Mix together 1 pint (or a 16 oz. can) tomato sauce, ½ cup chopped onions, 1 chopped green pepper, and 1 tsp. chili powder, then stir into drippings.

Celery: Add ½ cup chopped celery to the pan drippings and simmer until tender. Use ⅔ cup of casserole sauce mix mixed with 2 cups of water. Add to celery and pan drippings and simmer until thickened.

Onion: Add ½ cup chopped mushrooms to the pan drippings and simmer until tender. Use ⅔ cup of casserole sauce mix mixed with 2 cups of water. Add to 1 medium onion, sliced, and pan drippings and simmer until thickened.

You can use canned cream of mushroom or cream of celery soup.

Variation using canned pork slices:
Simply sear each side of all slices in frying pan, then proceed as above.

Barbecued pork

>2 CUPS LEFTOVER, SHREDDED PORK
>1 CUP BARBECUE SAUCE
>1 CUP WATER
>½ CUP CHOPPED ONIONS

In a saucepan, mix barbecue sauce, water, and onions. Heat to boiling and simmer until onions are tender. Add shredded pork. Simmer until thickened, stirring to prevent scorching. Serve hot on hot buns. If you like spicy barbecue sandwiches, add enough chopped jalapeño peppers to suit your taste.

Sweet and sour pork

>2 LBS. PORK LOIN OR BONELESS SHOULDER, CUT INTO ½-INCH CUBES
>1½ TSP. SOY SAUCE
>½ TSP. GROUND GINGER
>1 QUART VEGETABLE OIL FOR DEEP FRYING

In a large dish, toss pork with soy sauce and ginger. Let stand for 10 minutes.

Batter:
>3 EGGS, WELL BEATEN
>¾ CUP FLOUR
>3 TBSP. CORNSTARCH

Mix eggs very well; add flour and cornstarch; beat until smooth. In deep fryer, slowly heat oil to 375° F. Drain pork cubes well. Pour batter over them; mix well to coat evenly. Drop pork cubes into hot fat; do not crowd; fry about ¼ at a time. Fry about 5 minutes, moving them around and turning them until all sides are golden brown. Finish all pork cubes; drain on paper towels and keep warm.

Sauce:
>1 CAN (16 OZ.) PINEAPPLE CHUNKS, DRAINED AND JUICE RESERVED
>1 CUP SUGAR
>1 CUP VINEGAR
>2 LARGE GREEN PEPPERS, CUT IN ½-INCH STRIPS
>1 SMALL SWEET RED PEPPER, CUT IN ½-INCH STRIPS
>2 TBSP. CORNSTARCH
>¼ CUP WATER
>2 TSP. SOY SAUCE
>2 LARGE, FIRM TOMATOES, CUT IN EIGHTHS
>1 TSP. GROUND GINGER

Drain pineapple chunks, reserving juice. Add water to juice, if necessary, to make 1 cup. In large saucepan, mix juice, sugar, and vinegar; heat, stirring until boiling. Add green and red peppers. Boil 2 minutes and remove from heat. In a small bowl, mix cornstarch and ¼ cup water; stir until smooth. Add to pineapple juice. Mix in soy sauce, tomatoes, ginger, and pineapple chunks. Cook, stirring over moderate heat until thickened. Arrange pork cubes in serving dish; pour on the sweet and sour sauce. Serve over hot rice.

Variation using canned pork chunks:

While not as good as the recipe using fresh pork, this one still tastes good, although the meat is a little drier. Just gently coat pork pieces with batter, taking care not to break them. Deep fat fry just until they are getting golden and crusty. Drain and make the sauce as above.

Sweet and sour pork, quick method

1½ TSP. SOY SAUCE

½ TSP. GROUND GINGER

2 LBS. BONELESS PORK CHOPS, CUT INTO 1-INCH CUBES

2 TBSP. VEGETABLE OIL

In a bowl, combine soy sauce and ginger, tossing pork cubes in the mixture; let stand 10 minutes. Heat 2 Tbsp. vegetable oil in skillet and fry pork cubes until done. Keep warm.

Sauce:

JUICE FROM PINEAPPLE + WATER AS NEEDED TO MAKE 1 CUP

1 CUP SUGAR

1 CUP VINEGAR

1 GREEN PEPPER, SEEDED AND CUT INTO 1-INCH PIECES

1 SMALL SWEET RED PEPPER, SEEDED AND CUT INTO 1-INCH PIECES

1 MEDIUM ONION, CUT INTO SMALL CHUNKS

2 STALKS OF CELERY, CUT INTO 1-INCH SLICES

2 TBSP. CORNSTARCH

½ CUP WATER

2 TSP. SOY SAUCE

½ TSP. GROUND GINGER

1 CAN (14 OZ.) PINEAPPLE CHUNKS, DRAINED

Add pineapple juice, sugar, and vinegar; heat, stirring, until sugar is dissolved. Then bring to a boil. Add peppers, onions, and celery; boil 2 minutes or until just tender. In a small bowl, combine cornstarch and ½ cup water; stir until smooth. Add to pineapple juice mixture. Add soy sauce and ginger, finally pineapple chunks. Cook, stirring, over a medium heat until thickened and translucent. Add pork chunks and serve over hot rice.

You can easily substitute canned pork cubes, just lightly searing the meat, before adding to sauce with vegetables and pineapple.

Tamales

Dough and wrapping:
- 1 PKG. CORN HUSKS OR CLEAN DRIED CORN HUSKS FROM GARDEN
- 3 CUPS MASA HARINA (CORN FLOUR, NOT CORNMEAL, AVAILABLE AT MOST LARGE STORES)
- 1 CUP LARD OR VEGETABLE SHORTENING
- 1 TSP. SALT

Meat filling:
- 1 LB. COOKED PORK ROAST, GROUND WITH HAND MEAT GRINDER OR YOU MAY USE 2 PINTS CANNED PORK CHUNKS, DRAINED AND GROUND
- ½ CUP CHOPPED ONION
- 1 CLOVE GARLIC, MINCED
- 1 CAN (10 OZ.) TOMATO PUREE OR ¾-PINT CANNED TOMATO PUREE OR SAUCE
- 1 TBSP. VINEGAR
- 1 TBSP. SUGAR
- ¼ TSP. GROUND CUMIN
- 1 TBSP. GROUND CHILE PEPPER, MILD OR HOT **OR** 1 TSP. CHILI POWDER

Put corn husks in a bowl of water and press down with saucer. Soak overnight.

Mix masa harina and water to form a soft dough that can be handled. Cover and let stand 30 minutes. In a large bowl, beat lard and salt until very fluffy. Add dough, a little at a time, beating constantly. Heat meat, onion, and garlic in a large skillet. Add remaining ingredients. Cover and remove from heat.

Pat corn husks dry with paper towels. If they are not pre-trimmed, cut off the pointy ends square. Spread out husks and spread 2 Tbsp. dough, about ⅛-inch thick down the husk in a rectangle, leaving 1 inch as a border with no dough, all around. Top with 1 Tbsp. meat filling.

Roll husks around dough and fold up the bottom. Tie each rolled husk with a strip of corn husk. In a kettle, place a steam rack in the bottom or place an inverted plate held up off the bottom with four canning jar rings. Pour 1 cup of water or broth in the bottom of the kettle, then begin placing the tamales in the kettle, folded side down. Bring to a boil, covered, and steam for 45 minutes, adding liquid if needed to maintain steam. When done, husk should peel back easily from dough.

Baked ham

Because home-smoked hams are not precooked as are many store-bought hams, you must first soak the ham overnight in cold water, then place skin-side up in a large kettle, covering with water. Bring to a boil, then simmer, tightly covered, until tender. Allow 25-30 minutes per pound. Remove from water and cool. Trim off skin and any rusty-colored edges.

Place on a rack in a large roasting pan. Bake at 300° F until the interior temperature is 170 degrees for a whole ham that has been home cured (about 25 minutes per pound) or 150-160 degrees for a store-bought ham (about 15 minutes per pound). A home-cured half ham should have an internal temperature of 170 degrees (bake about 30 minutes per pound) where a store-bought ham should be 150-160 degrees (bake about 20 minutes per pound).

When the ham is about half done, I remove it from the oven and score the fat in diamond shapes and spread a glaze made of 1 cup brown sugar and ½ cup pineapple juice. To make a festive ham, pin pineapple slices onto the ham's surface with whole cloves and place a maraschino cherry in the center of each slice. Pour the glaze over the surface and baste with this juice. If the ham starts to get too dark before it is done, tent with foil to finish baking.

Another nice glaze is a pint of cherry or chokecherry jelly spread over the surface of the ham, about 30 minutes before it's done, then basted several times with the juice.

While you can't "bake" canned ham like this, you can enjoy the same flavor by arranging canned ham slices or pieces in a baking dish and pouring a glaze (even with the pineapple and maraschino cherries) over the ham. Bake uncovered for about 30 minutes, basting with the ham broth and glaze juice, as needed to prevent drying and to enhance the flavor.

Ham loaf

- 1 LB. GROUND HAM
- 1 LB. LEAN PORK SAUSAGE
- 2 CUPS SOFT BREAD CRUMBS
- 2 EGGS, BEATEN
- 1 CUP SOUR CREAM
- ⅓ CUP CHOPPED ONION
- 1 SEEDED AND CHOPPED SWEET GREEN PEPPER (SMALL)
- 2 TBSP. LEMON JUICE
- 1 TSP. DRY MUSTARD
- 1 TSP. GROUND GINGER
- ⅛ TSP. NUTMEG

In a large mixing bowl, mix all ham loaf ingredients. Form into a loaf. Place in a shallow baking pan. Bake at 350° F, uncovered, for 1 hour.

Basting sauce:
- ½ CUP FIRMLY PACKED BROWN SUGAR
- ¼ CUP WATER
- ¼ CUP VINEGAR
- ⅛ TSP. PEPPER

In a small saucepan, mix all ingredients for basting sauce; bring to a boil. Drain off any grease from ham loaf and pour basting sauce over it. Continue baking loaf, basting with pan juices, for 30 more minutes or until lightly browned.

Poultry

Oven-roasted stuffed turkey

    1 FRESH TURKEY (CHILLED 24 HOURS OR MORE) OR THAWED FROZEN TURKEY
    8 CUPS CUBED, STALE BREAD CHUNKS
    1 CUP CHOPPED CELERY
    ½ CUP CHOPPED ONION
    2 TSP. RUBBED SAGE
    ½ TSP. BLACK PEPPER
    1 TSP. SALT
    2 TBSP. MELTED BUTTER
    3 TBSP. BUTTER AND 3 TBSP. FLOUR FOR GRAVY

Rinse and dry turkey, paying special attention to the neck and body cavities. Mix bread chunks (you want larger pieces, about 1-inch square, approximately), chopped celery, onion, and seasonings well, then drizzle on melted butter and toss lightly. Just before baking, gently stuff the body and neck cavity, fastening openings closed with skewers or sew shut with a large needle and cotton twine. Do *not* ram the stuffing in or you will have soggy stuffing. Spoon it in and lightly pack it with your fingers. Tie drumsticks together and place on a rack in a roasting pan. (If you don't have a rack, you can sit the turkey on two large-mouth canning jar rings to hold the back up from the bottom of the pan so it doesn't stick to the pan when you try to lift the turkey out.) It is a good idea to make a cradle from two pieces of heavy cotton twine, running under the turkey, just in front of the wings and just behind the drumsticks (or wherever it seems best balanced), so you can lift the hot turkey out of the roaster to let it rest before carving. Bake the turkey at 350° F for about 3½ to 4 hours, basting the bird every hour with its own juices or added margarine, to keep it from drying out. If it is browning too quickly, make a tent of aluminum foil and place over the bird. When the turkey is done, the meat will shrink from the leg bones a bit and the meat will be fork tender. Let the turkey stand for 15 minutes so it doesn't fall apart when you cut it. Remove the dressing into a bowl for serving.

To make gravy, drain off the cooking juices, skimming off as much of the floating grease as you can. Pick out any clinging pieces of skin or meat in the roasting pan. Add 3 Tbsp. flour to a little cold water in a bowl. Make a paste, then add more water for a total of about 1 cup. Put roaster on stovetop and heat drippings in pan. Add water/flour and stir until heated. Add enough of the pan juices to make a nice, thick gravy. Add more water, if necessary. Season with salt, pepper, and herbs to taste. Serve strained gravy in a gravy boat.

Oven-roasted canned turkey dinner

Although you can't make a traditional stuffed, roasted turkey out of canned turkey, you can still have a roast turkey dinner, using home-canned turkey meat and broth. It might not be quite as elegant, but it is very good and it takes much less time to put on the table!

    1 QUART OR MORE CANNED TURKEY BREASTS AND/OR DARK MEAT, DRAINED AND
        LIQUID RESERVED

1 pint turkey broth
8 cups cubed, stale bread chunks
1 cup chopped celery
½ cup chopped onion
2 tsp. rubbed sage
½ tsp. black pepper
1 tsp. salt
2 Tbsp. melted butter
3 Tbsp. butter and 3 Tbsp. flour for gravy

Mix bread chunks (you want larger pieces, about 1-inch square, approximately), chopped celery, onion, and seasonings well, then drizzle on melted butter and toss lightly. Add 1 cup turkey broth and stir well. Butter a large, covered casserole dish and spoon stuffing into it. Drain canned turkey of your choice (all breast meat or a mix of dark and white meat) onto the stuffing, reserving canning broth. Place cover over casserole and bake at 325° F for 30 minutes. I like to lift off the turkey meat onto a warm serving dish, cover it and keep warm, then with the cover off the stuffing, return it to the oven for another 10 minutes to dry the top of the stuffing. In the meantime, in a saucepan, melt 3 Tbsp. butter and 3 Tbsp. flour together until smooth, then slowly add the canning broth and any additional broth/water, until the gravy is the right thickness. Stir well while heating. Season gravy with salt, pepper, and herbs (rubbed sage and thyme are nice) to taste. Arrange turkey around stuffing on a warm serving dish and pour gravy into a gravy boat to serve.

Turkey can be roasted with the above stuffing, but in many families and areas of the country, other dressings are commonly used. Here are a couple more for you to try and enjoy. The baking of the turkey is the same, but the recipes for the dressing vary widely.

Cornbread stuffing

2 cups chopped celery **or** ½ cup dehydrated celery
1 cup chopped onion **or** ¼ cup dehydrated onion
½ cup butter or margarine
6 cups cubed, day-old cornbread
2 cups soft bread crumbs
1 Tbsp. rubbed sage
½ tsp. thyme
½ tsp. black pepper
2 eggs, lightly beaten
1 cup chicken or turkey broth

In a skillet, sauté celery and onion in butter until tender. Place in a large mixing bowl with cornbread, crumbs, sage, and other seasonings. Mix eggs and chicken/turkey broth and add to cornbread mixture, tossing gently. Makes enough to stuff a 12-pound turkey.

Sausage stuffing

- 1 lb. bulk pork breakfast sausage
- 1 cup chopped onion OR ½ cup dehydrated chopped onion
- 2 cups chopped celery OR ¾ cups dehydrated chopped celery
- 1 cups chopped green pepper
- 10 cups day-old bread cubes
- 2 tsp. salt
- 1 egg, slightly beaten

In a large skillet, cook sausage, stirring until lightly browned. Remove from pan with slotted spoon; drain grease, reserving 2 Tbsp. of the drippings. In reserved drippings, sauté onion, celery, and green pepper until tender (about 5 minutes). In large mixing bowl, mix remaining ingredients and sausage until well combined. Makes enough to stuff a 12-pound turkey.

Wild rice stuffing

- 6 bacon slices
- 6 Tbsp. butter or margarine
- 1½ cups diced celery OR ¾ cup dehydrated celery
- 12 oz. sliced, canned (drained), or fresh mushrooms
- 1 cup chopped onion OR ½ cup dehydrated chopped onion
- 6 cups cooked wild rice
- 1 Tbsp. salt
- 1 tsp. pepper
- 2 tsp. dried rosemary

In a skillet, fry bacon over medium heat until crisp. Remove bacon from pan and add butter to grease. Add celery, mushrooms, and onion and sauté until tender; about 10 minutes. Add remaining ingredients, crumbling bacon. Toss gently with a fork to mix. Makes enough to stuff a 12-pound turkey.

Grilled turkey breasts

- 2 turkey breast tenderloins
- ¼ cup soy sauce
- ¼ cup vegetable oil
- ¼ cup apple juice
- 2 Tbsp. lemon juice
- 2 Tbsp. dried minced onion
- 1 tsp. vanilla
- ¼ tsp. ground ginger
- dash of garlic powder and pepper

In a shallow bowl, mix soy sauce, oil, apple juice, lemon juice, onion, vanilla, ginger, garlic powder, and pepper. Add turkey; cover and refrigerate for at least 2 hours. Discard marinade. Grill turkey, covered, over medium coals for 8-10 minutes on each side or until done. Cut into medallions and serve hot. These breasts may also be broiled or baked in a covered dish at 350° F until done.

You can also bake this recipe, using canned turkey breasts by gently pouring off the canning liquid (reserve), then adding the marinade to the canning jar (less handling of the meat, which means less coming apart!). Refrigerate the jar for 3 hours. Pour off marinade, then gently work turkey breasts out of jar and lay in casserole dish. Add canning liquid and cover, baking at 300° F for about 20 minutes.

Turkey a la king

> 1 CUP CANNED SLICED MUSHROOMS, DRAINED
> ¼ CUP CHOPPED GREEN PEPPER
> ½ CUP PIMENTO, SLICED OR CANNED RED PEPPER, SLICED AND DRAINED
> 1 MEDIUM ONION, CHOPPED
> 3 TBSP. BUTTER
> 3 TBSP. FLOUR
> 3 CUPS MILK (MAY USE RECONSTITUTED POWDERED MILK)
> 2 CUPS COLD COOKED OR CANNED DICED TURKEY, DRAINED
> SALT, PEPPER, AND PAPRIKA

Sauté mushrooms, green pepper, pimento, and onion in butter. Add flour and stir well. Slowly add milk, stirring as you do, to make mushroom white sauce, adding more or less milk to make a medium white sauce. Add turkey. Season to taste with salt, pepper, and paprika. Simmer slowly until blended. Serve on toast or over buttered biscuits.

Rustic country chicken

> 1 BROILER CHICKEN, CUT INTO SERVING PIECES
> ¼ CUP FLOUR
> 1½ TSP. SALT
> ¼ TSP. PEPPER
> ⅓ CUP VEGETABLE OIL
> ½ CUP CHICKEN BROTH
> 1 CAN (16 OZ.) CORN, DRAINED **OR** 1 PINT CANNED
> 1 CAN (16 OZ.) BUTTER BEANS, DRAINED **OR** 1 PINT CANNED
> 1 CAN (4 OZ.) SLICED MUSHROOMS **OR** ½-PINT, CANNED, DRAINED
> 1 TBSP. CHOPPED PIMENTO, OPTIONAL (MAY USE DEHYDRATED SWEET PEPPER)
> 1 CAN (16 OZ.) TOMATO SAUCE **OR** 1 PINT CANNED
> 1 TSP. DRIED BASIL

Mix flour, salt, and pepper. Lightly coat chicken with flour mixture. Heat oil in large skillet. Lightly brown chicken on all sides. Pour off excess grease. Add broth; cover and simmer 40 minutes. Add remaining ingredients and simmer 10 minutes or until chicken is tender.

Curried turkey with rice

1 CUP SLICED ONION
¼ CUP SLICED CARROTS
¼ CUP SLICED CELERY
1 MEDIUM APPLE, PARED, CORED, AND SLICED
1 CLOVE GARLIC, MINCED
¼ CUP BUTTER
⅓ CUP FLOUR
2½ TSP. CURRY POWDER
¼ TSP. GROUND GINGER
¼ TSP. GROUND MACE
¼ TSP. PEPPER
2 CUPS TURKEY OR CHICKEN BROTH
1 CAN (4 OZ.) SLICED MUSHROOMS (OR FRESH OR DEHYDRATED, REHYDRATED), UNDRAINED
3 CUPS CUBED, COOKED TURKEY
2 CUPS SOUR CREAM
HOT COOKED RICE

Sauté onion, carrots, celery, apple, and garlic in melted butter. Slowly blend in flour, curry powder, and spices. Gradually add broth and mushrooms (not drained). Cook over medium heat, stirring constantly until it comes to a boil. Simmer 5 minutes. Stir in turkey. Heat well to blend flavors. Stir in sour cream and heat two more minutes. Serve hot over hot, fluffy rice.

Serve with any of the following: chopped fresh onions, raisins, chopped green pepper, chopped tomato, chopped hard-boiled eggs, chopped peanuts, chile paste, coconut, and chutney.

This dish can be made using canned, cubed turkey in the same manner.

Dilled barbecued turkey breast

1 TURKEY BREAST HALF, BONE IN
1 CUP PLAIN YOGURT
¼ CUP LEMON JUICE
3 TBSP. VEGETABLE OIL
¼ CUP MINCED PARSLEY
¼ CUP CHOPPED ONION
1 GARLIC CLOVE, MINCED
2 TBSP. FRESH MINCED DILL WEED
½ TSP. DRIED BASIL
½ TSP. SALT
⅛ TSP. PEPPER

In a small bowl, combine ingredients, except for turkey breast. Mix well. Spread over turkey breast in large bowl, then cover and refrigerate overnight. Remove breast and reserve marinade. Grill turkey, covered, over medium coals for about 1 hour or until juices run clear, basting often with marinade. Or bake turkey, covered, in oven at 300° F, basting often, for about 1 hour or until juices run clear.

Roast chicken

Make ¼ recipe of turkey stuffing. Rinse and wipe inside and out of fresh, chilled chicken. (May use thawed, frozen chicken, as well.) Fill cavities with stuffing, packing lightly. Fold neck skin down over breast stuffing and tuck under, on rack, in roasting pan. Truss legs together. Cover and bake at 350° F, allowing about 25 minutes per pound. During the last 25 minutes, uncover and let brown. Baste with juices from time to time.

To roast a goose, fix the same as with chicken, but allow 20-25 minutes per pound. Be sure to use a rack to hold the goose up out of the grease that will cook out of the bird.

To roast a duck, allow 20-25 minutes per pound.

Chicken cordon bleu

3 BONELESS CHICKEN BREASTS, CUT IN HALF
6 SLICES SWISS CHEESE
6 SLICES BOILED HAM
½ CUP FLOUR
2 EGGS, LIGHTLY BEATEN
1 CUP FINE BREAD CRUMBS
2 TBSP. BUTTER
1 TBSP. VEGETABLE OIL

Flatten chicken breasts to ½-inch thick with mallet or the side of a knife. Top each with 1 slice of cheese, then ham. Roll each piece, then secure with a toothpick. Season flour with salt and pepper. Dip pieces in seasoned flour, then into egg. Roll in bread crumbs. Heat butter and oil in large skillet. Sauté about 6 minutes on each side. Place on baking dish and bake at 350° F for about 20 minutes or until done.

Virginia barbecued chicken

1 CUT UP BROILER OR FRYING CHICKEN
PAPRIKA
1 JAR (16 OZ.) OF BARBECUE SAUCE OR 1 PINT, HOME CANNED
GARLIC POWDER AND SALT TO TASTE
1 ONION, CHOPPED
½ GREEN PEPPER, CHOPPED

Sprinkle chicken pieces with paprika and lay on baking sheet in oven. Bake at 350° F for 1 hour. In a saucepan, mix barbecue sauce, garlic, salt, onion, and green pepper. Simmer until pepper and onion are tender, stirring to prevent scorching. Place browned chicken in large casserole dish. Cover with barbecue sauce and bake for 1 hour. If sauce is getting too dry, cover dish until finished baking.

Chicken cacciatore

    1 BROILER OR FRYER CHICKEN, CUT INTO SERVING PIECES OR USE 2 PINTS CANNED CHICKEN PIECES, BROTH RESERVED
    ¼ CUP OLIVE OIL
    SALT AND PEPPER
    1 CLOVE GARLIC, MINCED
    2 MEDIUM ONIONS, CHOPPED
    12 MEDIUM MUSHROOMS, SLICED
    1 SMALL SWEET GREEN PEPPER, SEEDED AND CUT INTO SLICES
    ½ CUP SLICED BLACK OLIVES
    1 CAN (8 OZ.) TOMATO SAUCE OR ½-PINT CANNED
    1½ CUPS CHICKEN BROTH
    1 TSP. OREGANO
    1 BAY LEAF
    COOKED NOODLES
    GRATED ROMANO CHEESE
    GRATED PARMESAN CHEESE

Heat oil in large skillet. Salt and pepper chicken pieces and brown on all sides. Remove chicken; sauté garlic and onions until golden brown. Add mushrooms, green pepper, and olives; place chicken on top of vegetables. Pour mixture of tomato sauce, broth, and herbs over chicken and bake at 350° F for 1 hour or until tender. Serve over hot pasta, sprinkled generously with cheese.

You may also make this with canned chicken, sautéing chicken chunks after onions and garlic, lightly. Proceed as above, but only bake for 20 minutes, covered.

Chicken and dumplings

This is one of our favorite dishes and one I serve a lot. It's an old-fashioned comfort food that really is easy, tastes wonderful, and sticks to your ribs on a cold fall or winter day! It's amazing how light and fluffy those dumplings are and so full of chicken flavor, too. We even take this in thermos jugs when we go hunting or out in the big woods to cut firewood.

    1 FRYING CHICKEN, CUT INTO SERVING PIECES
    1 ONION, CHOPPED
    SALT AND PEPPER
    ½ CUP CHOPPED GREEN PEPPER OR 1 TBSP. DEHYDRATED

Place clean chicken pieces in large kettle and partially cover with water. Add onion, salt, and pepper. Add green pepper. Simmer gently until tender (usually 1½ to 3 hours). Cool to warm, remove chicken pieces and remove bone and skin. Place meat back in kettle.

Dumplings:

    1½ CUPS FLOUR
    2 TSP. BAKING POWDER
    ½ TSP. SALT

MINCED PARSLEY, IF YOU WISH TO ADD COLOR
⅓ CUP MELTED BUTTER OR MARGARINE
½ CUP MILK

Mix flour, baking powder, salt, and parsley. Mix in butter. Add milk to make a thick batter that will just fall off spoon. Drop from spoon into simmering chicken broth. Cover tightly and cook for 15 minutes without raising lid. Place chicken on platter and surround by dumplings. I often also make a gravy from the chicken broth by mixing 3 Tbsp. flour with 3 Tbsp. cold milk or water then adding enough broth to make a nice gravy. Add salt and pepper to taste and serve over your chicken and dumplings.

Stir-fried chicken and vegetables

Marinade:
½ CUP CHICKEN BROTH
2½ TBSP. SOY SAUCE
1 TBSP. CHINESE FIVE SPICE OR CURRY POWDER
2½ TSP. GARLIC POWDER
SALT AND PEPPER
1 TBSP. CORNSTARCH

Stir-fry:
3 CHICKEN BREASTS (7-8 OZ.), SKINNED AND BONED
   OR 2 PINTS CANNED BONELESS CHICKEN, DRAINED
1 CARROT, DIAGONALLY CUT
3 STALKS CELERY, CUT INTO THICK SLICES
1 ONION, DICED
1 GREEN PEPPER, CUT INTO 1-INCH CHUNKS
1 RED SWEET PEPPER, CUT INTO 1-INCH CHUNKS
2⅓ CUPS CHICKEN BROTH, DIVIDED
1 MEDIUM-SIZE BOK CHOY, CUT INTO SMALL PIECES
1 LB. BEAN SPROUTS
1 CAN (8 OZ.) WATER CHESTNUTS OR ½ CUP *RAW* JERUSALEM ARTICHOKES, SLICED
1 TSP. GROUND GINGER

Mix a marinade ingredients. Cut chicken into strips and marinate 1 hour. Transfer to wok or deep large skillet. Bring liquid to boil and lower heat and stir-fry the chicken until tender. Put in covered container and set aside. Stir-fry vegetables, adding carrots first, then celery, onion, and peppers. Add ½ cup chicken broth at a time while stir-frying vegetables. Add bok choy, bean sprouts, and water chestnuts. Add powdered ginger. Make a paste of cornstarch and 3 Tbsp. broth. Add to vegetables, return cooked chicken, and mix gently. Heat well and serve hot over hot rice or noodles.

If you use home-canned chicken in place of raw, omit the precooking and just add to vegetables while stir-frying.

Parmesan chicken

- 2 lbs. boneless chicken (breasts or thighs)
- 4 Tbsp. butter
- 4 Tbsp. vegetable oil

Coating mix:
- ½ cup flour
- ½ cup fine cracker crumbs
- 3 Tbsp. grated Parmesan cheese
- 2 tsp. salt
- ¼ tsp. pepper
- ½ tsp. onion powder
- ¼ tsp. garlic powder
- ½ tsp. dry mustard
- ¼ tsp. paprika
- ½ tsp. dried basil, crushed
- 1 tsp. dried parsley, crushed

Wash and pat dry chicken. Cut into serving-sized pieces. Preheat oven to 350° F. On a cookie sheet with sides, melt oil and butter. Meanwhile, mix coating ingredients in a bowl and mix very well. Remove cookie sheet with hot butter/oil from oven. Dip chicken pieces, a few at a time, in butter mixture, then toss in bowl of coating mix. Return chicken pieces to pan. Bake until done (about 1 hour). If coating is getting done too quickly, cover chicken to finish baking.

Southern fried chicken

- 1 broiler, cut into serving-size pieces
- 1 tsp. salt
- ½ tsp. pepper
- ½ cup flour
- 1½ cups vegetable shortening or lard

Rinse and pat dry chicken pieces. Mix salt, pepper, and flour and dredge chicken in flour. Melt shortening or lard in large, deep skillet. Heat until hot but not smoking. Lay in thick, meaty pieces first, as they take longest to cook. Brown all pieces on one side, then turn and brown other side. Cover pan and lower heat, continue cooking until chicken is tender and no pink shows in meat.

Fried chicken tenders

- 2 lbs. boneless, skinless chicken breasts
- ½ cup flour
- ½ tsp. salt
- ½ tsp. pepper
- ½ tsp. dried basil
- ½ cup milk
- vegetable oil to fry

Rinse and pat breast halves dry. With a sharp knife, cut the breasts into 1-inch wide pieces, discarding any fat or gristle. Pound the breast strips flat, about ½-inch thick. Mix flour and seasonings in bowl. Dip each strip first in a bowl with milk, then in the bowl with the seasoned flour. In a large skillet, add about 1-inch of vegetable oil and heat until hot but not smoking. Place floured chicken strips in grease and fry on all sides until golden brown. Serve hot with roasted potato wedges or French fries and your favorite dipping sauce (barbecue, sweet and sour, hot mustard, ranch, or plum).

Sweet and sour chicken

2 LBS. BONELESS, SKINLESS CHICKEN, CUT INTO ½-INCH CUBES

1½ TSP. SOY SAUCE

½ TSP. GROUND GINGER

In a large dish, toss chicken with soy sauce and ginger. Let stand for 10 minutes.

Batter:

¾ CUP FLOUR

1 TBSP. SUGAR

3 TBSP. CORNSTARCH

1 QUART VEGETABLE OIL FOR DEEP FRYING

Mix flour, sugar, and cornstarch; beat until smooth. In deep fryer or large, deep skillet, slowly heat oil to 375° F. Drain chicken cubes well. Pour batter over them; mix well to coat evenly. Drop chicken cubes into hot oil (do not crowd); cook about ¼ at a time. Fry about 5 minutes, moving them around and turning them until all sides are golden brown. Drain on paper towels and keep warm.

Sauce:

1 CAN (16 OZ.) SMALL PINEAPPLE CHUNKS, RESERVE LIQUID

1 CUP BROWN SUGAR

⅓ CUP VINEGAR

2 LARGE GREEN PEPPERS, CUT IN ½-INCH STRIPS

1 SMALL SWEET RED PEPPER, CUT IN ½-INCH STRIPS

2 TBSP. CORNSTARCH

2 TSP. SOY SAUCE

Drain pineapple chunks, reserving juice. Add water to juice, if necessary, to make 1 cup. In large saucepan, mix juice, brown sugar, and vinegar; heat, stirring until boiling. Add green and red peppers. Boil 2 minutes and remove from heat. In a small bowl, mix cornstarch and ¼ cup water; stir until smooth. Add to pineapple juice. Mix in soy sauce and pineapple chunks. Cook, stirring over moderate heat until thickened. Arrange chicken cubes in serving dish; pour on the sweet and sour sauce. Serve over hot rice.

Fish

No homestead recipe book would be complete without a section of fish recipes. In almost every part of the country there are fish-laden lakes and streams ready to supply wonderful meals for your family. Fishing is one of my favorite pastimes, and when I have time, I find a little wild lake, a section of wilderness stream, or a remote pond. Not only do I have an enjoyable outing, but I also usually bring home enough fish for supper. Whether it might be fresh trout, northern pike, walleye, salmon, or even feisty (and tasty!) sunfish, they always make enjoyable meals on our homestead.

Generally, you can substitute different species of fish in the following recipes. When there is a recipe for salmon loaf, you can also substitute leftover northern pike or sunfish fillets, as well. I hope you enjoy your fish and see what a variety of recipes you can choose to use them in.

Pan-fried fish

2 LBS. CLEANED, SCALED FISH, CUT INTO SERVING-SIZED PIECES OR FISH FILLETS

1 EGG IN 1 CUP MILK, MIXED WELL

1 CUP FLOUR

½ TSP. SALT

½ TSP. PEPPER (I USE LEMON PEPPER)

VEGETABLE OIL FOR FRYING

Rinse and pat dry fish. Dip in egg/milk mixture, then roll in a bowl containing mixed flour, salt, and pepper. (For a crunchier batter, add ½ cup cornmeal with ½ cup flour.) Heat vegetable oil in large frying pan to hot, but not smoking. Fry the fish on one side, then gently flip and fry the other side. When both sides are golden brown, remove from pan, drain on paper towel, and serve.

Baked stuffed fish

1 LARGE (5-8 LB.) WHOLE FISH (WITH OR WITHOUT HEAD)

1 TSP. SALT

3 TBSP. LEMON JUICE

Clean and scale fish. Rub fish with salt, inside and out. Sprinkle with lemon juice.

1 CUP CHOPPED CELERY

1 MEDIUM ONION, CHOPPED

½ CUP BUTTER

½ CUP SLICED MUSHROOMS

4 CUPS COARSE BREAD CRUMBS

1 TSP. RUBBED SAGE

1 TSP. DRIED BASIL

½ TSP. PEPPER

Sauté celery and onion in butter until tender. Add mushrooms and cook 5 minutes longer. Combine with crumbs and seasonings. Place stuffing in fish and place on greased baking sheet. Bake at 425° F, allowing 10 minutes per pound of fish (weight of fish before stuffing). Baste frequently with lemon juice and butter.

Flaked fish in cream sauce

    2-3 cups home cooked or canned fish, liquid reserved
    ¼ cup butter or vegetable oil
    ¾ cup cream
    ¼ cup fish stock (the liquid from canned fish or substitute water)
    2 Tbsp. onion, minced finely
    3 Tbsp. minced parsley
    ½ tsp. salt
    ¼ tsp. pepper

Drain fish; remove any bones or dark skin. Flake into bowl coarsely.

Heat butter or oil; combine cream, stock, onion, parsley, and seasonings. Add to oil gently. Stir well. Add flaked fish and simmer for 15 minutes, stirring to prevent scorching. Serve over toast or with baked potato. You might like a sprinkle of fresh, chopped dill or chives over this.

Salmon patties

    16 oz. (about 2 pints) canned salmon or any other canned fish, drained
    3 eggs
    ½ tsp. salt
    ½ tsp. pepper
    ½ cup cracker crumbs, coarsely crushed
    4 Tbsp. vegetable oil
    2 Tbsp. butter

Flake fish into a bowl, removing any bones or dark skin. Add eggs, beating lightly. Add salt and pepper, then cracker crumbs, mixing well. With damp hands, form into balls, then patties about ½-inch thick. Heat vegetable oil and butter in large skillet until hot but not smoking. Place patties in pan and sauté until golden brown on both sides. Serve hot with lemon or catsup and horseradish.

Salmon loaf

    16 oz. (about 2 pints) canned salmon or any other canned fish, drained
    2 eggs
    ½ tsp. salt
    ½ tsp. pepper
    1 Tbsp. lemon juice
    ½ cup cracker crumbs, coarsely crushed

Flake the fish into a bowl, removing any bones or dark skin. Add eggs, beating lightly. Add salt and pepper and lemon juice. Mix well, then add cracker crumbs. Mix thoroughly. Grease a bread pan lightly, then pack the mixture into the pan, rounding the top slightly. Dot top with butter and bake uncovered at 350° F for 30 minutes or until the top is golden and drying. Serve with lemon juice, vinegar, or catsup.

Casseroles

Old-fashioned baked macaroni and cheese

    2 CUPS UNCOOKED MACARONI
    3 TBSP. BUTTER
    3 TBSP. FLOUR
    3 CUP MILK (MAY USE REHYDRATED POWDERED MILK)
    ½ LB. GRATED SHARP CHEDDAR CHEESE (YOU MAY USE POWDERED, RECONSTITUTED CHEESE SAUCE INSTEAD OF THIS CHEESE AND THE ABOVE 3 INGREDIENTS.)
    1 TBSP. ONION, FINELY CHOPPED (MAY USE 1 TSP. DEHYDRATED ONION)
    ½ TSP. DRY MUSTARD
    1 TSP. WORCESTERSHIRE SAUCE (OPTIONAL)
    ½ CUP BUTTERED BREAD CRUMBS

Cook macaroni in boiling water until tender; drain.

In a large saucepan, melt butter and work in flour until smooth. Gradually add milk, heating to thicken. Stir well, until a medium thin white sauce has formed. Add grated cheese, onion, mustard, and Worcestershire sauce, reserving a little of the grated cheese for topping. Add macaroni. Place in a buttered casserole. Top with buttered crumbs, remaining cheese, and a dash of paprika. Bake at 350° F about 25-30 minutes, until the top is browned.

Shepherd's pie

    1 SMALL ONION, CHOPPED
    1½ CUPS DICED COOKED HAM OR BEEF **OR** 1 PINT CANNED MEAT, DRAINED
    ½ CUP DICED, COOKED CARROTS **OR** ½-PINT CANNED CARROTS
    1 CUP LEFTOVER GRAVY
    ¼ TSP. SALT
    PEPPER
    1 CUP HOT MASHED POTATOES
    2 TBSP. BUTTER
    GRATED CHEESE TO TASTE

Sauté onion until golden and tender. Add meat, carrots, gravy, and seasonings. Mix together and pour into a greased baking dish. Cover with mashed potatoes. Top with dabs of butter and grated cheese. Bake at 400° F for 10-20 minutes or until golden brown.

Buttered noodle ring

Cook 1 package or 1 batch of homemade noodles in boiling broth or water. Add ¼ cup butter to hot, drained noodles; stir well. Pack into a ring mold about 9 inches in diameter. Let stand a few minutes to set up, then unmold onto a large platter; fill center with creamed meat or vegetables. Top with grated cheese. This is a tasty, filling, and easy dish to serve the family.

Spaghetti with meat sauce

½- ¾ lb. ground meat or 1 pint canned ground meat, drained
1 stalk celery, chopped
½ lb. chopped or sliced mushrooms (either fresh or canned)
1 medium onion, chopped
1 can/jar (16 oz.) tomato sauce
1 can/jar (8 oz.) chopped tomatoes
1 tsp. oregano
1 tsp. dried basil
1 tsp. garlic powder
½ cup brown sugar (if sauce is quite acidic)
salt and pepper to taste (optional)
½ lb. spaghetti noodles

In large skillet, brown ground meat, celery, mushrooms, and onion. Add tomato sauce, chopped tomatoes, and seasonings. Simmer over low heat until cooked down nice and thick. Taste and add brown sugar, if necessary.

Boil ½ lb. spaghetti noodles in lightly salted boiling water until tender but yet firm. Drain. Either pour spaghetti sauce over pasta and stir well or serve pasta hot with spaghetti sauce served over it. You may also add sliced ripe olives and Parmesan cheese.

Noodle and ham casserole

1 pkg. (8-9 oz.) wide noodles, cooked
2 Tbsp. butter
2 Tbsp. flour
⅔ cup milk (or more)
2 cups chopped ham, cooked or 1 pint canned ham pieces, undrained
2 Tbsp. finely chopped onion
½ cup buttered bread crumbs
salt
pepper
paprika

Cook noodles and drain. In a large saucepan, melt butter then mix in flour. While heating, add milk and stir constantly, to make a medium white sauce, adding more milk, as needed. Add cooked ham and onion. Put noodles in buttered casserole dish, then pour ham and sauce over them. Stir lightly to blend. Top with crumbs and salt, pepper, and paprika, to taste. Bake at 350° F about 25 minutes or until top is browned.

Steak pie

- 1 unbaked double-crust pie pastry
- 2 cups cooked cubed steak
- 2 cups gravy made from beef broth or leftover steak gravy
- 3 carrots, sliced and cooked **or** ½-pint canned carrot slices, drained
- 4 medium potatoes, cooked and diced **or** ½-pint canned potato chunks, drained
- ½ cup fresh or frozen peas **or** ½-pint canned peas, drained
- 1 small onion, sliced
- parsley, fresh or dried, chopped
- salt and pepper to taste
- 1 tsp. Worcestershire sauce (optional)

Mix all ingredients together and pour into an unbaked pie crust. Put top on and pinch edges together to seal. Tip edges upward to keep gravy in pie, not on oven bottom. Cut several slices into top crust so steam can vent. Bake at 375° F for 30 minutes on a cookie sheet to prevent spills.

Tip: If you brush the top crust with butter, you'll get a pretty, flaky crust.

Chicken or turkey pot pie

- 1 unbaked double-crust pie pastry
- 2 cups cooked boneless chicken, cut up **or** 1 pint boneless chicken meat, home canned, drained
- 3 carrots, cooked and sliced **or** ½-pint sliced canned carrots, drained
- 4 medium potatoes **or** ½-pint canned potato chunks, drained
- ½ cup fresh or frozen peas **or** ½-pint canned peas, drained
- 1 medium onion, chopped **or** 1 Tbsp. dehydrated onion flakes
- 2½ cups chicken gravy made from chicken broth or bouillon

Lay bottom crust in pie tin. Mix all ingredients together and pour into unbaked pie shell. Put top crust on. Pinch edges together to seal, turning up the outer edge so the gravy doesn't leak. Make a few slits in the top of the crust to let steam out. Put pie on cookie sheet and bake at 350° F until done.

Tip: If you brush the top with butter, you'll get a pretty, flaky top crust.

Tamale pie

Meat mixture:
- ½ lb. ground meat
- 1 medium onion, chopped
- 1 medium green pepper, seeded and chopped
- 2 tsp. mild powdered chile (not chili powder, but ground chile peppers, if available)
- 2½ cups tomato sauce
- 1 can (14 oz.) whole corn, drained **or** 1 pint whole corn, drained

In large frying pan, brown ground meat. Add chopped onions and green peppers. Stir in chile powder (or chili powder if you don't have powdered chiles). Drain off excess grease. Stir in tomato sauce and about ¾ of the drained corn. Remove from heat.

Topping:
- ½ CUP CORNMEAL
- ½ CUP FLOUR
- ¼ CUP WHITE SUGAR OR HONEY
- 2 TSP. BAKING POWDER
- 1 TSP. SALT
- 1 EGG, SLIGHTLY BEATEN
- 1 CUP MILK

Add dry ingredients together in bowl: cornmeal, flour, sugar, baking powder, and salt. Mix well. Stir in egg and milk. Add remaining drained corn. Add more milk, if necessary, to make a thick but pourable batter. Pour meat mixture into casserole and top with batter. Bake at 350° F until top turns a golden brown. Serve hot with butter, sour cream, and salsa if you wish.

Lasagna

- 1 LB. GROUND BEEF **OR** 2 PINTS CANNED GROUND MEAT, DRAINED
- ¾ CUP CHOPPED ONION
- 2 TSP. SALT
- 1 TSP. GARLIC POWDER
- 1 TSP. OREGANO
- 1 TSP. BASIL
- 1 CAN (16 OZ.) TOMATOES **OR** 1 PINT CANNED TOMATOES, UNDRAINED
- 1 CAN (16 OZ.) TOMATO SAUCE **OR** 1 PINT CANNED TOMATO SAUCE
- 8-10 OZ. WIDE LASAGNA NOODLES (ABOUT ⅔ PACKAGE)
- 1 LB. COTTAGE OR RICOTTA CHEESE
- ½ LB. MOZZARELLA CHEESE
- 1 CUP GRATED PARMESAN CHEESE

In a large skillet, brown meat and onion in a little oil. Add the spices, tomatoes, and tomato sauce. Simmer uncovered. Meanwhile, cook lasagna noodles in boiling water until just limp. Drain. Cool to handling. In a 13x9x2-inch pan, spread about 1 cup of sauce. Then layer lasagna noodles, sauce, ricotta (or cottage cheese), mozzarella, then a layer of noodles, then more sauce, ricotta, Parmesan cheese, more noodles, sauce, more cheese, and finally more sauce and top with mozzarella cheese. Bake at 350° F for 40-50 minutes until lightly browned. Allow to stand 15 minutes before cutting.

Jambalaya

Mom spent some of her younger years in Virginia, then Florida, before moving to Montana. Somewhere along the way, she picked up this recipe, which was written by hand on notebook paper, eighty years ago or longer. She gave this family recipe to me and we've enjoyed it for years. I never make it without wondering how her life in the South as a child was and how new and different her experiences must have been after growing up in Michigan.

> 2 Tbsp. cooking oil
> 1 cup minced onion
> 1 cup minced green pepper
> 4 garlic cloves, minced
> 12 small pork sausage links, cut into 1-inch lengths
> 1½ cups cubed cooked chicken **or** ½-pint canned chicken, drained
> 1½ cups cubed cooked ham **or** ½-pint canned ham, drained
> 1 can (28 oz.) tomatoes, cut up and juice reserved **or** 1 quart tomatoes with ½ cup juice discarded and the rest reserved
> 1 cup uncooked long grain rice
> 1 can (28 oz.) chicken broth **or** 1 pint canned broth
> 3 Tbsp. chopped parsley
> 1 tsp. salt
> 1 tsp. black pepper
> ¾ tsp. dried thyme

In a heavy skillet, heat oil over medium heat. Sauté onion, green pepper, garlic, and sausage until vegetables are tender. Add chicken and ham; cook 5 minutes longer. Add all remaining ingredients. Pour into a large casserole dish. Bake, covered, at 350° F for 1 hour or until rice is tender and liquid absorbed.

Chicken (or turkey) and biscuits

Biscuit dough:
> 2 cups flour
> 4 tsp. baking powder
> 2 Tbsp. sugar
> 1 tsp. salt
> ½ cups shortening
> 1 cup milk

Mix biscuit dough by mixing dry ingredients, then cutting shortening in to resemble coarse meal. Add milk to make a soft but workable dough. Roll out on floured surface and cut into rounds. (I use a regular canning jar ring.)

Filling:
> 1½ cups cubed, cooked chicken or turkey
> 2 cups mixed vegetables (carrots, onions, potatoes, peas, etc.)
> 2 cups chicken or turkey gravy from bouillon or broth

In a casserole dish, mix cooked chicken or turkey, drained vegetables, and gravy. Top with biscuits and bake, uncovered, at 350° F for 15 minutes or until biscuits are golden brown and the gravy is steaming.

Midwest corn and bacon casserole

1 LB. BACON, DICED (MAY USE ½ CUP BACON-FLAVORED BITS OR TVPs)
2 CUPS BREAD CRUMBS
¼ CUP CHOPPED ONION
½ CUP GREEN PEPPER, SEEDED AND CHOPPED
2 CANS (16 OZ. EACH) OF CREAM STYLE CORN **OR** 1 PINT HOME-CANNED CREAMED CORN, DRAINED
2 EGGS, BEATEN

In a skillet, fry the bacon until lightly browned. Remove and set aside. Pour ¼ cup bacon drippings over bread crumbs and toss. Set aside. Discard all but 2 Tbsp. of remaining drippings. In 2 Tbsp. bacon drippings, sauté onion and green pepper until tender. Add corn and bacon pieces, then eggs. Pour into a casserole dish and sprinkle with bread crumbs. Bake at 350° F for 25 minutes or until bubbly and bread crumbs are browned.

Turkey rice casserole

2 CUPS CUBED COOKED TURKEY OR CHICKEN **OR** 1 PINT CANNED TURKEY, DRAINED
3 CUPS HOT COOKED RICE
1 MEDIUM GREEN PEPPER, SEEDED AND CHOPPED
1 MEDIUM ONION, CHOPPED
1 CUP SHREDDED MOZZARELLA CHEESE OR MONTEREY JACK
4 EGGS, SLIGHTLY BEATEN
2½ CUPS MILK (MAY USE POWDERED MILK, RECONSTITUTED)
1 TSP. SALT
1 TSP. DRY MUSTARD
½ TSP. DRIED BASIL
½ TSP. RED PEPPER SAUCE
⅛ TSP. PEPPER
¼ CUP GRATED PARMESAN CHEESE

Mix turkey, rice, green pepper, onion, and mozzarella (or Monterey Jack) cheese. Spread into a casserole dish. Mix eggs, milk, seasonings and pour over rice mixture. Sprinkle top with Parmesan cheese and bake, uncovered, at 300° F for about 50 minutes until set and the top is nicely browned. Let stand 10 minutes before cutting.

Wild rice supreme

2 CUPS WATER

1 CUP CHICKEN OR TURKEY BROTH

1½ CUPS UNCOOKED WILD RICE

2 TBSP. BUTTER OR MARGARINE

½ LB. SLICED MUSHROOMS

½ CUP CHOPPED PARSLEY

½ CUP CHOPPED PEPPERS

½ CUP CHOPPED ONIONS

1½ CUPS CHICKEN OR TURKEY CUBES, COOKED OR 1 PINT CHICKEN OR TURKEY CUBES, DRAINED

1 CUP FRESH, FROZEN OR DEHYDRATED PEAS OR ½-PINT CANNED PEAS, DRAINED

1½ CUPS MAYONNAISE

Mix broth with water and add rice. Bring to a boil, covered, then reduce heat and simmer until moisture is absorbed. Meanwhile, sauté mushrooms in butter. Combine all ingredients when rice is tender and place in a casserole dish. Top with grated cheese if you wish and bake at 325° F for about 50 minutes or until top is nicely browned.

Chile relleno bake

½ LB. GROUND BEEF OR 1 PINT CANNED GROUND MEAT, DRAINED

½ LB. CHORIZO OR BULK PORK SAUSAGE OR 1 PINT CANNED GROUND SAUSAGE, DRAINED

1 CUP ONION, CHOPPED OR ¼ CUP DEHYDRATED ONION

2 CLOVES GARLIC, MINCED

2 CANS (4 OZ. EACH) WHOLE GREEN CHILES, DRAINED AND SEEDED OR 1 PINT CANNED CHILE PEPPERS, DRAINED

2 CUPS SHREDDED SHARP CHEESE, DIVIDED

4 EGGS

¼ CUP FLOUR

1½ CUPS MILK (MAY USE POWDERED MILK, RECONSTITUTED)

½ TSP. SALT

HOT SAUCE, TABASCO, OR CHILE PASTE TO TASTE

In a large skillet, crumble ground beef and chorizo or sausage. Fry over medium heat, stirring to brown meat and break into small pieces. Add onion and garlic; cook until onion is tender. Drain off excess grease. Lay half of the chiles in a casserole dish, top with 1½ cups of cheese. Add the meat mixture and top with remaining chiles; set aside. Beat eggs and flour together; add milk, salt, and hot sauce. Mix well. Pour egg mixture over casserole. Bake uncovered at 350° F for about 40 minutes. Spread the rest of the cheese on top and let melt. Let stand after removing from oven for a few minutes to let set well.

Homemade pizza

This pizza is a long-time homestead and neighborhood favorite. When visitors hear I'm making a pizza, they tend to hang around until supper time. I love this. In fact, a good friend and neighbor of ours, back in Sturgeon Lake, Minnesota, would come for a visit and ask, "When are you going to make another pizza?"

And, of course, I'd always answer, "Why, right now. You can stay for a little, can't you?"

Crust:
- 2 CUPS FLOUR
- 1 TBSP. SUGAR
- A PINCH EACH OF GARLIC POWDER, BASIL, AND OREGANO
- 1 PKG. (2¼ TSP.) DRY YEAST
- WARM WATER
- CORNMEAL
- OLIVE OIL

Mix all dry ingredients in mixing bowl. Slowly add warm water until dough hangs together in a soft, yet not sticky, ball. Knead in bowl for a few minutes. Toss a handful of cornmeal on the dough and in the bowl, then knead lightly again to coat dough ball. Cover with a warm, damp kitchen towel and let rise at least 15 minutes. Grease pizza pan or cookie sheet with olive oil, oiling your hands as well. Work dough into a circular piece with your hands, then place on pan and continue pressing the dough out to the edges of the pan. Make a small ridge on the outside of the crust to hold in any juices during baking.

Pizza sauce:
- 1 CAN (10-12 OZ.) OF TOMATO SAUCE **OR** ¾-PINT THICK TOMATO SAUCE
- 1 TBSP. BROWN SUGAR
- 1 TSP. GARLIC, MINCED
- 1 TSP. BASIL
- 1 TSP. OREGANO

Top dough with tomato sauce, then sprinkle on brown sugar, minced garlic, and spices. Blend slightly with the back of a spoon. Lay toppings on, and top with plenty of cheese. Bake at 375° F until topping is nicely brown in spots. Remove and let rest for 10 minutes before cutting or the cheese will pull away when you cut.

Toppings might include: black or green olives, mushrooms, sliced or sun-dried tomatoes, onion, sweet green pepper, pepperoni, Italian sausage crumbles, mozzarella, and Parmesan cheese.

Beef enchiladas

1 Tbsp. shortening
1 lb. ground beef OR 2 pints canned ground meat, drained
3 Tbsp. flour
1 can (8 oz.) tomato sauce OR ½-pint canned tomato sauce
1 cup water
2 Tbsp. chili powder or for hotter chile taste, use 1 Tbsp. chile paste
Salt to taste
¾ tsp. garlic powder
12 corn tortillas
1 lb. cheddar cheese, grated
1 large onion, finely chopped

Melt shortening in heavy skillet. Add the ground meat and brown. Sprinkle meat with flour; mix in skillet. Add tomato sauce and 1 cup water. Mix ½ cup water with the chili powder to form a smooth paste; add to the meat mixture. Add salt and garlic powder to taste. Cook over medium heat, uncovered, until it is of gravy consistency. Cover and simmer over very low heat. Add more water if the chili gravy becomes too thick.

Dip tortillas one at a time in the hot chili gravy with a wide metal spatula. The tortillas will become pliable almost immediately, which will make rolling the enchiladas easier. Soaking too long will cause the tortillas to fall apart.

Place a good sprinkling of grated cheese and minced onion and about a tablespoon of the meat mixture to one side of the center of the tortilla. Roll tortilla tightly around the filling and place loose side down in a glass casserole baking dish. For best results, place the enchiladas in a row with sides touching. When all enchiladas have been formed, pour the remaining hot chili gravy over all, and sprinkle generously with grated cheese, and top with chopped onion. Bake at 350° F until the cheese is melted and enchiladas are bubbling. Serve immediately. I serve them with fresh salsa and sour cream.

Tuna surprise

6 medium potatoes, sliced
1 medium can sliced mushrooms, OR ½-pint canned mushrooms, drained OR 1 cup fresh sliced mushrooms
1 tsp. salt
1 cup milk
1½ cups flaked, drained tuna
½ cup grated cheddar cheese
2 Tbsp. chopped green pepper
1 cup sweet corn, fresh or canned, drained
¼ tsp. pepper
1 cup buttered bread crumbs

Mix ingredients, except for bread crumbs, then pour into a greased casserole. Sprinkle crumbs over the top. Bake at 350° F for about 1 hour.

Baked Spanish rice

¼ CUP BUTTER OR MARGARINE
¾ CUP CHOPPED ONION
1 CUP CHOPPED GREEN PEPPER
1 CUP CHOPPED PIMENTO OR SWEET RED PEPPER, IF DESIRED
¾ CUP DICED CELERY
2¾ CUPS CANNED TOMATOES
¼ TSP. GARLIC POWDER
½ TSP. CHILI POWDER
1 TSP. SALT
2 TSP. BROWN SUGAR
⅛ TSP. RED PEPPER
2½ CUPS COOKED RICE

Melt butter in large skillet; add onion, green and red (or pimento) peppers, and celery and sauté until tender. Add tomatoes and simmer covered for 15 minutes. Add seasonings and rice and pour into a casserole dish. Bake at 350° F for about 20 minutes, covered.

Vegetable casserole

1 MEDIUM HEAD CABBAGE, COARSELY SLICED
3 MEDIUM POTATOES, PEELED AND SLICED THICKLY
4 CARROTS, PEELED AND SLICED
2 SMALL SUMMER SQUASH
3 MEDIUM ONIONS, SLICED THICKLY
½ LB. LEAN GROUND MEAT, RAW
SALT
PEPPER
CATSUP

In a roasting pan or casserole dish, put a thick layer of fresh, coarsely sliced cabbage. Next, a layer of potatoes, thickly sliced, followed by a layer of carrots, then summer squash, then onions; layer vegetables of your choice until dish is full. Top with crumbled uncooked ground meat. Sprinkle salt, pepper, and any other seasonings of your choice on top. Top with a layer of catsup. Cover tightly and bake at 300° F for about 1½ hours.

Hot Cha

Hot Cha was one of Mom's favorite recipes and one I loved as a child. It takes me back to the days when I'd come home from grade school, finding Hot Cha in the oven and Mom ironing clothes while listening to a Tiger's baseball game.

1 PKG. (8 OZ.) LARGE EGG NOODLES OR EQUIVALENT OF HOMEMADE NOODLES
1 LB. COOKED LEAN PORK, CUBED
1 GREEN PEPPER, SEEDED AND CHOPPED
1 SWEET BELL OR PIMENTO PEPPER, CHOPPED
1 CAN (16 OZ.) WHOLE KERNEL CORN OR 1 PINT CORN, UNDRAINED
1 CAN CHICKEN RICE SOUP OR 1 PINT CANNED CHICKEN BROTH WITH RICE
½ LB. SLICED MUSHROOMS
1 TBSP. BUTTER
1 CUP BUTTERED BREAD CRUMBS

Cook noodles in salted water; drain. Lightly brown pork in butter. Add peppers and sauté until tender. Add water from corn. Mix all ingredients except butter and breadcrumbs; season to taste. Put in greased casserole. Cover with buttered bread crumbs. Bake about 30 minutes until top is nicely browned.

Zella's Goo

This recipe came from my Dad's aunts Eloyda and Ada. We were served this yummy recipe when we went to visit, and even as a three year old, I still recall how good it tasted. When my hens are laying like mad, I make it often.

2 CUPS SLICED FRESH MUSHROOMS OR 1 PINT CANNED MUSHROOMS OR 2 SMALL STORE CANS, DRAINED
1½ CUPS CELERY, CHOPPED OR SLICED FINELY
1 GREEN PEPPER, CHOPPED
3 TBSP. BUTTER
3 TBSP. FLOUR
1 CUP MILK
½ LB. GRATED CHEDDAR CHEESE
4 EGGS, HARD-BOILED AND PEELED
BUTTERED BREAD CRUMBS

Sauté mushrooms, celery, and green pepper in small amount of butter until tender. Add 3 Tbsp. butter and melt; stir in flour. Add milk enough to make a medium white sauce. Add cheddar cheese and stir well, heating until melted. Add chopped hard-boiled eggs. Pour into a casserole if you wish and top with buttered bread crumbs, baking at 350° F for about 15 minutes or serve from the pan over crisp Chinese noodles.

Soups and stews

All winter long some type of soup or stew is found slowly cooking on the back of my wood-burning kitchen range. The old kitchen range is the forerunner of the crock pot. Folks come and go at our place, and there are always a couple of ladles of hot soup or stew, ready for whenever someone comes in from outdoors with a healthy appetite and cold fingers. The fun thing about soups and stews is that you can add what you want or what you have and keep adding ingredients as the pot gets low. I can dump in another quart of beef stock, another half head of shredded cabbage, a couple more carrots, another pint of canned meat, or more chopped onion. Whatever I add blends with the ingredients already simmering away merrily on the back of the stove. Soups and stews are especially good served with hot, homemade bread or rolls.

Buffalo Bill's chili

2 Tbsp. vegetable oil
2 cloves garlic, crushed
1-2 cups diced onion
1 cup green pepper, diced
2 cups cooked, diced beef or 1 pint cubed stewing meat with broth
½ lb. ground beef or 1 pint canned ground meat
2 cans (16 oz. each) diced or chopped tomatoes with liquid or 1 quart canned diced tomatoes
1 can (16 oz.) tomato juice or 1 pint tomato sauce
1 can (16 oz.) dark red kidney beans, drained or 1 pint canned kidney beans, drained
1 can (16 oz.) pinto beans, drained or 1 pint canned pinto beans, drained
2 tsp. chili powder (or more, to taste)
2 tsp. chile paste (optional)
1 tsp. salt (optional)

In a Dutch oven or heavy kettle, sauté garlic and onion in oil. Add green pepper and sauté until tender. Combine remaining ingredients and simmer for 30 minutes.

Hearty potato soup

6 Tbsp. butter or margarine
1 onion, chopped
6 Tbsp. flour
1½ cups milk
1 tsp. salt
½ tsp. pepper
4 cups cooked, diced potatoes
1 cup cooked, diced carrots
1 cup cooked, sliced or diced celery
grated cheese (optional)

In a large saucepan, sauté onions in butter, then add flour, stirring well. Slowly add milk, salt, and pepper to make a medium sauce. Gently stir in vegetables. Add more milk, if needed, to make the soup the desired consistency. You may also add grated cheese.

Hearty farm soup

2 Tbsp. olive oil or shortening
1 lb. stewing beef or 1 quart canned stewing meat with broth
2 cans (16 oz. each) whole tomatoes or 1 quart whole tomatoes with juice
4 cups thinly sliced cabbage or 1 quart drained, sliced cabbage
1½ cups chopped onion
2 cups sliced carrots or 1 pint canned sliced carrots, drained
1 cup sliced celery or ½ pint canned sliced celery
¼ cup green pepper, seeded and chopped
1 can (8 oz.) lima or butter beans, drained or ½ pint canned limas, drained
1 can (8 oz.) green beans, drained or ½ pint canned green beans, drained
1 can (16 oz.) peas, drained or 1 pint canned peas, drained
1 can (16 oz.) tomato sauce or 1 pint canned tomato sauce
2 Tbsp. chopped parsley
½ tsp. cloves
salt and pepper to taste

Brown stewing beef in oil. Add tomatoes, then the rest of the ingredients. Gently mix in a stockpot and simmer for 30 minutes.

Brunswick stew

¼ lb. thick sliced bacon, cut into 1-inch pieces
1 whole chicken
2 cups water
1 cup potatoes, cubed

    2 cans (16 oz. each) tomatoes with juice or 1 quart canned tomatoes with juice
    2 cups butter beans or limas or 1 pint canned butter beans or limas, drained
    2 Tbsp. onion, chopped fine
    1½ cups okra (optional)
    1 can (16 oz.) whole kernel corn or 1 pint canned corn
    4 tsp. salt
    1 Tbsp. sugar
    ½ lemon, seeded and sliced thin
    1 tsp. celery seed
    ½ tsp. ground cloves
    1 tsp. pepper
    ¼ tsp. cayenne pepper

Cut bacon in pieces and fry until crisp and brown. Cut chicken into pieces and put into kettle with water. Cover and cook slowly until chicken falls from bones, adding more water if necessary to prevent scorching. Remove chicken from bones; discard skin and bones. Add vegetables, bacon, and rest of ingredients to chicken broth. Bring to a boil and reduce heat; simmer for 30 minutes.

Old-fashioned cream of tomato soup

    2 cans (16 oz. each) diced tomatoes or 1 quart diced tomatoes
    1 cup chicken broth
    1 Tbsp. butter
    2 Tbsp. sugar
    1 Tbsp. chopped onion
    a pinch of baking soda
    2 cups cream (or milk)

Mix tomatoes, chicken broth, butter, sugar, onions, and soda in a large saucepan. Simmer about 30 minutes. Gently heat cream or milk; do *not* boil! Add cream to hot tomato mixture and serve.

Tomato corn chowder

    4 bacon strips, diced (may substitute 2 Tbsp. bacon bits or TVPs)
    1 large onion, chopped
    2 cans (15 oz. each) whole kernel corn, undrained or 2 pints canned whole corn, undrained
    2 cans (14 oz. each) diced tomatoes, undrained or 1 quart canned diced tomatoes, undrained
    4 medium potatoes, peeled and diced or 1 pint canned diced potatoes

In a large saucepan, sauté bacon pieces until crisp. Remove to paper towels. Drain off grease, reserving 1 Tbsp. In the drippings, sauté onion until tender. Add the corn, tomatoes, and potatoes. Cook over medium heat for 30 minutes or until potatoes are tender. Sprinkle with the bacon pieces.

Creamy wild rice soup

    4 cups water
    ½ tsp. salt
    ½ cup uncooked wild rice
    3 Tbsp. chopped green onions
    ¼ cup carrot, grated
    6 Tbsp. butter or margarine
    ⅓ cup flour
    2 cans (15 oz. each) chicken broth
    ½ cup cooked and diced ham
    ¼ tsp. pepper
    1 cup half and half, cream, or milk

In a large saucepan, bring water and salt to a boil. Add rice. Reduce heat to simmer, cover, and cook for 50-55 minutes or until tender. Remove from heat. Let stand for 10 minutes; drain and set aside.

In a Dutch oven, sauté the onions and carrot in butter for 1-2 minutes. Stir in flour until smooth. Gradually add broth. Heat while stirring until thickened. Reduce the heat. Add ham, pepper, and wild rice. Cover and simmer for 5 minutes. Add cream and heat (do not boil), then serve.

Italian vegetable soup

    2 cans (14 oz. each) chicken broth or 1 quart chicken broth
    1 medium potato, peeled and cubed
    1 medium onion, chopped
    1 medium carrot, chopped
    1 celery rib, chopped
    ½ cup peas (frozen or fresh)
    1 bay leaf
    ½ tsp. basil
    ½ tsp. oregano
    ½ tsp. garlic powder
    ⅛ tsp. pepper
    ½ cup small shell pasta, cooked and drained
    1 can (14 oz.) diced tomatoes, undrained or 1 pint canned diced tomatoes, undrained

In a large saucepan, combine all but pasta and tomatoes. Bring to a boil. Simmer for 15-20 minutes or until vegetables are tender. Add the pasta and tomatoes; heat thoroughly. Discard bay leaf before serving.

Split pea soup

    1 lb. dry split peas
    2½ quarts cold water

¼ cup diced ham or bacon or ½-pint canned ham or bacon

1 ham bone with meat

½ cup carrot, chopped

½ cup onion, chopped

2 tsp. salt

1½ tsp. sugar

1 Tbsp. butter

½ cup cream or milk (optional)

The night before: Place dried peas and cold water in a kettle; cover and soak overnight.

The next day, add ham/bacon, carrots, onions, and salt to peas and cook, covered, simmering gently for about 2 hours. Remove ham bone. Remove any meat from ham bone; dice and add to hot soup. Add sugar, butter, and cream or milk, if desired. Serve.

Homemade "cream of" soups

You can begin any "cream of" soup with the basic white sauce mix, found in the pantry mixes section, adding hot water to dry mix, and then adding any of the following: diced chicken (cream of chicken), chopped mushrooms (cream of mushroom), chopped tender asparagus (cream of asparagus), or chopped celery (cream of celery), etc. Add any seasonings you wish: salt, pepper, thyme, etc.

Or you can easily start from scratch; my homemade "cream of" soups are almost as fast to make from scratch as it is to open a can!

3 Tbsp. butter

3 Tbsp. flour

½ tsp. salt

milk

In a saucepan, melt butter then stir in flour and salt, stirring while heating to mix well. Add milk while continuing to heat, stirring to thicken. Add as much milk as you wish until the soup is the right consistency. Add cooked, chopped meat or vegetables to make whatever variety of soup you wish. Add any seasonings and heat thoroughly.

French onion soup

3 Tbsp. butter

2 cups onion, sliced

4½ cups beef stock or 1 quart canned beef stock

salt and pepper

Worcestershire sauce

Heat butter, add onions and sauté until lightly browned. Add beef stock and bring to a boil. Simmer 20 minutes. Season to taste with salt, pepper, and Worcestershire sauce. Serve with hot French bread.

Fish chowder

  2 lbs. boneless fish fillets
  ¼ cup bacon, diced
  ⅓ cup onion, chopped
  2 cups potatoes, diced
  1½ tsp. salt
  ⅛ tsp. pepper
  ⅛ tsp. thyme
  1½ cups water
  2 Tbsp. butter
  2 Tbsp. flour
  4 cups milk

 Remove any skin or bones from fish and cut into cubes. Fry bacon pieces in large saucepan until almost browned. Add onion and saute for about 5 minutes. Add fish, potatoes, seasonings, and water; cover and cook gently about 15-20 minutes or until fish and potatoes are tender. In another saucepan, melt butter and stir in flour to make a paste. Slowly add milk and stir to thicken. Add to fish mixture and heat well, stirring gently. Serve hot with crackers.

New England clam chowder

  2 lbs. clams, shelled
  ¼ cup bacon, diced
  ¾ cup onion, sliced
  3 cups potatoes, sliced or diced
  2 cups cold water
  2½ cups milk, scalded
  ½ cup cream
  2 Tbsp. butter

 Drain and chop clams, reserving liquid. Sauté bacon over low heat until almost crisp; add onions and continue cooking 3 minutes. Add potatoes, water, and clam liquid; cover and simmer for 10 minutes; add chopped clams, scalded milk, and cream. Cook gently about 20 minutes or until potatoes are tender; add butter.

Oyster stew

  1 lb. oysters, shelled
  ¼ cup butter
  ¼ cup cold water
  4 cups milk, scalded
  ½ tsp. salt
  ⅛ tsp. pepper
  1 tsp. Worcestershire sauce (optional)

Clean and pick over oysters, reserving liquid. Heat butter; add oysters, oyster liquid, and water; simmer gently until edges of oysters begin to curl. Add scalded milk, seasonings, and Worcestershire sauce. Serve at once. If a richer stew is desired, substitute ½ cup cream for ½ cup of the milk.

Minestrone

¼ CUP BACON, DICED
¾ CUP ONION, CHOPPED
¾ CUP CARROTS, DICED
¾ CUP TURNIPS, DICED
1 CUP CABBAGE, SHREDDED
½ CUP CELERY, SLICED
1 CLOVE GARLIC, MINCED
5 CUPS OR 2 QUARTS BEEF STOCK
1 TSP. SALT
¼ TSP. PEPPER
1½ CUPS POTATOES, DICED
¾ CUP PEAS
⅓ CUP MACARONI, BROKEN IN SMALL PIECES
2 CUPS TOMATOES, STEWED
1 CUP RED KIDNEY BEANS, COOKED OR CANNED
1 CUP PARMESAN CHEESE, GRATED

Sauté bacon slightly; add onion, cook 2 minutes longer, then add carrots, turnips, cabbage, tomatoes, kidney beans, celery, and garlic.

Add soup stock and seasonings; simmer for about 15 minutes. Add potatoes and continue cooking about 10 minutes longer. Add peas and macaroni pieces. Simmer 10-15 minutes until all vegetables and the macaroni are tender. Just before serving, add grated cheese; stir over low heat until cheese is melted.

Bean soup

2 CUPS NAVY OR GREAT NORTHERN BEANS (DRY)
½ LB. COOKED BACON, CUT INTO PIECES, OR DICED HAM
½ CUP ONION, CHOPPED
½ CUP DICED POTATOES
1 TSP. SALT
¼ TSP. PEPPER

Wash beans, cover with water, and soak overnight. Rinse and again cover with water. Add bacon pieces or diced ham. Add onion, potato, and seasonings. Bring to a boil, covered, then reduce heat and simmer until beans are tender. Add more water if necessary. If desired, milk or cream may be added just before bean soup is served.

Chicken noodle soup

For this recipe, you can either opt for regular wide store-bought noodles or easily make your own, which taste tons better and only contain three ingredients: flour, salt, and egg yolk, besides water. Homemade noodles tend to thicken the soup a little, which I love.

Noodles:
- 1 CUP FLOUR
- PINCH OF SALT
- 1 EGG YOLK, SLIGHTLY BEATEN
- 2 TBSP. WATER

Sift flour; measure; add salt and sift again. In bowl, mound flour, making an indentation in the top. Mix egg yolk and water and pour into the middle of the mound of flour/salt. Stir slowly into the flour mixture. If the dough seems too dry to handle, gradually add a little more water, just a bit at a time. When it forms a ball that holds together without being sticky, turn out on lightly-floured board and knead about 5 minutes or until smooth. Divide dough in 3 parts; cover 2 parts and roll out one quite thin. Roll up jelly-roll fashion then slice evenly into narrow strips. Separate and straighten strips; let stand until drying, then either hang over a dowel rack or lay on baking racks to finish drying. Repeat with other two balls of dough.

Soup:
- 6 CUPS CHICKEN BROTH OR 1 QUART PLUS 1 PINT HOME-CANNED BROTH
- ½ CUP DICED CARROTS
- 1 MEDIUM ONION, DICED
- ½ CUP CELERY, DICED
- ½ TSP. RUBBED SAGE
- ½ TSP. PEPPER
- SALT TO TASTE
- 1 SMALL BAY LEAF
- PARSLEY, CHOPPED OR CHIVES, CHOPPED FOR ADDITIONAL COLOR
- ½ CUP COOKED CHICKEN MEAT OR ½-PINT HOME-CANNED CHICKEN MEAT, UNDRAINED

Heat broth to boiling, then reduce to simmer. Add vegetables and seasonings. Simmer 5 minutes, then add cut up cooked chicken meat. Simmer for 10 minutes longer and remove bay leaf. Add as many noodles as you wish then turn up the heat and boil for 10 minutes, covered, or until noodles are tender.

Side dishes

Vegetables

Oven-roasted potato wedges

> 8 SMALL POTATOES, SCRUBBED WELL
> 2 TBSP. OLIVE OIL
> 1 TSP. GARLIC POWDER
> 1 TBSP. ONION POWDER
> ½ TSP. SALT
> ⅛ TSP. PEPPER

Cut potatoes, lengthwise, into wedges. Place in a greased casserole pan. Drizzle with olive oil. Mix seasonings and sprinkle on potatoes. Stir to coat all sides with oil and seasonings. Bake, uncovered, at 375° F about 45 minutes, turning once so all sides are crisp. When potatoes are tender, serve.

Creamed new potatoes

This recipe is sort of a tradition around here. I go out and "steal" a few new potatoes from around the edges of a potato plant or two, then go get my peas to top off the basket. I often toss in ⅔ cup of fresh peas to this, just as the potatoes finish simmering. It makes a perfect early summer garden meal and it's one of our very favorites. I can't imagine a summer without creamed new potatoes and peas!

> 10 SMALL NEW POTATOES, WELL SCRUBBED
> 2 TBSP. BUTTER OR MARGARINE
> 2 TBSP. FLOUR
> 1 CUP MILK (OR MORE)
> SEVERAL FRIED BACON STRIPS, CRUMBLED OR ¼ CUP BACON BITS OR TVPS
> 1 TSP. ONION POWDER

Boil new potatoes in salted water until tender. Meanwhile, fry bacon strips in skillet until crisp. Remove from skillet, cool, and crumble. To skillet, add butter and flour with drippings from bacon. Stir well to blend. Slowly add milk, stirring and heating, to thicken. Make a medium white sauce. Add onion powder. Pour over potatoes and slowly heat for a few minutes, add crumbled bacon, and serve.

Pan-fried potatoes

    5 strips of bacon, diced
    5 or 6 medium potatoes, peeled and sliced
    3 Tbsp. olive oil or shortening
    1 medium onion, sliced
    salt and pepper

Fry bacon dices until nearly crisp in large skillet. Remove from pan, reserving drippings. Peel and slice potatoes. Add oil or shortening to skillet. Heat to medium hot but not smoking. Slide potatoes in, being careful to avoid spatters. Arrange potatoes in layer covering all of the pan bottom. Fry until potatoes are just getting golden. Turn over and fry other side. Then stir several times to make sure all are cooked and tender. Add onions and bacon and continue cooking, just until onions are tender. Season to suit your taste.

Mashed potatoes

    6 medium potatoes, peeled
    1 tsp. salt
    2 Tbsp. butter or margarine
    ½ cup milk

Cut potatoes into large pieces. Put in large saucepan and cover well with water. Add salt and bring to a boil. Reduce heat and simmer until potatoes are tender but not breaking apart. Drain well. Return to pan and mash. Add butter and continue mashing to eliminate chunks. Add milk and whip potatoes well so they are fluffy and light.

Baked mashed potatoes

    3 cups leftover mashed potatoes
    ½ cup sour cream
    2 Tbsp. melted butter or margarine
    2 Tbsp. chopped chives
    ½ cup shredded cheddar cheese

Mix leftover mashed potatoes and sour cream until smooth. Spoon into greased casserole dish. Drizzle melted butter over potatoes. Sprinkle chopped chives and cheese on top and bake at 350° F until golden brown.

Twice-baked potatoes

    5 medium-sized baking potatoes, scrubbed well
    3 Tbsp. butter
    ½ cup cream or milk
    ½ cup cheddar cheese, grated
    Toppings also may include chopped chives, bacon bits, or herbs

Pierce each potato several times to let steam escape (to avoid exploding potatoes in the oven). Bake at 375° F until done (sharp slender knife pierces potato easily). Let cool a few minutes, then cut each potato in half. Scoop inside out of each potato into a bowl. Mash, adding butter, cream, cheese, and any seasonings to suit your taste. Refill potato shells and return to oven for 5 minutes or until top is starting to brown a little. Before serving, top with more cheese, bacon bits, herbs, or sour cream.

Potato cakes

2 CUPS LEFTOVER MASHED POTATOES
1 EGG, BEATEN
1 TBSP. FLOUR
2 TBSP. CREAM
1 TBSP. MINCED ONION (OR 1 TSP. DEHYDRATED ONION FLAKES)
FLOUR TO COAT
4 TBSP. COOKING OIL OR SHORTENING

In a mixing bowl, mix potatoes, egg, flour, cream, and onion into flat cakes about ½-inch thick. Dip in flour on both sides, then transfer to skillet with hot cooking oil in it. Fry to a golden brown on both sides.

Cheesy potatoes

6 MEDIUM POTATOES, PEELED OR NOT, AS YOU WISH
2 CUPS RECONSTITUTED CASSEROLE MIX
2 CUPS SHREDDED CHEESE
½ CUP BUTTER
1 CUP SOUR CREAM
¼ TSP. PEPPER
1 TSP. ONION POWDER
½ TSP. CELERY SALT

Slice or shred potatoes. Simmer potatoes in water until almost soft, yet firm. Drain. Mix the rest of the ingredients together and fold in potatoes. Put in greased casserole dish and bake at 350° F for 45 minutes. You may top with buttered bread crumbs, before baking, for a crunchy top.

French fries

5 LARGE POTATOES, PEELED OR NOT, AS YOU WISH
OIL OR SHORTENING FOR DEEP FRYER

Scrub or peel potatoes and pat dry with towel. Cut into French fries. Rinse them in a bowl of cold water, then drain. Soak in a bowl of ice water, covered, in the refrigerator for an hour. Drain well and toss dry in clean toweling. Heat deep fryer oil to 350° F. Frying at a lower temperature results in soggy, grease-laden French fries. Fry potatoes until they are golden brown. Dip out and drain on a cookie sheet lined with paper towels. Sprinkle with salt if you wish.

Deep-fried potato boats

 5 LARGE POTATOES, SCRUBBED WELL
 ½ CUP CHEDDAR CHEESE
 ½ CUP BACON BITS OR DICED, CRISP FRIED BACON (OR BACON-FLAVORED TVPs)
 OIL OR SHORTENING FOR DEEP FRYER

Cut raw potatoes in half and with a spoon, scoop out the middle, reserving the "chips." Heat oil in deep fryer to 350° F. Fry a few of the "boats" at a time until they are just starting to become golden on the edges. Drain on paper towels and finish frying the rest of the "boats." Place all of the boats on a cookie sheet. Mix bacon bits and cheddar cheese and put a spoonful in each boat. Put the filled potatoes in the oven and bake at 350° F for 20 minutes or until the cheese is starting to brown and the potatoes are tender. Serve hot with sour cream, if you wish.

Hash brown potatoes

This is an old-time favorite of ours. I always boil a lot more potatoes than I need for a meal so I have plenty of extras left over for hash browns. Luckily, potatoes have always been a bounteous crop for us, so I use a lot of them. And the family always makes short work of these great hash browns. They're so much better than frozen store-bought ones!

 5 MEDIUM POTATOES, PEELED
 3 TBSP. COOKING OIL OR SHORTENING
 1 SMALL ONION, CHOPPED
 SALT AND PEPPER

Boil potatoes and cool or use leftover firm boiled potatoes. Dice or shred. Add oil to large skillet and heat to a medium heat; don't let it smoke. Put potatoes in pan and lightly pack down in a single layer. Sprinkle chopped onion on top and season to taste. Fry bottom layer, then carefully turn the potatoes over to brown the other side. (Sometimes cutting the layer into more easily handled wedges works best for turning.) Serve hot with sour cream or catsup.

Candied carrots

 8 MEDIUM CARROTS, SCRAPED OR PEELED OR 1 QUART CANNED CARROT SLICES
 WATER TO BOIL
 2 TBSP. BUTTER
 ¼ CUP BROWN SUGAR

Slice carrots and simmer in boiling water until tender. Drain off most of the water, saving about ½ cup. Add butter and brown sugar to carrots and simmer, covered, for about 10 minutes. Remove cover and continue cooking. The liquid will cook down, leaving the carrots coated with a glaze. Be sure to stir them so they don't scorch.

Spiced carrots

 6 MEDIUM CARROTS
 2 TBSP. VINEGAR

2 Tbsp. sugar

¼ cup butter

4-5 whole cloves

Wash, scrape, or peel carrots. Cut into chunks and boil until tender. Meanwhile, combine vinegar, sugar, butter, and cloves. Heat to boiling, then reduce heat to simmer. Remove from heat and cover. When carrots are done, pour this hot sauce over carrots.

Flemish carrots

6 medium carrots, scraped or peeled, cut into thin, 2-inch strips

2 Tbsp. butter or margarine

½ tsp. salt

1 tsp. sugar

½ cup water

½ cup cream

1 tsp. lemon juice

In saucepan, sauté carrots in melted butter or margarine about 5 minutes. Stir in salt, sugar, and water. Simmer, covered until carrots are tender. Add cream and lemon juice, stirring until a coating forms. Serve.

Boston baked beans

1 lb. navy or Great Northern beans or 3 pints canned navy beans (see variation)

1 medium onion, sliced

½ lb. ham or bacon chunks

¼ cup brown sugar

1 tsp. dry mustard

3 Tbsp. molasses

1 tsp. salt

⅛ tsp. pepper

Place beans in large saucepan and cover with water. Heat to boiling; boil 2 minutes. Remove from heat and let stand 1 hour. Add water, if necessary to cover beans. Simmer uncovered 50 minutes or until tender. Cut ham or bacon into pieces. Layer together with beans in ungreased 2-quart bean pot or casserole. Stir together remaining ingredients and 1 cup of the reserved cooking broth. Pour over beans. Add enough of the remaining reserved broth to almost cover beans. Cover and bake at 350° F for 3½ to 4 hours, stirring if beans are looking too dry during the latter part of baking. Remove the cover 30 minutes before beans are due to be done baking.

Variation using canned beans: Mix all ingredients together. Add enough water to just cover beans. Bake at 350° F until thoroughly heated and top is drying (about 30 minutes).

Carrot mushroom stir-fry

- 6-8 medium carrots, scraped or peeled and thinly sliced
- 2 Tbsp. butter or margarine
- 2 tsp. olive or vegetable oil
- 6 oz. can sliced mushrooms, drained
- 5 green onions with tops, thinly sliced
- 1 Tbsp. lemon juice
- ½ tsp. salt
- ¼ tsp. pepper

In a large skillet, over medium heat, stir-fry carrots in butter and oil for 7 minutes. Add mushrooms and onion. Stir-fry for 4-6 minutes until vegetables are tender. Stir in lemon juice. Season with salt and pepper if desired.

Frijoles con queso

- 1 lb. pinto beans
- 5 strips bacon, diced
- 1 clove garlic, minced
- 1 small onion, minced
- 2 tsp. chili powder
- ¼ cup cheddar cheese, diced

Wash and pick over beans. Cover with cold water and soak overnight. Rinse and add water to cover beans. Cook slowly, adding more water, as needed until beans are tender. Drain. Mash beans in pot. Fry bacon until crisp; sauté garlic and onion briefly and add to beans along with chili powder and cheese. Mix until cheese is melted. Add salt to taste, if you wish.

Bean bake

- 5 cups cooked or 2 pints canned navy beans
- 1 cup cream or milk
- ½ cup brown sugar
- 1 tsp. dry mustard
- ½ cup catsup
- 2 Tbsp. onion, chopped
- ½ cup chopped cooked ham or bacon pieces
- ½ cup cheddar cheese, grated
- 2 Tbsp. butter or margarine

Mix all ingredients together and put into an ungreased casserole. Bake at 350° F until heated thoroughly (about 20 minutes).

Tip: To make barbecued baked beans, just substitute 1 cup barbecue sauce for the catsup and exchange water for the cream or milk.

Refried beans

I am not a "bean" person, but I can eat these all day! I never liked store-bought refried beans, but these, like most homemade foods, are a "whole 'nother ball game!" I fried up one batch just as my son, David, came home. He ate the whole batch and asked for more. (I didn't tell him that beans are good for you, too!)

2 TBSP. SHORTENING OR VEGETABLE OIL
1 CLOVE GARLIC, MASHED
½ SMALL ONION, CHOPPED
1 TSP. POWDERED CHILE PEPPER OR CHILI POWDER
3 CUPS COOKED DRY PINTO BEANS OR 1 PINT CANNED PINTOS

Heat shortening in large skillet. Sauté onions, garlic, and pepper. Pour beans into pan, including liquid. With potato masher or fork, mash most of the beans while they begin to heat. When finished mashing, press down into a single layer and cook uncovered. When liquid has been absorbed and the beans are starting to brown, turn over with spatula. Fry other side, adding a bit more shortening, if necessary. When dry and just a little golden brown in spots, turn out and serve.

Note: I often toss in a little chopped, leftover ham for extra flavor.

Laredo pinto beans

2 CUPS PINTO BEANS OR 2 PINTS CANNED PINTO BEANS
8 CUPS WATER (OMIT IF USING CANNED BEANS)
½ LB. SALT PORK, CUT IN PIECES
2 ONIONS, FINELY DICED
1 GREEN PEPPER, FINELY DICED
1 CAN (17-18 OZ.) TOMATOES
1 CLOVE GARLIC, FINELY DICED
¼ TSP. DRY MUSTARD
¼ TSP. CHILI POWDER
WORCESTERSHIRE SAUCE
SALT AND PEPPER

Clean beans. Place in large kettle with the water. Simmer for 2 hours. (If using canned beans omit this step.) Drain. Add remaining ingredients. Boil slowly about 2 hours (30 minutes for canned beans) or until beans are tender, adding more water if necessary.

Red beans and rice

¾ LB. LARGE RED KIDNEY BEANS
½ LB. SALT PORK OR HAM HOCK
1 TBSP. SHORTENING
1 TBSP. FLOUR
1 LARGE ONION, CHOPPED
1 CARROT, SLICED
3 PINTS BEEF STOCK OR BOUILLON
2 STALKS AND LEAVES OF CELERY
1 BAY LEAF
⅛ TSP. THYME
PINCH OF SAGE
SALT AND PEPPER TO TASTE
4 CUPS HOT, COOKED RICE

Soak kidney beans overnight in cold water. Brown meat in shortening. Remove meat from pan. If using ham hock, pick meat off bone; discard bone. Stir flour into grease in pan; brown lightly. Add onion and cook 3 minutes. Add beans, carrot slices, meat, and stock. Cook slowly for 1 hour. Add celery, herbs, salt, and pepper. Cook until gravy is thick and dark. Serve over hot rice.

Cuban-style black beans

1 LB. BLACK BEANS OR BLACK-EYED PEAS
1 TBSP. SALT
1 CLOVE GARLIC, CUT IN HALF
½ CUP COOKING OIL
3 CLOVES GARLIC, MASHED
3 GREEN PEPPERS, CHOPPED
3 MEDIUM ONIONS, CHOPPED
½ TSP. GROUND SAGE
2 BAY LEAVES, CRUSHED
3 TBSP. CIDER VINEGAR
1 TSP. SALT
PEPPER

Wash and pick over beans. Cover with water and soak overnight. Drain and place in kettle with fresh water to cover. Add salt and garlic halves. Cook beans until tender (about 3 hours), adding more water as needed. Just before serving, heat oil in skillet. Add mashed garlic, green pepper, onion, sage, and bay leaves. Cook until vegetables are soft. Add vinegar, salt, and pepper to taste. Place beans in serving dish and pour vegetable mixture over all.

Baked lima beans and ham

> 3½ cups cooked lima beans
> ¼ lb. diced ham
> 1 small onion, minced
> 1 Tbsp. molasses
> 2 cups drained, canned tomatoes (or 1 pint)
> 1 Tbsp. brown sugar
> 1 tsp. salt
> ¼ tsp. pepper

Combine all ingredients. Place in a 2-quart baking dish and bake at 375° F for 45 minutes.

Corn salsa

> 1 can (15 oz.) whole kernel corn, drained
> ½ cup chopped green pepper
> ½ cup chopped sweet red pepper
> ½ cup chopped onion
> 1 medium tomato, chopped
> ¼ cup sliced ripe olives (optional)
> 2 Tbsp. chopped pickled jalapeño peppers
> 1 tsp. pickled jalapeño pepper juice
> 2 Tbsp. vinegar
> 2 Tbsp. lemon juice
> ½ tsp. garlic salt
> ½ tsp. pepper

Combine all ingredients in large bowl. Cover and refrigerate for several hours. If you like a milder salsa, omit the jalapeños and their juice.

Dilled corn and peas

> 2½ cups fresh or frozen sugar snap peas
> 2 cups fresh or frozen corn
> 1 small sweet red pepper, sliced
> ¼ cup water
> 1 Tbsp. butter or margarine
> 1 tsp. fresh dill, minced
> ⅛ tsp. salt, optional
> ⅛ tsp. pepper

Place peas, corn, red pepper, and water in a saucepan; cover and cook over high heat until vegetables are crisp-tender. Drain. Add butter, dill, salt, and pepper. Toss to coat well.

Old-time succotash

¼ LB. BACON, DICED
2 CUPS FRESH CORN OR 1 PINT CORN, DRAINED
½ LB. GREEN LIMA BEANS OR BUTTER BEANS
1 MEDIUM GREEN PEPPER, CHOPPED
1 MEDIUM ONION, CHOPPED

In a large skillet, cook the bacon until crisp. Remove bacon to paper towels; drain, reserving 1 Tbsp. drippings. Add corn, beans, green pepper, and onion to drippings. Cook slowly for 10-15 minutes until vegetables are almost tender, adding water if necessary. Stir in bacon and serve.

Corn pudding

3 EGGS, LIGHTLY BEATEN
4 TBSP. SUGAR
1 CUP MILK
2 CUPS WHOLE KERNEL CORN OR 1 PINT, DRAINED
1 TBSP. BUTTER, MELTED

Combine eggs, sugar, and milk. Mix in rest of ingredients. Turn into a buttered baking dish and bake at 350° F for 30-35 minutes or until set.

Campfire-roasted corn on the cob

One of the meals of roasted corn I remember best was long ago when I worked at a riding stable called Longhorn Ranch. We "hands" foraged some fresh ears of green corn from the field corn next to the pasture. We built a fire in the parking lot and roasted our corn. (It didn't matter to us that we dipped our corn into the stock tank, complete with water bugs and algae!) I can still remember those charred ears and the wonderful meal we had...even though a customer's car ran right over our fire!

6 EARS OF FRESH SWEET CORN
WATER

Burn campfire wood until only coals remain. Peel back husks of corn and pull off silks. Fold husks back in place. Plunge ears into cold water and shake off. Put next to hot coals and roast until husks are blackened. Turn, if necessary, to heat other side of ears. Remove hot husks carefully and serve with butter and salt.

Onion rings

1 CUP FLOUR
½ TSP. SALT
1 TSP. SUGAR
1 TSP. BAKING POWDER
MILK
3 LARGE ONIONS, SLICED AND SEPARATED INTO RINGS
COOKING OIL OR SHORTENING FOR DEEP FRYER

Mix flour, salt, sugar, and baking powder. Add enough milk to make a thick batter. Heat oil in Dutch oven or deep fryer to 350° F. Place some onion rings in the batter bowl and stir around with a fork. One at a time, pick one ring out and let it drip briefly to get rid of excess batter. Place in hot oil. Repeat until you have a single layer of onion rings. Move them around with a fork as they fry to keep them from sticking together. Turn over to make sure they fry equally on both sides. When light golden, lift them out of the oil, drain on paper towels, then hold in the oven on a towel-lined cookie sheet, with the heat at its lowest setting. Be sure the oil has returned to 350° F before putting in your next batch. Serve hot or slowly dry in the oven on low to use in such dishes as green bean casserole.

Onion patties

- ¾ cup flour
- 1 Tbsp. sugar
- 1 tsp. salt
- 2 tsp. baking powder
- 1 Tbsp. cornmeal
- ⅔ cup milk (you may use powdered, reconstituted)
- 1 egg, lightly beaten
- 2½ cups onions, finely chopped (you may also use dehydrated, reconstituted onions)

Mix dry ingredients, then add milk and egg. Batter should be fairly thick; add onions, mix well. Drop by spoonful into hot cooking oil in skillet. Flatten slightly when you turn them over to fry other side.

Glazed onions

- 24 small onions
- 1½ cups sugar
- ⅓ cup water
- ⅓ cup butter or margarine
- ½ tsp. salt

Parboil onions about 10 minutes and drain. Combine sugar and water and cook until sugar has dissolved. Add butter and salt, stirring until melted. Cook 5 minutes. Arrange onions in pan and pour syrup over them. Place under broiler until lightly browned, basting frequently with the sugar syrup. If you have no broiler, just hold in a skillet on medium heat and simmer, basting frequently, until liquid absorbs and onions begin to brown; turn frequently.

Stuffed onions

6 medium large onions
4 bacon strips, cut into 1-inch pieces
¼ cup dry bread crumbs
2 Tbsp. fresh parsley
1 Tbsp. butter
1½ cups sliced fresh mushrooms or 1 small can store-bought mushrooms, drained
¼ tsp. salt
⅛ tsp. pepper
½ cup beef broth
grated cheese (optional)

In a Dutch oven, bring a small amount of water to a boil. Peel onions. Place onions in boiling water and cover. Cook for 4-6 minutes or until softened. Remove and cool enough to handle. Cut a ¼-inch slice off the top of each onion. Remove center, leaving a ½-inch onion shell. Chop onion centers and tops; set aside. In a skillet, fry bacon until crisp. Remove to a paper towel to drain. In the drippings, sauté chopped onion until tender. Stir in bread crumbs and parsley. Add the butter and mushrooms; cook until mushrooms are tender. Add bacon, salt, and pepper. Stuff onion shells; place in an ungreased shallow baking dish. Pour broth around onions. Bake uncovered at 375° F for 40-45 minutes, basting occasionally. Serve topped with cheese if you wish.

Onions au gratin

6 medium yellow or white onions
¼ cup butter or margarine
½ cup beef broth
½ cup cream
2 Tbsp. flour
¼ tsp. salt
⅛ tsp. pepper
½ cup shredded Swiss cheese
½ cup grated Parmesan cheese

Slice the onions and separate into ½-inch rings. Sauté in butter until tender. Place in a greased baking dish. In a bowl, stir broth, cream, flour, salt, and pepper until smooth; pour over onions. Sprinkle with cheeses. Bake, uncovered, at 350° F for about 30 minutes or until cheese is golden brown.

Green bean casserole

2 cans (15 oz. each) green beans or 2 pints canned green beans
1 can cream of mushroom soup
½ soup can of milk (you can substitute reconstituted homemade casserole mix from the pantry mixes section; 2 cups of casserole mix plus ½

CUP CHOPPED MUSHROOMS FOR THE MUSHROOM SOUP AND MILK, ABOVE)

1 LARGE CAN FRENCH FRIED ONION RINGS OR USE YOUR OWN LEFTOVER DRIED ONION RINGS, USING 2 CUPS, BARELY CHOPPED

Drain green beans. Mix mushroom soup with milk or make 2 cups casserole mix with ½ cup chopped mushrooms. Pour over green beans in casserole dish. Add ½ the can of the onion rings or 1 cup of home-fried onion rings. Mix lightly with beans and soup mixture. Sprinkle salt and pepper on top and bake, uncovered, for 20 minutes. Remove from oven and spread remaining onion rings over bubbly surface. Return to oven and bake for another 10 minutes or until onion ring top is hot and sizzly.

Creamed beans and potatoes

4 MEDIUM RED POTATOES, CUT INTO CHUNKS

1 CAN (15 OZ.) GREEN BEANS OR 2 CUPS FRESH GREEN BEANS OR 1 PINT CANNED GREEN BEANS

2 TBSP. BUTTER OR MARGARINE

2 TBSP. FLOUR

1 CUP MILK (MAY USE POWDERED, RECONSTITUTED MILK)

½ TSP. SALT

⅛ TSP. PEPPER

Scrub potatoes well and cut into wedges or medium-sized pieces. Place in a saucepan with water covering them and bring to a boil. Cook until tender (about 10 minutes). Cook beans, if fresh, until tender, in boiling water; about 10 minutes. Drain potatoes. In saucepan, melt butter and work flour, salt, and pepper into it until smooth. Gradually add milk, heating and stirring to make a medium white sauce. Add more milk, if necessary. Drain beans. Put potatoes and beans in saucepan with white sauce and stir gently. Serve hot.

Sesame green beans

3 CUPS FRESH OR FROZEN GREEN BEANS, CUT INTO 1-INCH PIECES OR 1 PINT CANNED, DRAINED GREEN BEANS

1 CLOVE GARLIC, FINELY CHOPPED

2 TSP. SESAME SEED

2 TBSP. BUTTER OR MARGARINE

2 TBSP. SOY SAUCE

Boil green beans in salted water until tender. Simmer until tender. Drain. If using canned green beans, omit this step. In a small amount of butter or margarine, sauté garlic and sesame seeds until garlic is tender and sesame seeds are golden. Add more butter and the soy sauce. Toss with green beans and serve.

Green beans with tomatoes

> 3 CUPS FRESH OR FROZEN, CUT GREEN BEANS OR 1 PINT CANNED, DRAINED GREEN BEANS
>
> 4 LARGE TOMATOES, PEELED AND CHOPPED
>
> 1 CUP ITALIAN DRESSING

Place beans in a saucepan and cover with water. Boil until tender. Drain. Add tomatoes and salad dressing. Lightly mix and serve.

Baked squash with brown sugar

> 1 MEDIUM-LARGE SQUASH OR 2 ACORN-SIZED SQUASH
>
> 4 TBSP. BUTTER OR MARGARINE
>
> 4 TBSP. BROWN SUGAR

Cut squash in two, lengthwise (from stem to blossom end). Remove seeds and strings. Scrape inside with a large spoon to smooth the meat and remove stringy pulp. If these are smaller squash, cut a small flat spot on the rounded side of each one so they'll sit flat on a baking sheet. If it is a large squash, cut it into serving-sized pieces, trimming each one a little flat on the rounded bottom. Place on a baking sheet. Rub butter liberally on the squash meat, then sprinkle generously with brown sugar. Bake at 350° F until very tender; about 50 minutes, depending on how thick the squash is.

Baked spaghetti squash

> 1 MEDIUM-SIZED RIPE SPAGHETTI SQUASH
>
> ½ LB. GROUND MEAT OR 1 PINT CANNED AND DRAINED
>
> 1 CLOVE GARLIC, MINCED
>
> 1 MEDIUM ONION, CHOPPED
>
> 1 JAR (15 OZ.) OF SPAGHETTI SAUCE OR 1 PINT CANNED
>
> 1 TSP. BASIL
>
> 1 TSP. OREGANO
>
> 1 CUP MOZZARELLA CHEESE, GRATED

Cut squash in half, lengthwise (from stem to blossom end). Lightly fork through strands to separate them and check for any seeds; remove seeds.

Place squash on cookie sheet and bake at 350° F until tender (about 50 minutes). Remove from oven. Meanwhile, brown ground meat in skillet with onion and garlic. Drain off any excess grease. Add spaghetti sauce and seasonings. Heat for 10 minutes. Remove from heat and wait until squash is tender. Pour sauce over squash strands, then top with grated mozzarella cheese. Return to oven and bake for another 15 minutes or until cheese is browning.

Apricot baked squash

> 1 MEDIUM WINTER SQUASH, SEEDED AND CUBED INTO 2-INCH CUBES OR 2 QUARTS CANNED, DRAINED.
>
> ½ CUP APRICOT OR PEACH PRESERVES

¼ cup brown sugar

¼ cup cream

Peel, seed, and cube winter squash, such as butternut, buttercup, or Sunshine. Place cubes in a large saucepan with an inch of water. Cover and heat. Steam squash until tender. Mash squash and add preserves, brown sugar, and cream. Mix well and turn out into a greased baking dish. Bake at 350° F until nicely dry and thoroughly heated.

Summer and winter squash stir-fry

2 Tbsp. butter or margarine

2 Tbsp. olive oil or vegetable oil

1 medium young yellow summer squash, sliced

1 medium young green or black zucchini, sliced

½ small butternut or buttercup squash, seeded, peeled, and julienned

1 large onion, sliced

1 green pepper, seeded and sliced

1 sweet red pepper, seeded and sliced

2 cloves garlic, minced

⅛ tsp. pepper

2 Tbsp. soy sauce

In a large skillet or wok, heat butter and oil over medium heat. Add vegetables, garlic, and pepper. Stir fry until tender, moving the vegetables around to evenly cook. Sprinkle on soy sauce. Serve hot. I usually serve this over rice with sweet and sour sauce. It makes great use of end-of-the season squash, using both the last of the summer squash and the not-quite-mature winter squash that won't keep in storage.

Asparagus with sesame seeds

2 lbs. fresh asparagus spears

boiling water

½ tsp. salt

1 Tbsp. cornstarch

¼ cup cold water

¼ cup butter or margarine

3 Tbsp. sesame seeds, toasted

Cut off tough ends of asparagus spears and place in a large skillet with boiling water to cover. Add salt and simmer until spears are tender (about 6 minutes). Remove, cover and keep warm. Drain cooking liquid, reserving ½ cup in a small pan. Combine cornstarch and cold water; stir into reserved liquid. Cook and stir over medium heat until thickened. Stir in butter until melted. Spoon over asparagus, set out on serving plate, and then sprinkle with sesame seeds; serve immediately.

Asparagus popovers

Popover:

>1 cup flour, sifted twice
>
>½ tsp. salt
>
>2 eggs, beaten well
>
>1 cup milk

Sift flour, then add salt and sift again. Mix eggs and milk into dry ingredients. Beat well. Fill well greased muffin tins or popover cups half full. Bake at 425° F for about 40 minutes. Don't peek until the very last or your popovers may fall!

Filling:

>1 pound fresh asparagus, cut into 1-inch pieces or 1 pint canned, drained
>
>¼ cup diced onion
>
>2 Tbsp. butter or margarine
>
>2 Tbsp. flour
>
>1½ cups milk
>
>½ tsp. salt
>
>¼ tsp. pepper
>
>½ cup shredded Swiss cheese
>
>2 Tbsp. grated Parmesan cheese
>
>2 cups diced, cooked ham or 1 pint canned, drained
>
>½ tsp. paprika

Make popovers and while they are baking, make the filling. Simmer raw or frozen asparagus until tender. Skip this part if you are using canned asparagus. In a saucepan, sauté onion in butter until tender. Stir in flour until mixed well. While still heating, slowly stir in milk to make a medium white sauce. Add the salt and pepper. Reduce the heat and add cheeses until melted. Stir in ham and asparagus. Heat thoroughly. Remove popovers from pan and cut off tops. Fill popovers with asparagus mixture and sprinkle paprika on top; serve hot.

Creamed asparagus on toast

This is one of our old family favorites. Each and every new garden that Grandma, Mom, and I have started always had asparagus roots planted in it, right from the start. Just our immediate family has planted asparagus in Michigan, Virginia, Florida, Montana, New Mexico, Minnesota, and Saskatchewan, Canada! Just think of all of that asparagus! And here on our homestead in northern Minnesota, we have more than 150 asparagus plants growing. Every spring, I just can't wait until those fat green spears come poking up through the ground like magic. And I feel sure that my homesteading grandparents felt the same as I do. The very first meal of fresh asparagus is always, without fail, asparagus on toast. I could eat it for three meals, every day!

>6 slices toast, preferably made from homemade bread
>
>1 lb. fresh or frozen asparagus spears or 1½ pints canned, drained
>
>2 Tbsp. butter or margarine

2 Tbsp. flour
1½ cups milk
½ Tsp. salt (optional)

Cut asparagus into 1-inch pieces, discarding tough ends. Simmer raw or frozen asparagus in a saucepan with boiling water until tender. Skip this part if you are using canned asparagus. In a saucepan, melt butter and stir in flour to make a smooth paste. Slowly add milk, stirring while heating, to make a medium white sauce. Add more or less milk, as needed. Add salt, if you wish. Add drained asparagus to white sauce and gently mix. Butter hot toast. Put on plates (2 pieces is a serving), and top with creamed asparagus.

Sweet and sour garlic mushrooms

1 lb. fresh smaller mushrooms
¼ cup vinegar
1 Tbsp. cornstarch
2 Tbsp. soy sauce
½ cup brown sugar
1 clove garlic, mashed or minced

In a saucepan, simmer mushrooms until tender; drain. In same saucepan, before mushrooms are returned, mix vinegar with cornstarch, making a smooth paste. Heat while stirring until it thickens. Add soy sauce and brown sugar. Mix well. Add garlic and continue heating and stirring. Add drained mushrooms and slowly simmer until thoroughly heated. If you must thin sauce, add a little water. Serve mushrooms over hot rice.

Mushrooms over toast

¼ cup butter or margarine
½ lb. fresh sliced mushrooms
2 cloves garlic, minced
¼ cup cream
2 tsp. lemon juice
½ tsp. salt
pepper to taste
4 slices of bread, toasted and buttered (homemade bread is best)
2 Tbsp. fresh chopped parsley or chives (optional)

In skillet, melt butter; sauté mushrooms until browning. Add garlic, cream, lemon juice, and salt and pepper to taste, stirring to prevent scorching. When cream has thickened, spoon mushroom mixture over toast and sprinkle top with fresh parsley or chives, if desired.

Stuffed mushrooms

> 1 LB. FRESH BUTTON MUSHROOMS OR MORELS
>
> 1 PKG. (8 OZ.) OF CREAM CHEESE OR 1¼ CUPS HOMEMADE CREAM CHEESE
>
> ¼ CUP BACON BITS OR BACON-FLAVORED TVPs

Soften cream cheese to room temperature.

Rinse mushrooms and pat dry. Pull stems out. If using morels, cut mushrooms in half. Lay mushrooms out in a single layer on a baking dish. In a small mixing bowl, mix softened cream cheese with bacon bits or TVPs with fork, mashing well to mix thoroughly. Stuff mushrooms with plenty of cream cheese mixture, mounding it up a bit. Bake mushrooms at 350° F until tender (about 30 minutes).

Creamed peas over tuna sandwiches

> 2 CUPS FRESH OR FROZEN PEAS OR 1 PINT CANNED PEAS, DRAINED
>
> 2 TBSP. BUTTER OR MARGARINE
>
> 2 TBSP. FLOUR
>
> 1½ CUPS MILK
>
> WHITE BREAD, SLICED
>
> 1 CAN (5 OZ.) LIGHT TUNA, DRAINED OR ½-PINT CANNED TUNA OR SALMON, DRAINED
>
> SALT AND PEPPER TO TASTE

In a saucepan, simmer fresh or frozen peas until just done (about 10 minutes). If using canned peas, put in saucepan with canning liquid and heat to simmer for 10 minutes. Drain well. In saucepan, melt butter and stir in flour to make a thick paste. While heating, slowly add milk, stirring constantly until thickened; add more or less milk to make a medium white sauce. Add peas to white sauce and gently mix. Butter white bread and add drained tuna in a light layer, between slices. Then ladle peas over sandwiches. Top with a dab of butter, season with salt and pepper if you wish, and serve hot.

Pea patties

Line muffin tins with pie pastry, rolled out and cut with a large-mouth canning jar ring. Push the pastry down into the tin, then pinch the edges to ruffle them nicely. Use your favorite pastry recipe or look in the pie section for one. Bake pastry shells until just golden brown.

Filling:

> 1 CUP FRESH OR FROZEN PEAS OR USE 1 PINT CANNED PEAS
>
> 2 TBSP. BUTTER OR MARGARINE
>
> 2 TBSP. FLOUR
>
> 1 CUP MILK
>
> ½ CUP CHOPPED HAM
>
> SALT AND PEPPER
>
> PAPRIKA OR GRATED CHEESE TO TOP

While baking pastry shells, simmer fresh or frozen peas in boiling water until just done; about 10 minutes or heat canned peas and their liquid for 10 minutes, simmering. Drain well. In saucepan, melt butter and stir in flour to make a thick paste. Slowly add milk, heating and stirring to make a thick white sauce. Add more milk, if necessary. Add peas and ham. Salt and pepper to taste. Then fill hot pastry shells with pea filling. Serve with a sprinkle of paprika or grated cheese.

Parmesan peas

> 1 LB. OR 4 CUPS FRESH OR FROZEN PEAS
> 2 TBSP. GRATED PARMESAN CHEESE
> 1/8 TSP. GRATED LEMON PEEL
> 1 TBSP. LEMON JUICE
> 1 SMALL CARROT, GRATED

In saucepan, simmer peas until tender; drain. Toss with remaining ingredients and serve with additional Parmesan cheese.

Marinated fresh tomatoes

> 3 LARGE, FRESH TOMATOES, SLICED THICKLY
> 1/3 CUP OLIVE OIL
> 1/4 CUP VINEGAR
> 1/2 TSP. GARLIC CLOVE, MINCED
> 2 TBSP. CHOPPED ONION
> 1 TBSP. CHOPPED FRESH PARSLEY
> 1 TBSP. CHOPPED FRESH BASIL OR 1 TSP. DRIED BASIL

Place tomatoes in large, shallow bowl. Combine remaining ingredients in a bowl and mix very well. Ladle over tomatoes. Cover and refrigerate for at least 1 hour.

Tuna-stuffed tomatoes

> 2 CANS (5 OZ. EACH) TUNA IN WATER, DRAINED
> 4 TBSP. MAYONNAISE
> 1 MEDIUM ONION, CHOPPED
> 1/4 TSP. DRIED BASIL
> 1 TBSP. CHOPPED GREEN OLIVES
> 1 TBSP. LEMON JUICE
> LETTUCE
> 6 LARGE TOMATOES, SLICED THICKLY
> 24 PITTED SMALL RIPE OLIVES

Mix drained tuna with mayonnaise, onion, basil, olives, and lemon juice. Arrange lettuce leaves on large serving dish. Lay half of the tomato slices down on the lettuce. Top each with about 1/4 cup of tuna filling, then top with other tomato slice. Pin together with toothpicks and slide two ripe olives down on toothpick. Drizzle with a little light salad dressing and serve.

Fried green tomatoes

    1 Tbsp. brown sugar
    1 cup flour
    4-6 medium green tomatoes
    1 egg, beaten
    ¼ cup milk
    1 cup seasoned dry bread crumbs
    3 Tbsp. butter or margarine
    1 Tbsp. cooking oil

Mix sugar and flour in shallow bowl. Dip both sides of each tomato slice into the mixture. Combine egg and milk. Dip each tomato slice in that, then into bread crumbs. In a skillet, heat butter and oil over medium-high heat. Fry tomatoes until brown on both sides, but still firm.

Cauliflower au gratin

    1 head of cauliflower, broken into florets
    6 Tbsp. butter or margarine
    4 oz. cooked, chopped ham or ½-pint canned ham pieces, drained
    2 Tbsp. flour
    1½ cups cream
    ½ tsp. salt and pepper
    1½ cups shredded cheddar cheese

In large saucepan, bring cauliflower to a boil, then reduce heat and simmer until just tender. Melt butter in large skillet. Sauté ham for 2 minutes. Add drained cauliflower. Mix well. Combine flour and cream; stir into skillet and blend well. Add salt and pepper if you wish. Cook, stirring until thickened. Pour into a baking dish and sprinkle with cheese. Bake at 350° F for about 12 minutes or until cheese is starting to brown.

Baked cauliflower

    1 head cauliflower, broken into florets
    1½ cups drained, canned tomatoes
    ½ cup chopped onion
    ½ tsp. dried oregano
    ½ tsp. salt
    ⅛ tsp. pepper
    ¾ cup grated cheese
    ¾ cup coarse cracker crumbs

Simmer cauliflower florets, covered, until just tender. In greased baking dish, mix tomatoes, onion, oregano, salt, and pepper. Add cauliflower and mix gently to coat with above mixture. Mix cheese and crumbs; sprinkle over cauliflower. Bake at 350° F for about 30-40 minutes.

Country cauliflower

- 1 LARGE HEAD CAULIFLOWER, BROKEN INTO FLORETS
- 3 TBSP. BUTTER OR MARGARINE
- 6 TBSP. DRY BREAD CRUMBS OR CRACKER MEAL (I USE CHEESE CRACKERS)

Cook cauliflower in salted boiling water, covered, until tender. Drain and place on a warm platter. Melt butter in pan and add crumbs. Sauté until it reaches a caramel color. Spread over cauliflower and serve.

Fry-steamed cabbage

- 2 TBSP. BUTTER OR MARGARINE
- 1 TBSP. COOKING OIL
- 1 SMALL HEAD OF CABBAGE, SLICED
- ½ TSP. SALT
- ½ CUP MILK

In large skillet, heat oil and butter to medium heat and add cabbage slices. Sprinkle with salt and cover. Cook slowly until tender. When tender, remove cover and stir until liquid is nearly gone. Add milk and continue cooking on low heat until milk is reduced. Serve hot with butter.

Scalloped cabbage

- 1 MEDIUM HEAD OF CABBAGE, SLICED
- 2 CUPS THIN WHITE SAUCE
- 1 CUP BUTTERED BREAD CRUMBS
- 1 TSP. PAPRIKA

Arrange layers of sliced cabbage and white sauce in buttered baking dish. Top with bread crumbs and sprinkle with paprika. Bake at 350° F, covered, for 35 minutes.

Glazed sweet potatoes

- 2 LBS. MEDIUM-SIZED SWEET POTATOES OR 1 QUART OR 2 CANS (18 OZ. EACH) SWEET POTATOES, DRAINED
- ¼ CUP BUTTER OR MARGARINE
- ¼ CUP PINEAPPLE JUICE
- ¼ CUP FIRMLY PACKED BROWN SUGAR
- ⅛ TSP. GROUND CINNAMON
- ⅛ TSP. GROUND CLOVES

If using fresh sweet potatoes, peel and cut into large pieces and cook, covered with water, in large saucepan, until tender. Drain. If using canned sweet potatoes, just drain. Place in a baking dish. In a small saucepan, combine butter, pineapple juice, brown sugar, and spices. Cook until syrup boils. Pour over potatoes and bake, uncovered, at 350° F for about 30 minutes, basting with the syrup several times.

Sweet potato casserole

- 2½ lbs. sweet potatoes (about 4 cups) peeled, cooked and mashed or 1 quart canned sweet potatoes, drained
- ⅓ cup butter or margarine, melted
- 2 eggs, beaten
- ½ cup milk (or powdered, reconstituted)
- ½ cup sugar

In large mixing bowl, mash sweet potatoes and add butter, eggs, milk, and sugar. Mix well. Put in greased baking dish.

Topping:
- ½ cup chopped nuts (pecans are great!)
- ½ cup firmly packed brown sugar
- 3 Tbsp. butter or margarine, melted

In small bowl, mix chopped nuts, brown sugar, and melted butter or margarine. Sprinkle over sweet potatoes. Bake, uncovered, at 375° F for about 25 minutes or until thoroughly heated.

Baked sweet potatoes with apples and raisins

- 2½ lbs. medium-sized sweet potatoes or 1 quart or 2 cans (18 oz. each) sweet potatoes, drained
- 2 tart pie apples (peeled, cored, and cut into ¼-inch rings)
- ½ cup seedless raisins
- 2 Tbsp. butter or margarine
- ½ cup pineapple juice
- ¼ cup firmly packed brown sugar
- ¼ tsp. ground cinnamon
- ¼ tsp. ground cloves

In large saucepan, cook peeled, cut sweet potatoes, covered, in boiling water until tender. Drain. Cut into slices and lay in greased 13x9x2-inch baking dish. Alternate layers of sweet potatoes and apples, sprinkling raisins on top of the top layer of potatoes, ending with apple slices. In a small saucepan, mix butter, pineapple juice, sugar, and spices. Heat to boiling and stir well. Drizzle over apples. Bake, uncovered, at 350° F until apples are tender (about 40 minutes).

Chiles rellenos

- 1 can (15 oz.) tomatoes or 1 pint canned tomatoes, undrained
- 1 small onion, finely chopped
- 1 tsp. beef bouillon granules
- dash of cumin
- dash of cinnamon
- 8 large Big Jim, Poblano, or Relleno chile peppers, green and roasted
- 4 cups shredded cheddar or Monterey Jack cheese

- 8 EGG YOLKS (WHITES RESERVED)
- 2 TBSP. WATER
- ¼ CUP FLOUR
- ½ TSP. SALT
- 8 EGG WHITES, BEATEN UNTIL FLUFFY
- SHORTENING OR OIL FOR FRYING

Make a tomato sauce from undrained tomatoes, onions, bouillon, cumin, and cinnamon; heat thoroughly, then let simmer while fixing the peppers.

Remove seeds and veins from peppers, slitting each carefully on one side only. Stuff liberally with cheese without straining walls of pepper. Set aside on a plate.

Slightly beat egg yolks and water. Add flour and salt and beat until thick. Whip egg whites. (If you use a mixer, first clean blades after mixing egg yolk and dry them.) Fold stiff egg whites into the yolk/flour mix.

In a large skillet, heat ½-inch of shortening until hot but not smoking. For each serving, spoon about ⅓ cup of batter into hot fat, spreading it in a circle. Fry 3-4 at a time. As the batter begins to set, gently place a stuffed chile on top of each. Cover it with another ⅓ cup of batter. Continue cooking until the underside is browning nicely. Turn carefully and brown other side. Drain on paper towels and keep warm on a cookie sheet, in a 300° F oven, until all are finished. Serve with tomato sauce.

Harvard beets

- 3 CUPS COOKED, DICED BEETS OR 1 PINT DICED CANNED BEETS, DRAINED
- 6 TBSP. SUGAR
- 3 TBSP. CORNSTARCH
- 3 TBSP. MELTED BUTTER
- ¼ CUP WATER
- ½ CUP VINEGAR

Combine all ingredients but beets. Cook slowly until smooth and thick, stirring constantly. Add beets. Heat thoroughly. Serve at once.

Vegetables in beet cups

- 6 MEDIUM-SIZED BEETS, COOKED UNTIL TENDER AND PEELED
- ½ CUP FRESH OR FROZEN WHOLE KERNEL CORN
- ½ CUP FRESH OR FROZEN PEAS
- ½ CUP FRESH OR FROZEN DICED CARROTS

Cut a slice from the root of each beet, then cut the top off and scoop out the center. Cook vegetables, mix, and fill in beet cavities. Sprinkle a little grated cheese over the tops if you wish and bake at 375° F until cheese is browning.

Mom's pickled beets

2 CANS (14 OZ. EACH) SLICED BEETS OR 2 PINTS CANNED BEETS, SLICED
¼ CUP WATER
¾ CUP VINEGAR
¾ CUP SUGAR
1½ TSP. SALT
¾ TSP. PEPPER
1 LARGE ONION, SLICED THINLY

In a saucepan, combine water, vinegar, sugar, and spices. Bring to a boil; simmer until sugar is dissolved. Remove from heat; add drained beets. Let stand at room temperature for 1 hour. Cover and refrigerate overnight.

Stuffed eggplant

1 SMALL TENDER EGGPLANT
¼ CUP CHOPPED GREEN PEPPER
2 TBSP. ONION, CHOPPED
1 CLOVE GARLIC, FINELY CHOPPED
¼ CUP BUTTER OR MARGARINE
½ CUP SEASONED BREAD STUFFING
1 JAR (2 OZ.) DICED PIMENTO, DRAINED
¼ CUP GRATED PARMESAN CHEESE

Cut eggplant lengthwise into halves. Remove eggplant, leaving a ½-inch shell. Cut eggplant into 1-inch cubes. Sauté pepper, onion, and garlic in butter in medium skillet until tender. Stir in cubed eggplant and continue cooking about 5 more minutes. Stir in stuffing and pimento. Fill eggplant halves with stuffing and sprinkle with cheese. Bake, uncovered, at 350° F until shell is tender and cheese is golden. Serve by cutting each stuffed shell in half.

Eggplant Parmigiana

Italian sauce:

1 CLOVE GARLIC, MINCED FINELY
1 MEDIUM ONION, CHOPPED
1 SMALL GREEN PEPPER, CHOPPED
2 TBSP. OLIVE OIL
1 CAN (16 OZ.) WHOLE TOMATOES, UNDRAINED OR 1 PINT WHOLE TOMATOES, UNDRAINED
1 CAN (8 OZ.) TOMATO SAUCE OR ½-PINT CANNED TOMATO SAUCE
1 TSP. DRIED BASIL
½ TSP. SALT
½ TSP. DRIED OREGANO
⅛ TSP. PEPPER

Sauté garlic, onion, and pepper in olive oil until tender. Add the rest of the ingredients. Break up the tomatoes and simmer gently for 45 minutes, covered.

Eggplant:
- 2 SMALL EGGPLANT
- 1 EGG
- 2 TBSP. WATER
- 1 CUP BUTTERED DRY BREAD CRUMBS
- ¼ CUP OLIVE OIL
- 2 CUPS MOZZARELLA, SHREDDED
- ¼ CUP PARMESAN, GRATED

Cut each eggplant crosswise into ¼-inch slices. Mix egg and water. Dip eggplant into egg mixture; coat with bread crumbs. Heat oil in large skillet until hot but not smoking. Fry 3-4 slices of eggplant at once, turning once until both sides are golden brown. Drain. Repeat, adding more oil if necessary. Place half of the eggplant in ungreased baking dish, overlapping slices a little. Spoon half of the Italian sauce over eggplant; sprinkle with 1 cup of the mozzarella cheese. Repeat with the rest of the eggplant, then more sauce. Sprinkle with Parmesan cheese. Bake, uncovered, at 350° F until sauce is bubbly and cheese is browning.

Glazed parsnips

- 2 LBS. PARSNIPS, CUT INTO STRIPS
- 2 TBSP. BUTTER OR MARGARINE
- 1 TBSP. FIRMLY PACKED BROWN SUGAR

Heat water to boil. Add parsnip strips. Cover and heat to boiling; reduce heat and simmer until tender. Drain. Heat margarine over medium heat until melted and stir in brown sugar. Mix parsnips and brown sugar mixture until parsnips are coated.

Salads

Waldorf salad

- 2 CUPS COARSELY CHOPPED APPLES (ABOUT 2 MEDIUM APPLES)
- 1 CUP CHOPPED CELERY
- ½ CUP MAYONNAISE, OR TO TASTE
- ⅓ CUP COARSELY CHOPPED WALNUTS
- MIXED SALAD GREENS OR LETTUCE
- SEEDLESS RED OR GREEN GRAPES IN SEASON

Toss all ingredients together in a serving bowl.

Cantaloupe salad

We really love this fresh salad, especially when we have just harvested the fruits from our garden. It's one reason I always grow some day-neutral strawberries, so we have strawberries all summer...even though the plants aren't always winter hardy here in the Northwoods of Minnesota. This will make six side salads, but we just about make a meal out of this so we always end up making two salads and serving them with some fresh cheese and crackers.

> 2 SMALL CANTALOUPE
> 1 CUP SLICED STRAWBERRIES
> 1 CUP SEEDLESS GREEN GRAPES
> LETTUCE LEAVES

Cut off about 1 inch from ends of each cantaloupe. Peel and reserve. Cut up end pieces; mix with strawberries and grapes. Remove seeds from cantaloupe. Cut each cantaloupe into 3 even rings. Place rings on lettuce leaves on each of 6 plates; cut each ring into 1-inch pieces, keeping the ring shape. Spoon mixed fruit into each ring.

Dressing:
> ½ CUP SOUR CREAM
> ¼ CUP MAYONNAISE
> 1 TSP. LEMON JUICE
> 2 TBSP. FIRMLY PACKED BROWN SUGAR
> ¼ CUP CHOPPED NUTS

Mix sour cream, mayonnaise, lemon juice, and brown sugar until sugar is dissolved. Stir in nuts. Spoon sour cream dressing on each individual salad.

Vegetable pasta salad

> 2 CUPS COOKED SHELL MACARONI
> 2 MEDIUM TOMATOES, CHOPPED (ABOUT 1½ CUPS)
> 1 SMALL ONION, SLICED
> ½ CUP SLICED RIPE OLIVES
> ½ CUP MAYONNAISE OR SALAD DRESSING
> 1 TBSP. LEMON JUICE
> ½ TSP. DRIED BASIL LEAVES
> ½ TSP. SALT
> 1 LARGE CLOVE GARLIC, CRUSHED
> 2 CUPS SHREDDED LETTUCE

Mix macaroni, tomatoes, onion, and olives. Stir mayonnaise, lemon juice, basil, salt, and garlic. Toss with macaroni mixture until well coated. Cover and refrigerate overnight. Just before serving, add lettuce and toss lightly to coat.

Three-bean salad

- 1 can (15 oz.) cut green beans or 1 pint canned green beans
- 1 can (15 oz.) cut wax beans or 1 pint canned wax beans
- 1 can (15 oz.) red kidney beans, drained or 1 pint canned red kidney beans, drained
- ½ cup onion, thinly sliced
- 1 clove garlic, mashed
- 1 green pepper, sliced thinly
- ½ cup salad oil
- ⅔ cup vinegar
- ½ cup sugar
- 1 tsp. celery seeds

In large salad bowl, mix beans, onion, garlic, and green pepper. In a mixing bowl, mix oil, vinegar, sugar, and celery seeds. Pour over bean mix; mix to coat beans well. Cover and refrigerate overnight or at least 3 hours. Serve cold.

Cold cabbage salad

- 1 small head of firm cabbage
- 3 carrots, peeled or scraped and grated coarsely
- ¼ cup celery, sliced
- 1 medium onion, sliced finely
- 1 cup sugar
- ½ tsp. celery seeds
- 1 cup vinegar

Remove core from cabbage and shred. Grate carrots; slice celery and onions. Mix together in large bowl with cover. Mix sugar, celery seeds, and vinegar together well. Pour over vegetables and toss thoroughly to mix well. Cover and refrigerate.

Creamy coleslaw

- 1 small head cabbage, finely shredded
- 2 carrots, shredded
- ½ cup mayonnaise
- 2 Tbsp. white vinegar
- 2 Tbsp. sugar
- ¼ cup sour cream
- ½ tsp. celery seed

Mix vegetables together in bowl. In a small mixing bowl, mix remaining ingredients and pour over vegetables. Toss well to coat and cover bowl; refrigerate for at least 1 hour.

Farmstead potato salad

4 cups diced cooked potatoes
2 hard-boiled, peeled, diced eggs
½ medium onion, diced
½ cup diced celery

Dressing:
1 cup mayonnaise or salad dressing
1 Tbsp. mustard
1½ Tbsp. vinegar
1¼ tsp. salt
a splash of milk
¾ cup sugar

Pour dressing over salad ingredients in large bowl. Toss lightly to coat then refrigerate overnight or for at least 2 hours.

Layered lettuce salad

1 head lettuce, broken
1 green pepper, chopped
3 eggs, hard-boiled and diced
1 cup celery, diced
1 cup baby spinach leaves
2 cups fresh raw or frozen peas (don't cook peas; if frozen, thaw under running water)
1 medium sweet onion, sliced
8 slices bacon, fried crisp and diced or bacon bits (or bacon-flavored TVPs)
2 cups mayonnaise or salad dressing of your choice

Layer ingredients in order, making sure all are dry. Cover and refrigerate for up to a week.

Cucumber and onion sour cream salad

4½ cups thinly sliced peeled cucumbers
2 medium onions, peeled and sliced into rings or slices
1 cup sour cream
2 Tbsp. white vinegar or lemon juice
1 Tbsp. sugar

Put cucumbers and onions into a salad bowl, then blend dressing ingredients together in small bowl and pour over cucumber mix. Cover and refrigerate at least 1 hour.

Tuna salad

2 cans (5 oz. each) light chunk tuna in water, drained or ½-pint canned tuna (or salmon)

1 LARGE ONION, CHOPPED
2 MEDIUM TOMATOES, DICED
2 TBSP. GREEN OLIVES, SLICED
1 CUP MAYONNAISE
1 TBSP. VINEGAR OR LEMON JUICE
½ CUP FRESH OR FROZEN PEAS, BARELY BOILED TENDER

In a medium bowl, lightly mix all ingredients until well coated. Serve immediately over lettuce. Or omit the peas and use as a sandwich filling between thick slices of nice homemade bread.

Taco salad

4 LARGE FLOUR TORTILLAS
½ LB. GROUND BEEF OR 1 PINT CANNED GROUND MEAT
1 MEDIUM ONION, CHOPPED
1 TSP. GARLIC POWDER
1 TBSP. CHILI POWDER
½ TSP. SALT
1 SMALL HEAD OF LETTUCE, CHOPPED
2 MEDIUM TOMATOES, CHOPPED
½ CUP GRATED CHEDDAR CHEESE
1 CUP TACO-FLAVORED CORN CHIPS

Dressing:
1 CUP MAYONNAISE
½ CUP CATSUP
1 TSP. ONION POWDER
½ TSP. GARLIC POWDER
2 TSP. MILD (OR HOT) POWDERED CHILE PEPPER OR CHILI POWDER
2 TBSP. SUGAR

Mix ingredients of dressing together in bowl and reserve for your salads.

In hot vegetable oil, fry tortillas until they start to puff, but *not* until crisp. Quickly remove from oil, drain, and place upside down over appropriate-sized baking dish to make the bowl of the taco salad, placed on a cookie sheet. When all tortillas have been placed, put in oven at 300° F and bake until crisp and golden, not browned.

Meanwhile, in a small amount of oil, brown ground meat. Break into small bits. Add onion, garlic powder, chili powder, and salt. Drain excess grease. In baked taco bowls, add chopped lettuce, then add a layer of the taco meat, tomatoes, dressing, then grated cheese. Sprinkle corn chips on top.

Tip: In place of baked taco shells, you can purchase a taco bowl form from several restaurant supply catalogs, which holds the tortilla in shape in a deep fryer, making a quick, perfectly-shaped bowl every time. I finally broke down and bought one and I truly love it.

Mandarin chicken salad

- 2 Tbsp. butter or margarine
- 2 cups cooked or canned chicken, cut into strips
- ½ cup toasted, slivered almonds
- 1 small head lettuce or mixed red and green leaf lettuce, torn
- 1 small onion, sliced
- 1 can (11 oz.) mandarin oranges, drained
- ½ cup toasted croutons (I make mine from buttered bread)
- sesame seeds (optional)

Dressing:
- ¼ cup vegetable oil
- 2 Tbsp. vinegar
- 2 Tbsp. sugar
- ⅛ tsp. hot pepper sauce
- ⅛ tsp. powdered ginger

In small skillet, melt butter, then lightly sauté chicken and almonds. Cool. Break lettuce into bowl; add onions and toss. Add cooled chicken and almond slivers. Toss again. Add mandarin oranges and croutons. In a jar, mix dressing ingredients, cover and shake well. Pour over salad and lightly toss. I sprinkle sesame seeds over the salad just before serving. You can also add Chinese noodles for extra crunch.

Oriental chicken salad

- 3 cups diced cooked or canned chicken, drained
- 1 can (13 oz.) pineapple tidbits, drained
- 1 can (5 oz.) water chestnuts, drained and sliced or ½ cup raw kohlrabi or Jerusalem artichokes, sliced
- 2 Tbsp. sliced green onion
- ¾ cup sour cream
- 1 tsp. powdered ginger
- dash salt and pepper
- greens for serving
- ¼ cup toasted slivered almonds

Combine first 4 ingredients. Chill. Blend sour cream, ginger, salt, and pepper. Add to chicken mix. Toss lightly. Serve on greens and sprinkle with almonds.

Spinach crunch salad

- 5 cups fresh torn spinach leaves
- 1 can (16 oz.) bean sprouts or 1 pint canned bean sprouts, drained
- 1 can (8 oz.) sliced water chestnuts, drained or ½ cup raw kohlrabi or Jerusalem artichokes, sliced
- 4 eggs, hard-boiled, peeled, and chopped

6 bacon strips, fried and crumbled

1 small onion, thinly sliced

Dressing:

½ cup firmly packed brown sugar

½ cup vegetable oil

⅓ cup vinegar

⅓ cup catsup

1 Tbsp. Worcestershire sauce

Toss salad ingredients in large bowl. In a jar, combine all dressing ingredients. Cover and shake until blended well. Pour over salad ingredients and serve immediately.

Mom's lemon/lime cottage cheese salad

1 box (3 oz.) lime Jello

1 cup pineapple juice

1 box (3 oz.) lemon Jello

1 cup whipped cream

1 cup cottage cheese

Dissolve lime Jello in 1 cup boiling water. Mix well. Cool to lukewarm and add 1 cup pineapple juice. Pour into mold. Refrigerate until set. Dissolve lemon Jello in 1 cup boiling water. Let start to set, then fold in 1 cup whipped cream and 1 cup of cottage cheese. Mix well and pour on top of lime Jello. Refrigerate until firm.

Five-fruit salad

1 can (20 oz.) pineapple chunks, drained, reserving ¾ cup juice

½ cup sugar

2 Tbsp. cornstarch

⅓ cup orange juice

1 Tbsp. lemon juice

3-4 unpeeled apples, chopped

2 bananas, sliced

1 cup seedless red grapes, halved

1 can (11 oz.) mandarin oranges, drained or 1¾ cups fresh orange slices, seeded

Drain pineapple, reserving ¾ cup juice. In a saucepan, mix sugar and cornstarch and stir in pineapple juice, orange juice, and lemon juice slowly. Heat, stirring, until thickened. Cook, stirring, 1 minute longer. Set aside. In a salad bowl, combine fruits. Pour warm sauce over fruit, stirring gently to coat. Cover and refrigerate. Serve with fresh, sweetened whipped cream if you wish.

Sunray salad

> LETTUCE LEAVES
> 8 OZ. CREAM CHEESE, SOFTENED
> ½ CUP POWDERED SUGAR
> 2 CUPS SMALL-CURD COTTAGE CHEESE
> 4 PEACH HALVES
> 1 SMALL CAN MANDARIN ORANGE SLICES, OR FRESH PEELED ORANGE SLICES

On four salad plates, arrange lettuce leaves. In small mixing bowl, mix softened cream cheese, powdered sugar, and cottage cheese. Place a circular layer on each plate, in the center of the lettuce leaves, about 5 inches in diameter. In the center of each, place a fresh, peeled peach half (or canned peach half). Around each "sun," arrange drained orange slices for the "sunrays." It's an easy salad, very tasty, and so pretty for special occasions. My kids always liked a surprise under each peach half — seedless grapes, hidden from view like little treasures.

Cranberry salad

This cranberry salad has graced our family's holiday tables for two generations now. A holiday wouldn't be the same without it. I'd rather eat my turkey or ham with this salad than "traditional" cranberry sauce. It's so sweet/tart and freshly chunky; I just love it. It molds well, too, so if you wish you can create little cranberry molds for each plate.

> 2 CUPS FRESH CRANBERRIES
> 1 CUP CHOPPED WALNUTS
> ½ CUP SUGAR
> 2 BOXES (3 OZ. EACH) CHERRY JELLO
> 8 OZ. CREAM CHEESE, SOFTENED

Grind fresh cranberries and walnuts together. Add sugar and set aside. Make Jello according to directions on box, only add the softened cream cheese to the Jello just after you add the boiling water. Mix very well until cream cheese has melted and mixed with the Jello. Then add the cold water according to directions and again mix well. Add the ground cranberries and walnuts. Refrigerate until Jello is just starting to set. Mix once more and refrigerate. Serve with sweetened whipped cream.

Fresh fruit salad

> 3 FIRM APPLES, PEELED AND SLICED
> 2 FRESH PEACHES, PEELED AND SLICED
> 2 CUPS SEEDLESS GRAPES, HALVED
> 1 CUP FRESH STRAWBERRIES, SLICED OR HALVED
> 1 CUP FRESH CHERRIES, PITTED AND HALVED
> ½ CUP CHOPPED NUTS
> 1 CUP MAYONNAISE
> ½ CUP SUGAR

2 Tbsp. milk
LETTUCE LEAVES

In salad bowls, arrange lettuce leaves. In a medium mixing bowl, mix all fresh fruits. In a small mixing bowl, add mayonnaise, sugar, and milk. Mix well until sugar is dissolved. Spoon fresh fruit out onto lettuce leaves and top with dressing.

Turkey salad

3½ cups diced cooked or canned turkey
4 celery stalks, sliced
1 medium onion, sliced
½ cup sweet red pepper, chopped
½ cup pecans, toasted and chopped
½ cup mayonnaise
1 Tbsp. lemon juice
½ tsp. celery seed
lettuce leaves, optional

In a large mixing bowl, combine turkey, celery, onions, red pepper, and pecans. In a small mixing bowl, combine mayonnaise, lemon juice, and celery seed. Stir well and mix with turkey mixture. Refrigerate for at least 1 hour. Serve on a bed of lettuce leaves or use as a sandwich filling. Of course, thick slices of homemade bread make this even better.

Grilled chicken salad

6 boneless skinless chicken breast halves
½ cup sliced green olives
1 medium red onion, chopped
2½ cups sliced celery
1 medium sweet red pepper, chopped
1 small head lettuce or mixed greens for salad
2 Tbsp. lemon juice

Dressing:
½ cup mayonnaise
3 Tbsp. vinegar
2 Tbsp. sugar
1 Tbsp. Dijon mustard (optional)
½ cup olive oil

Grill or sauté chicken breasts, turning once, until tender and done. Remove from grill. In large bowl, toss greens with green olives, onion, celery, and pepper. In a jar, mix dressing ingredients. Shake well. Lay warm chicken breasts over bed of greens and sprinkle with lemon juice. Pour dressing over salad and toss. You may add ½ cup of buttered, toasted bread croutons if you wish.

Gram Richards' sweet potato salad

> 2 LBS. SWEET POTATOES, BOILED AND MASHED
> 5 STALKS CELERY, CUT FINELY
> 1 LARGE BUNCH GREEN ONIONS, CHOPPED FINE
> 4 HARD-BOILED EGGS, PEELED AND MASHED
> 2 CUPS MAYONNAISE
> 2 TBSP. CATSUP
> 1 TBSP. SUGAR
> 1 TBSP. SWEET RELISH

Mix mashed sweet potatoes and mashed hard-boiled eggs. Add chopped celery and chopped onions. Add remaining ingredients, cover, and refrigerate.

Rice

I have adopted children from India and Korea, and we once sponsored a Vietnamese family of nine at our farm, so I learned to appreciate rice in all its glory, from main dishes to sweets. Some folks have never cooked rice that was not "instant" or precooked. My kids always told me instant rice was "yucky," and I have to agree. It's so easy to make do-it-yourself rice that I can't imagine paying a premium for an inferior product.

White rice (long grain and broken)

Although some cookbooks still say to add rice to boiling water, boil, then drain, I've found I don't like the results, so this is how I cook white rice:

> 1 CUP RAW REGULAR WHITE RICE
> 2½ CUPS COLD WATER OR COLD BROTH

Add rice and cold water or broth to large saucepan with tight lid. Bring to a boil, then cover and reduce heat to just simmering. Cook without "peeking" for 12 minutes. Then lift lid, stir, fluffing with a fork. Return cover and turn off heat and let stand for 5 minutes longer. Serve hot.

Tip: By adding seasonings, bouillon, powdered soup base, chopped vegetables, or herbs to the boiling rice, you can quickly turn plain old rice into something truly magnificent. I often add chopped chicken, ham, or bacon bits (TVPs), as well as using tomato juice instead of water and adding chopped green sweet peppers and seasonings to make a quick and easy Spanish rice. My Indian children loved rice with curry paste over it, but would also eat it with 1 Tbsp. curry powder and 2 Tbsp. butter melted in the boiling rice. All the rest of us, me included, preferred our rice with soy sauce, sweet and sour sauce, or with butter and brown sugar melted into the top.

Brown rice

Brown rice is whole grain rice, much as whole wheat flour is whole grain flour, compared to white flour, which is processed (the wheat germ removed and sometimes bleached unless you use unbleached flour). Because brown rice is whole grain rice, it will quickly get rancid unless it is packaged very tightly and used quite soon after opening. It also takes longer to cook. But it *does* taste very good and most people prefer brown rice, once they have tasted it.

    1 CUP RAW BROWN RICE
    2½ CUPS COLD WATER
    ½ TSP. SALT (OPTIONAL)

Add brown rice to cold water and salt in large saucepan with tight-fitting cover. Bring to a boil, then cover and reduce heat to barely simmering. Simmer for 30 minutes without peeking. Lift cover, fluff with fork. If getting very dry, add just a little more boiling water and fluff again. Mash a grain to see if it is nearly tender. If so, cover and let stand for 10 minutes. If still fairly hard, return to simmer for 10 minutes longer, then take off heat and let stand for 10 minutes.

Jasmine rice

Jasmine rice is a processed white rice with a very nice fragrance. It's often used in Oriental cooking, in place of long grain or brown rice. It does require a little longer cooking than long grain rice, however.

    1 CUP RAW JASMINE RICE
    2 CUPS COLD WATER
    ½ TSP. SALT

Rinse rice in cold water. Place 2 cups cold water and salt in large saucepan with a tight cover. Bring water to a boil and add rinsed rice. Cover and reduce heat to barely simmering. Cook without peeking for 20 minutes. Turn off heat and let stand, covered for 5 more minutes. Fluff with fork and serve hot.

Basmati rice

Basmati rice is a common fragrant rice, often used in Indian cooking. It is high in starch and can stick together if not presoaked.

    1 CUP RAW WHITE BASMATI RICE
    2 CUPS WATER
    ½ TSP. SALT

Rinse rice in bowl with cold water, using fingers to help with rinsing process. Drain and cover with cold water and let stand for 1 hour or longer. This rinsing and draining helps keep the rice nice and fluffy, fat and tender. After soaking, drain off water. Add 2 cups of water to a large saucepan with a tight fitting lid. Add salt. Bring to a boil and add rice. Cover and reduce heat to barely simmering. Simmer for 12 minutes. Do not open cover. Turn off heat and let stand for 10 minutes longer. Fluff with fork and serve.

Wild rice

Although wild rice is a grass seed, not a true rice, it is cooked like brown rice and has its own distinctive nutty flavor and a puffy, curly, black and white appearance. Wild rice is a traditional Native American crop, growing chiefly in northern Minnesota and Wisconsin. In any recipes, you may substitute broth for the water and add any seasonings you choose to suit your use and taste.

> 1 CUP WILD RICE
>
> 3 CUPS BOILING WATER
>
> ½ TSP. SALT

Rinse wild rice well in cold water to remove any chaff or dust. Bring 3 cups water and salt to a boil in a heavy saucepan with a tight-fitting cover. Add wild rice and bring to a boil. Cover and reduce heat to a slow simmer. Cook for 50 minutes. Remove cover and test rice; if tender, drain any remaining water and serve. If not, continue simmering, covered, for another 10 minutes. Drain, if necessary, and serve.

Pasta

When I was raising my large family on a small income, I quickly learned to include inexpensive pasta dishes frequently in my daily cooking.

Nearly all pasta is cooked the same way — boiled in plenty of slightly salted water. It is said that if you add olive oil to the boiling pasta it won't boil over. True, but it also coats the pasta so that the sauce doesn't stick well to it. So I never use oil and have never had pasta boil over. Of course, I use a very large pot and always am there to keep an eye on it! Never cover a pot of boiling pasta; that's not only asking for boil-overs, but it can also make your pasta sticky. Likewise, always make sure your pot of water is boiling heartily before you add your pasta. Adding pasta to water that is not boiling is asking for sticky, clumpy pasta.

The thicker your pasta is, the longer it will need to boil. Very small pastas, such as small shell macaroni, thin noodles, acini di pepe, or alphabet pasta need only a few minutes of boiling, where thicker pasta, such as lasagna, rigatoni, or manicotti need longer boiling.

Be sure to separate the pasta while boiling in plenty of water, so it doesn't clump together, especially when first adding it to the water.

No pasta should be boiled too long! Pasta should be firm, yet tender. This is called *al dente*. Properly boiled pasta shouldn't be like canned SpaghettiOs. That is mush, not pasta.

Pasta should be drained as soon as it becomes tender, but not rinsed. The only exception to this is if the pasta is going to be used in a cold salad. Then it should be rinsed to prevent it from sticking together in a lump or having the pasta break apart when mixed with the other ingredients.

Homemade Rice-A-Roni

> 2 TBSP. BUTTER OR MARGARINE
>
> ½ CUP ANGEL-HAIR PASTA, BROKEN INTO SMALL PIECES, OR VERMICELLI IF YOU CAN FIND IT
>
> ¾ CUP LONG GRAIN WHITE RICE
>
> 1 CUBE BOUILLON, BEEF OR CHICKEN

¼ CUP DICED ONION (FOR BEEF VERSION)

2⅔ CUPS HOT WATER

Melt butter in a large saucepan. Add pasta and rice, stirring to lightly brown. Add onion, if used. Add hot water and bouillon. Stir to dissolve. Cover well and turn down heat to slow simmer. Simmer, covered, for 20 minutes or until rice is tender and water is absorbed. If necessary, add a bit more boiling water and cover; cook 5 minutes longer. Keep cover on, remove from heat, and allow to stand for 10 minutes. You can also add chopped, dried parsley leaves, chopped chives, or minced garlic for added flavoring. Who needs store-bought? And this version is much cheaper, too. Did I mention it's *so* much better?

For the Spanish rice version, just substitute tomato juice for the water and add dehydrated green peppers, chopped onion, minced garlic, and a bit of chili powder and you've got it!

Pasta salad

2 CUPS UNCOOKED ELBOW OR SHELL MACARONI

1 CUP MAYONNAISE

2 TBSP. LEMON JUICE

1 TBSP. SUGAR (OPTIONAL)

⅛ TSP. PEPPER

1 CUP DRAINED LIGHT TUNA OR HAM, CUBED

1 MEDIUM ONION, DICED

½ CUP FRESH OR FROZEN PEAS (UNCOOKED; IF FROZEN, THAW UNDER RUNNING WATER)

In salted water (1 tsp. salt to 2 quarts boiling water), simmer pasta until tender. Drain. Add pasta to bowl. Mix in mayonnaise, lemon juice, sugar, and pepper. Add tuna or ham cubes. Toss lightly to coat. Add onion and peas. Toss lightly again. Refrigerate, covered for at least 1 hour. I often add fresh, uncooked asparagus tips to this salad when the first asparagus is popping out of the ground; there aren't enough spears for a meal, but there's plenty for this recipe!

Breads

Nothing, absolutely *nothing*, you buy in a store or bakery can come close to homemade baked breads. When you serve your own breads, rolls, coffee cakes, and more, your family's mouths will water even before the meal is. While breads have gotten an ill-deserved name for being hard to bake and taking lots of work and elbow grease to turn out, actually they are quite easy and quick to make, especially when you bake them often and develop the knack for baking. Like anything else, the more you do it, the better you'll get. And I promise your family will love your results! Besides, you'll save a ton of money, too. I call that a total win-win situation, don't you?

Note: Today you can buy pre-sifted flour in the stores, so most people have gotten out of the habit of sifting flour. When flour has been in storage for a long time, it needs to be sifted at least once, and preferably twice. This will make it fluffy and light and remove any lumps. Measure flour for these recipes after you have sifted it.

Biscuits, rolls, and tortillas

Tip: For any of these rolls and flat breads you may use dehydrated, reconstituted shortening, milk, or eggs in place of fresh.

Baking powder biscuits

- 2 CUPS FLOUR
- 4 TSP. BAKING POWDER
- 1 TSP. SALT
- 2 TBSP. SHORTENING
- ¾ CUP MILK

Sift dry ingredients, then cut in shortening until it is in small pieces. Add milk (a little more if necessary) and form into a ball. Lightly knead in bowl, then roll out to about ½-inch thick on a lightly-floured surface, cut (I use a regular-sized canning jar lid), place on greased baking sheet and bake at 400° F until light golden on top. Or use homemade biscuit mix in the pantry mix section. You may also use reconstituted powdered milk and dehydrated shortening in this recipe.

Buttermilk biscuits

- 2 CUPS FLOUR
- ½ TSP. BAKING SODA
- 2 TSP. BAKING POWDER
- 1 TSP. SALT

¼ CUP COLD SHORTENING

¾ CUP BUTTERMILK

Sift dry ingredients together. Cut in shortening until mixture resembles coarse crumbs. Add buttermilk. Stir until dough clings together. Knead lightly, then lay ball out on lightly-floured surface. Roll ½-inch thick and cut with biscuit cutter (or canning jar lid). Place on greased baking sheet and bake at 450° F for about 12 minutes until golden on top. You may also use reconstituted powdered buttermilk and dehydrated shortening in this recipe.

Grandma's light biscuits

1 PKG. (2¼ TSP.) DRY YEAST

¼ CUP WARM WATER

1 CUP WARM BUTTERMILK

2½ CUPS FLOUR

1 TBSP. SUGAR

1½ TSP. BAKING POWDER

1½ TSP. BAKING SODA

1 TSP. SALT

½ CUP SHORTENING

Dissolve yeast in warm water; let stand 5 minutes. Stir in the buttermilk. Set aside. In a large mixing bowl, combine flour, sugar, baking powder, baking soda, and salt. Cut in shortening until mixture resembles coarse crumbs. Stir in yeast/buttermilk mixture; mix well. Turn out onto a lightly-floured surface. Knead lightly 3-4 times. Roll out to ½-inch thickness and cut with biscuit cutter. Place on a lightly-greased baking sheet. Cover with a warm, moist, clean kitchen towel and let rise in a warm place about an hour or more. Bake at 450° F for 8-10 minutes. Lightly brush tops with melted butter. You may also use reconstituted powdered buttermilk and dehydrated shortening in this recipe.

Cheese biscuits

1 CUP FLOUR

¼ TSP. SALT

1 TBSP. BAKING POWDER

1 TBSP. BUTTER OR MARGARINE

½ CUP GRATED CHEDDAR CHEESE

½ CUP MILK

Sift dry ingredients. Work in butter or margarine and cheese, until mixture resembles coarse crumbs. Add milk. Mix quickly and lightly. Drop by spoonfuls on well-greased baking sheet. Bake at 450° F for 12 minutes. You may also use reconstituted dehydrated butter, milk, and cheese in this recipe.

Cornbread

¾ CUP CORNMEAL
1 CUP FLOUR
2 EGGS
¼ CUP MELTED SHORTENING
2 TBSP. SUGAR
1 CUP MILK
3 TSP. BAKING POWDER
1 TSP. SALT

Beat all ingredients until smooth. Grease the bottom of a 9-inch square pan and pour batter into it. Bake at 400° F for about 20 minutes. For variation, you may also add ½ cup drained corn kernels or ½ cup shredded cheese. You may also use reconstituted dehydrated eggs, shortening, and dry milk for this recipe. *Or* you can use the homemade cornbread mix on page 264.

Tip: You can also use this recipe to make cornbread muffins or corn sticks. If you use a corn stick mold, grease and preheat it in your oven until very warm before putting batter in it, to make releasing the sticks easier after baking. To grease a cast iron corn stick pan, either spray a baking spray on it or lightly brush melted shortening into each mold.

Spoonbread

2 CUPS MILK, SCALDED
1 CUP CORNMEAL
1 TBSP. SUGAR
4 BEATEN EGGS.
2 TSP. BAKING POWDER
1 TSP. SALT
2 TBSP. MELTED SHORTENING

Scald milk and pour immediately over cornmeal. Cool and add sugar and eggs. Stir in baking powder, salt, and shortening. Beat well. Bake in greased pan at 350° F for about 45 minutes. This is like an eggy cornbread; not at all grainy, like most cornbread. It's moist and smooth. Serve hot with butter.

Double-quick dinner rolls

1 PKG. (2¼ TSP.) DRY YEAST
¾ CUP WARM WATER
¼ CUP SUGAR
2¼ CUPS SIFTED FLOUR
¼ CUP SOFT SHORTENING OR BUTTER
1 TSP. SALT
1 EGG, BEATEN

Dissolve yeast in water, add sugar, salt, and about half the flour. Beat thoroughly 2 minutes. Add egg and shortening. Then beat in the remaining flour gradually until smooth. Spoon out, half filling lightly-greased muffin tins. Bake at 400° F for about 10 minutes.

Half-time spoon rolls

This is one of our family's old, long-time favorite recipes, handed down from cook to cook. It shows up at all of our holiday feasts. Not only does it taste great, but it's very easy and quick to make. I also use it frequently to make my own hamburger and hot dog buns by just adding an extra ½ cup of flour, making it easier to handle and shape into buns on a greased cookie sheet. (Remember that this dough rises a lot, so make your buns on the small side!)

1 PKG. (2¼ TSP.) DRY YEAST
¼ CUP WARM WATER
⅓ CUP SHORTENING
¼ CUP SUGAR
1 TSP. SALT
¾ CUP HOT SCALDED MILK
½ CUP COLD WATER
1 EGG
3½ CUPS SIFTED FLOUR

Stir yeast into water and let sit. Combine shortening, sugar, and salt into hot milk. Cool to lukewarm by adding ½ cup cold water, then add egg and yeast. Beat in 2 cups flour until smooth, then mix in the rest of the flour (1½ cups). Let rise in warm place, covered, until doubled. Stir down dough, then spoon into well-greased muffin tins, filling half full. Let rise and bake at 400° F for about 15 minutes. Brush tops with melted butter. I often sprinkle sesame or poppy seeds on after I butter the tops for extra sparkle and taste.

Dinner rolls

⅓ CUP MILK
⅓ CUP SUGAR
1 TSP. SALT
2 TBSP. BUTTER OR MARGARINE
1 TBSP. DRY YEAST
⅓ CUP WARM WATER
2 EGGS, BEATEN
3¼ CUPS FLOUR

Scald milk; cool to lukewarm. Add sugar, salt, and melted butter or margarine. Add yeast and warm water and stir until yeast dissolves. Add beaten egg and stir in flour. Let rise until double, covered in a warm place. Divide dough into 12 equal parts and form into balls. Place two inches apart on greased cookie sheet. Brush with melted margarine or butter and let rise 1 hour or until doubled. Bake at 400° F for 20 minutes.

Butter horns (crescent rolls)

These are so much better than the "rolls in a can" from the dairy section of your store. When my youngest son, David, was about 6 years old, his grandma gave him a roll of these refrigerated crescent rolls as a "treat." Of course, he had always eaten homemade butter horns and biscuits, so he was not familiar with them. When I thunked the roll on the countertop to open it, he stood by, fascinated. But when it exploded with a loud BANG, he jumped back with huge eyes. "I'm not eating exploding rolls, Mom! Make me some homemade ones. Please?"

Mix these ingredients in bowl and let stand 15 minutes:
- 1 PKG. (2¼ TSP.) DRY YEAST
- 1 CUP WARM WATER
- 1 TBSP. SUGAR
- 3 EGGS

Add:
- ½ CUP SUGAR
- ½ CUP SHORTENING, MELTED
- ½ TSP. SALT
- 5 CUPS FLOUR

Mix well, then knead well. Let stand in refrigerator overnight. Divide in 2 parts and roll out on a lightly-floured surface, into a 12-inch circle. Cut into 16 wedges by cutting into half, quarters, eighths, then sixteenths. Roll up each triangle, starting with wide edge. Lay on greased cookie sheet and let rise 3-4 hours, covered. Bake at 400° F for 15 minutes until golden on tops. Brush with butter and serve while warm.

Easy potato rolls

- ⅔ CUP SUGAR
- ⅔ CUP SHORTENING
- 1 CUP MASHED POTATOES (OR RECONSTITUTED DRY POTATO FLAKES)
- 2 TSP. SALT
- 2 EGGS
- 2 PKGS. (4½ TSP.) DRY YEAST
- 1⅓ CUPS WARM WATER, DIVIDED
- 6-6½ CUPS FLOUR

In a large mixing bowl, cream sugar and shortening. Add potatoes, salt, and eggs. Mix well. In a small bowl, dissolve yeast in ⅔ cup of warm water; add to creamed mixture. Beat in 2 cups flour and remaining water. Add enough remaining flour to form a soft dough. Shape into a ball; do not knead. Place in a greased bowl, turning once to grease the top. Cover and let rise in a warm place until doubled (about 1 hour). Punch down; divide into thirds. Shape each portion into 15 balls and arrange in 3 greased 9-inch round baking pans. Cover and let rise until doubled (about 30 minutes). Bake at 375° F for 20-25 minutes. Remove from pans to cool on wire racks.

Whole wheat rolls

2 pkgs. (4½ tsp.) dry yeast
½ cup warm water
1¾ cups milk, scalded
½ cup sugar
1 Tbsp. salt
3 Tbsp. shortening
4 cups whole wheat flour
3 cups white flour
2 eggs, beaten

Soften dry yeast in warm water. Combine hot milk, sugar, salt, and shortening and cool to lukewarm. Add 1 cup whole wheat flour and eggs. Beat well. Add yeast. Stir in remaining flour or enough to make a soft, yet not sticky, dough. Knead lightly on lightly-floured board. Place in greased bowl, turning once to grease top. Cover and let rise in warm place until double. Punch down and form in rolls. Place in greased round cake pan. Let rise in warm place until double (about 1½ hours). Bake at 400° F for 15-20 minutes. Brush tops with butter. Makes 4 dozen rolls. If you want less, simply halve recipe amounts.

Flour tortillas

4 cups flour
1 tsp. salt
2 tsp. baking powder
2 Tbsp. lard or shortening
1½ cups water

Mix dry ingredients in bowl and cut in lard/shortening until mixture resembles dry meal. Then add water and mix well. Knead well on lightly-floured surface. Divide dough into 24 equal pieces and roll into balls. Preheat a large cast iron frying pan, without grease. (You bake tortillas, not fry them!) Roll out a ball with a rolling pin, making a nice, thin tortilla. Put it onto the hot griddle and bake until bubbly and just getting golden brown. Turn onto the other side and bake. Put into a tortilla warmer to keep warm and repeat with the rest of the dough. While you may substitute shortening for lard, tortillas made with lard taste much better and are flakier. These tortillas are *very* easy to make and taste much better than their cardboard-like store-bought counterparts.

Corn tortillas

    2 CUPS MASA HARINA (CORN FLOUR, NOT CORNMEAL)
    1 TSP. SALT
    1¼ CUPS (PLUS 2 TBSP.) HOT WATER
    1 TSP. SHORTENING

Mix masa harina and salt in medium bowl and set aside. Pour 1¼ cups boiling water in another bowl and add shortening. Add to masa harina and mix well. If it is too dry, add 1 Tbsp. more of hot water at a time until the dough seems a bit dry but will still cling together. You don't want it to get too sticky. When the dough clings together, knead lightly into a ball. Divide the dough into golf ball-size pieces and roll into balls and gently flatten them a little with your hands. If you have a tortilla press (a *real* handy gadget), cut a piece of plastic or slip a bag over the top and bottom pieces. Place a flattened ball between the bags, a bit closer to the hinge part and close the press firmly. I like my tortillas thinner still, so I roll each one a little with a rolling pin before slipping them into a preheated cast iron frying pan, without grease or cooking spray. I bake my tortillas. Of course, you *can* fry them too! I often cut my tortillas into wedges and deep fry them for nacho chips or leave them round and deep fry them, to serve them with melted cheese and salsa mixed. Add a dish of refried beans and you have a great, filling meal. To use these tortillas in enchiladas, bake them first, then dip and roll them up. Again, homemade corn tortillas are so much more flavorful than store-bought ones. Even the aroma is way better!

Chapatis (Indian flatbread)

    1 CUP FLOUR
    1 CUP WHOLE WHEAT FLOUR
    ½ TSP. SALT
    2 TBSP. PEANUT OIL (PLUS A LITTLE EXTRA FOR GREASING YOUR BOARD) MAY SUBSTITUTE OLIVE OIL OR VEGETABLE OIL
    ½-¾ CUP WATER

In a medium-sized bowl, mix flours and salt. Mix in 2 Tbsp. oil. Add ½ cup water. If dough breaks up, add more water so it holds together and is slightly sticky.

Grease a board with a little oil. Knead the dough on this until smooth (about 10 minutes). The more you knead, the lighter the chapatis will be. Cover the dough with a moist, warm kitchen towel. Let rest 30 minutes.

Break dough into 12 equal parts. Keep unused dough balls under the towel so they remain moist. Press one ball flat by hand. Lightly flour the board and roll the ball out to about 6 inches in diameter. Bake on an ungreased cast iron frying pan, shaking it back and forth or moving it with your fingers so it doesn't stick. When the bottom is lightly brown, turn the chapati over. When that side is lightly brown, turn it again. It should puff up with large bubbles.

Chapatis are easy and are great with just about any meal, from Indian curries to just eating for breakfast, in place of toast.

Ada's finger rolls

This recipe was given to my grandmother by her sister, Ada, and we've used it for a long, long time in our family. These rolls are very tender and different, pulling apart in yummy layers that are oh-so-good.

> 2 PKGS. (4½ TSP.) DRY YEAST
> ¼ CUP WARM WATER
> 2 CUPS MILK, SCALDED AND COOLED
> 3 TBSP. MELTED SHORTENING
> 2 EGGS, WELL BEATEN
> ¾ TSP. SALT
> ½ CUP SUGAR
> 6-6½ CUPS FLOUR

Add yeast to ¼ cup warm water and mix. Let stand. Add lukewarm scalded milk, melted shortening, eggs, salt, and sugar together in large bowl. Add yeast mix. Stir well. Add flour (you want enough flour to make a soft, yet not sticky ball, so adjust as needed). Knead into loaf for 10 minutes on lightly-floured board. Grease bowl, wipe top of dough in grease, then flip over. Cover with damp kitchen towel and let rise in warm place until double. Punch dough down and repeat. Again punch dough down and let rise until double. (This makes *very* light rolls.) Break off finger-sized dough. You want Tootsie roll-like pieces, as fat as a finger. Dip in melted butter and crowd pieces together, next to each other, like logs, in lightly-buttered bread pan. Let rise and bake at 350° F for 30 minutes, then reduce heat to 300° for another 20 minutes or until light golden brown on top.

Quick breads

Hush puppies

> 2 CUPS CORNMEAL
> 2 TBSP. FLOUR
> 1 TSP. BAKING SODA
> 1 TBSP. BAKING POWDER
> 1 EGG
> 2 CUPS BUTTERMILK
> 2 TSP. SALT
> 8 TBSP. GRATED ONIONS

Mix all of the ingredients in a bowl. Drop the batter by spoonfuls into hot oil. They will be crisp and will float when they're done. Be sure the oil is *hot* or the hush puppies will become grease-soaked and heavy. Drain well on paper towels and serve hot.

Corn fritters

½ cup milk
2 cups cooked corn (can use reconstituted dehydrated corn)
1½ cups flour
2 tsp. baking powder
1 tsp. salt
1 Tbsp. melted shortening

Mix milk and corn together, then add dry ingredients and melted shortening. Fry by dropping spoonfuls in hot oil.

Cornmeal corn fritters

1 cup flour
½ cup cornmeal
2 tsp. baking powder
½ tsp. salt
½ tsp. sugar
⅛ tsp. ground red pepper
¾ cup milk
1 large egg
2 Tbsp. melted butter
1 cup cooked corn
thinly sliced garlic, if desired
vegetable oil for frying

In medium bowl, mix dry ingredients. Add milk, egg, and butter. Stir. Fold in corn and garlic. In large skillet, heat ½-inch of oil to 375° F. Spoon batter by heaping tablespoonfuls into hot oil. Fry on one side until golden brown, then turn and do other side. You may substitute dehydrated, reconstituted corn and garlic for fresh or canned.

Indian fry bread

3 cups unbleached flour, sifted
½ cup dry powdered milk
1 Tbsp. baking powder
½ tsp. salt
½ cup warm water or milk
1 quart oil for deep frying

Combine the first 5 ingredients in a large mixing bowl and knead until smooth and soft, but not sticky. Add more flour if necessary. Be careful not to overwork the dough, or it will become tough and chewy. Brush a tablespoon of oil over the finished dough and allow it to rest 20 minutes to 2 hours in a bowl covered with a damp cloth. After the dough has rested, heat the oil in a broad, deep frying pan or kettle until it reaches 375° F. Pull off egg-sized balls of dough and quickly roll, pull, and pat them out into large, plate-sized rounds. They should be thin in the middle and about

¼-inch thick at the edges. Carefully ease each piece of flattened dough into the hot boiling oil, one at a time. Using a long-handled cooking fork or tongs, turn the dough one time. Allow about 2 minutes cooking time per side. When golden brown, lift from oil, shake gently to remove bulk of oil, and place on layered brown paper or paper towels to finish draining. The secret of the fry bread not absorbing grease is to always fry it quickly in *hot* oil. Be sure the oil stays hot between fry breads so it doesn't give you grease-soaked food.

You can serve these hot with honey, sugar and cinnamon, or taco filling over the top and cheese grated on them.

Popovers

Popovers are crispy and tender shells around a hollow center. I really like to serve these a different way; I cut into the top, then fill, while steaming hot, with sloppy joe mix and top with shredded cheese, which instantly melts. This makes a really different, quick meal that fills those hungry people up!

1 CUP FLOUR, SIFTED TWICE
½ TSP. SALT
2 EGGS, BEATEN WELL
1 CUP MILK

Sift flour, then add salt and sift again. Mix eggs and milk into dry ingredients. Beat well. Fill well-greased muffin tins or popover cups ½ full. Bake at 425° F for about 40 minutes. Don't peek until the very last or your popovers may fall!

Tropical bread

⅓ CUP SHORTENING
⅔ CUP SUGAR
2 EGGS
1 CUP MASHED RIPE BANANA (OR RECONSTITUTED, DEHYDRATED BANANA CHIPS)
¼ CUP BUTTERMILK OR SOUR MILK
1¼ CUPS FLOUR
1 TSP. BAKING POWDER
½ TSP. SALT
½ TSP. BAKING SODA
1 CUP BRAN
¾ CUP CHOPPED, DRIED APRICOTS
½ CUP COARSELY CHOPPED WALNUTS

Cream shortening and sugar. Add eggs and beat well. Mix bananas and buttermilk (or sour milk). Sift together dry ingredients and add alternately with banana mixture to creamed mixture. Stir in bran, apricots, and nuts. Pour into a greased bread pan and bake at 350° F about 1 hour or until done.

Sopapillas (Mexican fry bread)

I learned about sopapillas when we lived in New Mexico. Nearly every Mexican restaurant there serves sopapillas with every meal. I really love them, and each time I make them, I remember the warm sun and warm people of the state.

> 3 CUPS FLOUR
> 2 TSP. BAKING POWDER
> 1 TSP. SALT
> 4-6 TBSP. LARD OR SHORTENING
> 1¼ CUPS WARM MILK (APPROXIMATELY)
> VEGETABLE OIL

In a large bowl, combine dry ingredients, then cut in shortening until it resembles large crumbs. Mix in milk. Turn out onto a well-floured board and knead until it is no longer sticky. Cover and let rest for 15 minutes. Divide the dough in half and keep one half covered to keep it from drying out. Roll remaining half of dough to a ¼-inch thick rectangle, using light strokes; do not overwork it or it will become tough. Cut dough into squares or triangles. Heat vegetable oil in deep fryer to 400° F. This is important to get the sopapillas to puff. You want them to look like little pillows. Slide one at a time into the hot oil. They should puff nearly at once. Add a couple more, then with a slotted spoon, turn the first, as they'll often want to float with only one side down. As they get golden, dip them out onto paper towels to drain. Keep hot in the oven at 200° F and cut and cook remaining dough. Serve hot with warm honey. These are very good!

Pumpkin bread

> 3½ CUPS FLOUR
> 2 TSP. BAKING SODA
> 1 TSP. SALT
> 1 TSP. CINNAMON
> 1 TSP. NUTMEG
> 1½ CUPS SUGAR
> 1 CUP VEGETABLE OIL
> 4 EGGS, BEATEN
> 1 PINT PUMPKIN CHUNKS, DRAINED AND MASHED OR 16-OZ. CAN PUMPKIN
> ¾ CUP BUTTERMILK OR SOUR MILK
> 1 TSP. VANILLA
> 1 CUP RAISINS
> 1 CUP CHOPPED PECANS

In a large bowl, sift dry ingredients together. Add sugar, oil, eggs, pumpkin, and buttermilk (or sour milk). Mix well and stir in vanilla, raisins, and pecans. Pour into 2 greased bread pans. Bake at 350° F for 1 hour or until done. Let stand 10 minutes before removing from pans. Cool on a wire rack.

Banana nut bread

½ cup shortening
½ cup sugar
2 eggs
1¾ cups flour
2 tsp. baking powder
½ tsp. salt
¼ tsp. baking soda
1 cup mashed bananas (or reconstituted, dehydrated banana chips)
½ cup walnuts, chopped coarsely

Cream shortening and sugar together. Add eggs and beat well. Sift dry ingredients together. Add to creamed mixture, alternately with banana, beating well after each addition. Stir in walnuts. Pour into well-greased loaf pan. Bake at 350° F for about an hour or until done. Remove from pan while hot and cool on rack.

Cranberry bread

1½ cups chopped raw cranberries
4 tsp. grated orange peel
3 Tbsp. sugar
3 cups flour
1¼ cups sugar
3 tsp. baking powder
½ tsp. baking soda
¾ tsp. nutmeg
2 eggs, beaten
¾ cup orange juice
¾ cup water
½ cup melted shortening
1 cup chopped walnuts

Mix cranberries, orange peel, and 3 Tbsp. sugar. Sift dry ingredients. Add eggs to orange juice and water. Mix. Add cranberries and shortening to dry ingredients with eggs, water and orange juice. Mix just enough to moisten. Fold in nuts. Turn into greased bread tin and bake at 350° F about 1½ hours. If the top tries to get too dark toward the end, quickly slip a piece of aluminum foil over the loaf.

Lemon bread

This is another of our family's favorites, especially during the holidays. It is sweet and moist, yet lemony tangy. It makes a very thoughtful holiday gift.

⅓ cup melted butter
1¼ cups sugar, divided
2 eggs
¼ tsp. almond extract
1½ cups flour
1 tsp. baking powder
½ cup milk
1 Tbsp. grated lemon peel
½ cup nuts
3 Tbsp. lemon juice

Blend butter and 1 cup sugar; reserve the ¼ cup. Beat in eggs, one at a time. Add almond extract. Sift and add dry ingredients alternately with egg mixture and milk. Blend just until mixed. Fold in chopped nuts and lemon peel. Turn into a greased bread pan and bake at 320° F about 70 minutes. Watch carefully as it tends to scorch. Mix lemon juice and ¼ cup sugar and spoon over loaf when taken from oven. Let set for 24 hours before slicing.

Tip: For orange bread, substitute orange peel and juice for the lemon peel and juice.

Orange date bread

2 cups flour
½ cup sugar
1 tsp. baking powder
½ tsp. baking soda
1 cup chopped dates
½ cup boiling water
1½ tsp. grated orange rind
¼ cup orange juice
1 egg, beaten
3 Tbsp. melted shortening
1 tsp. vanilla
½ cup chopped nuts

Sift dry ingredients twice. Chop dates very fine and add boiling water. Mix and cool to lukewarm. Add orange rind, juice, egg, shortening, and vanilla. Mix well, stir in nuts, and pour into sifted dry ingredients. Stir just until moistened. Turn into a greased bread pan and bake at 350° F for about 1 hour.

Mom's brown bread

This bread is very good with butter, sprinkled with cinnamon sugar, or spread lightly with mild goat cheese or cream cheese. A can goes pretty quickly around here!

> 1 CUP WATER
> 1¼ CUPS RAISINS
> 3 TBSP. BUTTER OR MARGARINE
> 1½ TSP. BAKING SODA
> 2 EGGS
> 1 CUP SUGAR
> 1¾ CUPS FLOUR
> 1 TSP. VANILLA EXTRACT
> ½ TSP. SALT

In a saucepan, bring water to a boil. Add raisins, butter, and baking soda. Remove from heat. In a mixing bowl, beat eggs, add sugar, flour, vanilla, and salt. Stir into raisin mixture. Grease 3 vegetable or fruit cans (16 oz.), with the labels removed. Divide the batter between the cans and place on a cookie sheet in the oven. Bake at 350° F for 35 to 40 minutes. Let stand 5 minutes before removing from cans. If necessary, you can remove the end of the can, then use it to push the bread through. Cool on a wire rack.

Yeast breads

Yeast bread basics

Yeast is a living plant and must be softened in warm (110 degree) water to activate. Water hotter than this will kill it, and water that is too cool will make it grow slower and not be as active. The active yeast produces the gas that causes bread dough to rise. Sugar or honey is usually used to feed the yeast, and salt controls the fermentation, so the gas bubbles don't get too large and make huge holes in the bread.

When mixing the dough for the first time in the bowl, add enough flour to keep the dough from sticking to your hands. Bread dough should not be so sticky that it is yucky to knead; it should be moist, yet smooth and firmly yielding to your hands.

To knead bread dough, lightly flour a surface (bread board or countertop) and flour your hands so the dough won't stick to them. I partially knead my dough in the bowl so this won't happen. If I must add a bit more flour I do it in the bowl, so when it's turned out, it is no longer sticky. You knead bread with the heel of your hands. With one hand, pull the rear of the dough into the middle and push down with the heel of your hand. Turn the entire dough ball slightly, then again pull the rear to the middle and push down. Push hard! Then again turn the dough in the same direction and again pull the rear to the middle. This is repeated for several minutes. You'll develop a rhythm. Add a bit of flour from your hands if the dough still seems sticky. Pretty soon, the dough ball will seem smooth and elastic. A good kneading usually takes about 10 minutes. When the dough is very smooth and feels alive, it is ready for the first rising.

Lightly grease or oil a large bowl and place the dough in it, then flip the dough over so the top is greased. Cover the bowl with a moist, warm kitchen towel and let sit in a warm place until double. This can take from 45 minutes to an hour. When it has risen enough, you can push a finger down in the top and the dent will remain.

Now it is ready to be punched down. Turn it out onto a lightly-floured surface and hit it. When they say "punch it down," they mean get aggressive! This distributes the gluten and gas bubbles before the next rise. Knead it and punch it again, pulling it in to the center, then smacking it down. Then work it back into a nice ball, divide, and shape your loaves. To make traditional bread loaves, divide the dough, then form each into a ball. One good method to ensure even baking is to roll each ball out, one at a time, into a 15x7-inch rectangle, then roll the dough up like a jellyroll, sealing at each turn with fingertips or the edge of the hand. Press down on the ends of the loaf with the sides of your hands to make a sealed edge on each end, then turn these strips under the loaf as you put it in the pan. This ensures that the loaf will be smooth and will rise evenly.

Cover the bread dough in the pans and let sit in a warm place until doubled. Again, press down gently in the top of the dough. If the finger dent remains, it's ready to bake. Bread rises and bakes best in a fairly hot oven (most recipes call for 375° to 400° F). Peek in at your loaves after 15 minutes. If the tops are browning too quickly, cover them with foil. Brush the tops of your hot loaves with butter for a soft shiny crust. If you like a softer crust, put a pan of water in your oven when you bake your bread. The steam will keep your crust softer.

Note: In any of these bread recipes you may substitute reconstituted dehydrated powdered milk, eggs, shortening, or buttermilk for fresh.

Perfect white bread

1 PKG. (2¼ TSP.) DRY YEAST
¼ CUP WARM WATER
2 CUPS MILK, SCALDED
2 TBSP. SUGAR
2 TSP. SALT
1 TBSP. SHORTENING
6-6¼ CUPS FLOUR, DIVIDED

Soften dry yeast in warm water. Mix scalded milk, sugar, salt, and shortening. Cool to lukewarm. Stir in 2 cups of the flour and beat well. Add the softened yeast. Mix. Add enough of the remaining flour to make a moderately stiff dough. (Not sticky; not too firm.) Turn out onto lightly-floured board and knead until smooth and satiny (about 10 minutes). Shape dough into a ball. Place in a lightly-greased bowl, turning once to grease surface of the ball. Cover with a moist kitchen towel and let rise in a warm place until double (about 1½ hours). Punch down. Let rise again until double (45 minutes). Cut in 2 portions. Shape each in a smooth ball. Cover. Let rest 10 minutes. Shape into 2 loaves and place in a greased bread pan. Let rise until double. Bake at 400° F for about 35 minutes or until done. Peek in oven after 15 minutes; if tops are browning too fast, cover with foil. Brush the tops of your loaves with butter for soft shiny crusts.

Mom's best-ever white bread

2 cups milk, scalded
2 Tbsp. sugar
2 tsp. salt
1 Tbsp. shortening
1 pkg. (2¼ tsp.) dry yeast
¼ cup warm water
about 6 cups flour

Scald milk, then add sugar, salt, and shortening. Cool to lukewarm. Sprinkle yeast on warm water and stir in. Add yeast and 3 cups flour to milk mix. Beat until smooth. Add rest of the flour, turn out on a floured board, and let rest 10 minutes. Knead about 10 minutes. Form into a ball and turn into a greased bowl. Turn the dough over, cover with a moist, warm kitchen towel, and let rise in a warm place until double. Punch down and let rise again. Divide into 2 loaves. Put in greased bread pans and let rise until double. Bake at 400° F for about 35 minutes.

Homemade bread

1 pkg. (2¼ tsp.) dry yeast
1 tsp. sugar
2 cups warm water, divided
6½ cups flour
⅓ cup softened shortening, butter, or margarine,
1 Tbsp. salt

Dissolve yeast and sugar in ½ cup warm water. Let stand 5 minutes. Add remaining water and 3 cups flour. Beat until smooth. Cover for 6 to 24 hours. Add shortening and salt. Stir in enough remaining flour to make a soft dough. Knead on a lightly-floured board about 8 minutes. Place in a greased bowl, turning once to grease top. Cover and let rise in a warm place until doubled (about 1 hour). Punch dough down. Divide into 2 parts. Form into loaves and place in greased bread pans. Let rise in a warm place, covered, until doubled. Bake at 400° F until golden brown, about 35 minutes. Remove from pans soon after baking and cool on a wire rack.

Honey whole wheat bread

This is one of my favorite bread recipes — one that I've used for more than 40 years. You need the 3 loaves because your family will beg for a loaf, right out of the oven, steaming hot, to eat right away. Try to hold them off for about 20 minutes or it doesn't cut very well. But oh how good it is! When my youngest son, David, was little, he would help me grind the wheat that went immediately into this bread. And, of course, he was always right there to get his share when it came out of the oven!

- 2 PKGS. (4½ TSP.) DRY YEAST
- 5 CUPS WARM WATER, DIVIDED
- 6 TBSP. SHORTENING
- ¼ CUP HONEY
- 4 CUPS WHOLE WHEAT FLOUR
- ½ CUP INSTANT POTATOES (DRY) NOTE: YOU CAN SUBSTITUTE 1 CUP MASHED POTATOES FOR DRY.
- ½ CUP POWDERED MILK
- 1 TBSP. SALT
- ABOUT 7 CUPS UNBLEACHED FLOUR

Sprinkle yeast on ½ cup warm water. Melt shortening in large pan. Add honey and 4½ cups warm water. Mix dry ingredients, except for white flour, and add to shortening/honey/water mix. Mix until smooth. Add yeast and beat well. Add enough white flour to make a medium dough. Turn out and knead on a lightly-floured surface for about 10 minutes. Place in a greased bowl, turn over once to grease top. Cover with a warm, moist kitchen towel and let rise until double. Punch down and divide into 3 loaves. Form loaves and place in greased bread pans. Let rise, covered, until doubled. Bake at 375° F for about 50 minutes. Peek after 30 minutes and if the tops are getting too brown, cover with foil. Turn loaves out after baking and cool on wire racks. Brush tops with butter while warm for a nice, shiny, soft top.

Whole wheat bread

- 5-6 CUPS WHOLE WHEAT FLOUR, DIVIDED
- 1 TSP. SALT
- 2 PKGS. (4½ TSP.) DRY YEAST
- 1¼ CUPS MILK
- ¾ CUP HONEY
- ⅓ CUP VEGETABLE OIL
- 2 EGGS

Mix 2½ cups flour, salt, and yeast. In a saucepan, heat the milk to scalding, then add the honey and oil. Cool to lukewarm and add eggs. Mix well. Add the liquid mixture to the flour/yeast. Beat well. Stir in the rest of the flour. This batter does not need to be kneaded. Cover the bowl and place in a warm spot to rise until double (1-2 hours). Turn out onto a lightly-floured bowl and punch down and knead for a few minutes. Add a little flour if the dough is too sticky to handle. Shape into loaves (any shape you wish or traditional bread loaves to go in bread pans). Put round or free-form loaves onto greased cookie sheet or one regular loaf into a greased bread pan. Cover and let rise until doubled. Bake at 375° F for about 35 minutes or until done.

Potato bread

    1 PKG. (2¼ TSP.) DRY YEAST
    ⅓ CUP WARM WATER
    1 CUP MILK, SCALDED
    1 TBSP. GRANULATED SUGAR
    1½ TSP. SALT
    1½ TBSP. BUTTER
    1½ TBSP. SHORTENING
    1 CUP LEFTOVER MASHED POTATOES
    5 CUPS FLOUR

Mix yeast and warm water. Scald milk and mix sugar, salt, butter, and shortening. Cool to lukewarm. Add potatoes and mix. Add flour and mix well. Turn out onto lightly-floured surface and knead 10 minutes. Form into a ball. Place in a greased bowl, turning once to grease top. Cover with a warm, moist kitchen towel and let rise in warm place for about ½ hour. Punch down and briefly knead. Form a loaf and place in a greased bread pan. Cover and let rise for about 45 minutes or until nearly doubled. Bake at 350° F for about 30 minutes or until bread sounds hollow when tapped.

Grandma's oatmeal bread

    2 PKGS. (4½ TSP.) DRY YEAST
    ½ CUP WARM WATER
    1½ CUPS BOILING WATER
    1 CUP ROLLED OATS
    ½ CUP LIGHT MOLASSES
    ⅓ CUP SHORTENING
    1 TBSP. SALT
    6-6½ CUPS FLOUR, DIVIDED
    2 EGGS, BEATEN

Soften yeast in warm water. Mix boiling water and rolled oats. Add molasses, shortening, and salt. Cool to lukewarm. Stir in 2 cups sifted flour. Beat well. Add eggs and the yeast. Beat again. Add enough remaining flour to make a soft dough. Mix well. Turn out on a lightly-floured surface. Cover and let rest 10 minutes. Knead until smooth. Place in a lightly-greased bowl, turning dough once to grease top. Cover with moist, warm kitchen towel and set in warm place to rise until double. Punch down. Coat 2 well-greased bread pans with 2 Tbsp. rolled oats each. Divide dough in half. Shape into loaves. Place in pans. Cover, let double (45-60 minutes). Brush with a mixture of 1 beaten egg white and 1 Tbsp. water; sprinkle lightly with rolled oats for picture-perfect loaves. Bake at 375° F for 40 minutes. Cover with foil after baking 15 minutes if the tops are browning too soon. Remove from pans and cool on wire rack.

Cornmeal loaves

2 PKGS. (4½ TSP.) DRY YEAST
½ CUP WARM WATER
1¾ CUPS MILK, SCALDED
⅓ CUP SUGAR
½ CUP SHORTENING
1 TBSP. SALT
6½-7 CUPS FLOUR, DIVIDED
2 EGGS, BEATEN
1 CUP CORNMEAL

Soften yeast in water. Mix milk, sugar, shortening, and salt. Cool to lukewarm. Add 2½ cups flour. Beat well. Add softened yeast and eggs. Beat until smooth. Add cornmeal and remaining flour to make a soft dough. Place on lightly-floured surface. Knead until smooth (10 minutes). Place in a greased bowl, turning once to coat top. Cover with a warm, moist kitchen towel and let rise in warm place until double (1½-2 hours). Punch down. Divide in half. Let rest 10 minutes. Shape into 2 loaves. Place in 2 greased bread pans. Cover and let rise until double. Brush the loaves with milk, then sprinkle with cornmeal. Bake at 375° F for 45 minutes. Remove hot loaves from pans and cool on wire racks.

Cinnamon bread

This beautiful, tasty, iced cinnamon bread has a swirl of sugar and cinnamon in the middle!

1 PKG. (2¼ TSP.) DRY YEAST
¼ CUP WARM WATER
2 CUPS MILK, SCALDED
½ CUP SUGAR
½ CUP SHORTENING
2 TSP. SALT
7½ - 8 CUPS FLOUR, DIVIDED
2 EGGS, SLIGHTLY BEATEN
¾ CUP BROWN SUGAR
1½ TBSP. CINNAMON
SOFT BUTTER

Soften yeast in warm water. In another bowl, mix scalded milk, sugar, shortening, and salt. Let cool to lukewarm. Add 3 cups flour, beat well. Stir in softened yeast and eggs, beat again. Add enough remaining flour to make soft dough that is not too sticky. Turn out onto lightly-floured surface. Knead until smooth (10 minutes). Place in lightly-greased bowl, turning once to grease top. Cover with a moist, warm kitchen towel and let rise in warm place until double (1½-2 hours).

Punch down and divide dough in half. Cover and let rest 10 minutes. Roll each half in a 15x7-inch rectangle, about ½-inch thick. Mix brown sugar and cinnamon. Spread a layer of the brown sugar/cinnamon mix on each rectangle, reserving 2 Tbsp. of the sugar mix. Sprinkle 1 tsp. water over each; smooth with spatula.

Roll each as for jelly roll, beginning with narrow side. Seal long edge by pinching it together. Place sealed edge down in 2 greased bread pans. Let rise until almost double. Just before baking, brush loaves with soft butter and sprinkle with remaining cinnamon-sugar. Bake at 375° F for 35-40 minutes or until done. If crust browns too quickly, cover with aluminum foil the last 15-20 minutes of baking. Turn out of pans and cool on a wire rack. Makes 2 loaves.

Swedish rye bread

While this recipe is very good, and is the one I use, it isn't as good as our neighbor, Ervin Dahlen's sister Lila's rye bread. It was famous, and she would never tell her secret! I whined and begged to no avail. One year I even raised a small rye crop, thrashed and ground my own rye, giving her a nice sack, thinking I could weasel the recipe out of her. Good try, but no luck! (Her brother, Ervin, thought that it might be the molasses from the feed mill that did it, but we never found out for sure.)

- 1 PKG. (2¼ TSP.) DRY YEAST
- ¼ CUP WARM WATER
- ¼ CUP MEDIUM BROWN SUGAR
- ¼ CUP LIGHT MOLASSES
- 1 TBSP. SALT
- 2 TBSP. SHORTENING
- 1½ CUPS HOT WATER
- 2½ CUPS RYE FLOUR
- 3 TBSP. CARAWAY SEED
- 3½-4 CUPS WHITE FLOUR

Soften yeast in warm water. In big bowl, mix brown sugar, molasses, salt, and shortening, then add hot water and stir until the sugar dissolves. Cool to lukewarm. Stir in the rye flour and beat well. Add the softened yeast and caraway seed; mix well. Reserving some of the white flour for kneading, add enough to make a soft dough. Mix well. Cover and let rest 10 minutes. Turn out on a lightly-floured surface and knead about 10 minutes. Place dough in a lightly-greased bowl, turning dough once to grease the top. Cover with a moist, warm kitchen towel and let rise in a warm place until double (about 1½-2 hours). Punch down. Turn out on a lightly-floured surface and divide into 2 portions. Round each piece of dough in a ball. Cover and let rest for 10 minutes. Pat balls of dough into 2 rounded balls and place on opposite corners of a greased cookie sheet or shape into loaves and place in 2 greased bread pans. Cover and let rise in a warm place until almost double (about 1-1½ hours). Bake at 375° F for 25-30 minutes. Place foil over tops the last 10 minutes, if they are browning too quickly. Brush tops of bread with butter when removed from oven. Turn out and cool on wire rack.

Multigrain bread

I often grind a handful of dehydrated pumpkin or squash and toss it into this recipe. Nobody but me knows it's there and the bread tastes moist and nutty.

    2 PKG. (4½ TSP.) DRY YEAST
    ⅓ CUP WARM WATER
    2⅓ CUPS HOT WATER
    ½ CUP BROWN SUGAR
    ¼ CUP OIL
    1 TSP. SALT
    1 CUP RYE FLOUR
    2 CUPS WHOLE WHEAT FLOUR
    2 CUPS WHITE BREAD FLOUR
    1 CUP DRY MILK POWDER
    1 CUP OATMEAL
    ½ CUP SUNFLOWER SEEDS
    ½ CUP CORNMEAL
    ½ CUP WHEAT GERM

Mix yeast and 1/3 cup warm water. Add brown sugar to 21/3 cups hot water and ¼ cup oil. Let cool to lukewarm. Add softened yeast. Mix, then add all dry ingredients. Turn out onto a lightly-floured surface. Knead well for 10 minutes. Form into a ball and place in a greased bowl, turning once to grease top. Cover with warm, moist kitchen towel and place in a warm area. Let rise to double in bulk. Punch down and shape into 2 loaves and cover; rise again. Bake at 375° F for 1 hour or so. Bread that is done should make a hollow sound when tapping the top crust.

Salt-rising bread

This is an old-time recipe that requires no yeast, using only the soured cornmeal as a leavening agent. This bread is wonderfully different and your family will love it.

    1 CUP MILK, SCALDED
    ½ CUP SIFTED CORNMEAL
    4 CUPS MILK
    1 TBSP. SUGAR
    14-16 CUPS SIFTED ALL-PURPOSE FLOUR, DIVIDED
    ¾ CUP SHORTENING
    ½ CUP SUGAR
    1 TBSP. SALT
    MELTED BUTTER TO BRUSH TOPS OF LOAVES

Scald 1 cup milk. Add sifted cornmeal and cook until thick. Place in a quart jar with top and place in warm place to sour overnight. (Starter can be stored in the refrigerator for 1-2 weeks.) When bubbles form, it is ready to use. In a saucepan, combine 4 cups of milk and 1 Tbsp. sugar and heat to scalding. Cool slightly and add to the cornmeal mixture in a large mixing bowl. Gradually stir in 6 cups of flour. Set in warm place to rise until double (approximately 2 hours). Next, add shortening, sugar, and salt. Mix well. Gradually add 6 more cups of flour and work in. Put a generous dusting of flour on board and turn dough mixture onto board. Work in more flour and knead for about 20 minutes.

Divide into 4 equal parts and put in greased and floured bread pans. Brush tops of loaves with shortening and place in warm place to rise double (takes approximately 2 hours). Place in preheated 200° F oven. Turn heat up to 300° F. Bake for 45 minutes. Take loaves out and brush tops with butter. Continue baking until done. Loaves will sound hollow when lightly tapped on bottom. Turn out on rack to cool.

Jeri's no-knead bread

2½ Tbsp. dry yeast
4½ cups warm water
1½ Tbsp. salt
9-10 cups unbleached flour

Mix together with a spoon and let rise, covered, for 2-4 hours or until doubled. Butter or put water on hands then divide dough into 4 greased bread pans. Cover and let rise in warm place for 45 minutes. Bake at 450° F for 25-30 minutes. Put a pan of water on the rack below the bread pans when baking.

Old-time Italian bread

3 cups flour
2 tsp. sugar
½ tsp. salt
1 pkg. (2¼ tsp.) dry yeast
1 cup warm water
2 Tbsp. olive oil
1 egg white, beaten

In large bowl, mix flour, sugar, salt, and dry yeast. Add warm water and oil. Mix well. Turn dough out onto lightly-floured surface. Knead dough 10 minutes. Place dough in lightly-greased bowl, turning once to grease top. Cover with a warm, moist kitchen towel and let sit in warm place for about 30-40 minutes. Sprinkle ungreased cookie sheet with cornmeal. Punch dough down and cover; let rest 15 minutes. Shape dough into long loaf, about 12 inches long, and place on cookie sheet. Cover and let rise in warm place for 35 minutes, or until doubled. With a sharp knife, make a deep lengthwise cut in the top of the loaf. Brush the loaf with egg white and bake at 375° F for 30 minutes or until it sounds hollow when tapped and is a golden brown. Cool on wire rack. You can also sprinkle sesame or poppy seeds on the egg white after it is brushed on for a "fancier" loaf.

Glazed raisin bread

1 pkg. (2¼ tsp.) dry yeast
¼ cup warm water
1 cup raisins
¼ cup butter, softened
¼ cup sugar
1½ tsp. salt
½ cup buttermilk or scalded milk
3¾ cups flour, divided
2 eggs, beaten

Soften yeast in warm water. Mix raisins, soft butter, sugar, salt, and scalded milk or buttermilk. Cool to lukewarm. Add 1½ cups of flour and beat well. Add softened yeast and eggs; beat again. Stir in remaining flour or enough to make a soft but not sticky dough. Turn out on a lightly-floured surface and knead about 10 minutes. Place dough in a lightly-greased bowl, turning once to grease the top. Cover with a moist, warm kitchen towel and let rise in warm place until double. Punch down. Round into ball, cover, and let rest 10 minutes. Shape in a loaf and place in a greased bread pan. Cover and let rise in a warm place until almost double. Bake at 375° F about 30 minutes or until done. Remove from pan. Cool on rack. Drizzle with glaze when nearly cool.

Glaze: 1 cup sifted confectioners' sugar and 1½ Tbsp. milk, mixed well.

Butter braid

1 pkg. (2¼ tsp.) dry yeast
¼ cup warm water
1 cup scalded milk
2 Tbsp. sugar
½ cups butter
2 tsp. salt
5-5½ cups flour
2 eggs, beaten

Soften yeast in warm water. Mix milk with sugar, butter, and salt. Cool to lukewarm. Stir in 2 cups flour and beat well. Add yeast and eggs; mix well. Add enough remaining flour to make a soft, yet not sticky, dough. Turn out on floured surface. Knead until smooth (8 minutes). Place in lightly-greased bowl, turning dough once to grease top. Cover with moist, warm kitchen towel and set in warm place to rise until double. Punch down. Turn out on lightly-floured surface; divide into 6 parts and form into balls. Cover and let rest 10 minutes. Shape each ball into a 13-inch strip 2 inches thick. For each braided loaf, place three strips side by side on a greased cookie sheet. Braid. Don't stretch the dough. Pinch the ends and turn under. Repeat with other loaf. Brush with beaten egg for a shining crust before baking or brush with butter after baking for a soft, shining crust. Bake at 375° F for 30-35 minutes or until done. Makes 2 braided loaves.

Sourdough baking

Sourdough breads are wonderfully tangy and tasty. They get their leavening from a perpetual starter that can be made and kept alive for generations with good care. Some sourdough starters are known to be more than 100 years old and are still going strong! While you use yeast to begin the initial starter, you never need to add yeast again, so these breads are very economical, as well as being yummy.

With a good sourdough starter, covered and kept in the fridge or other cool, dark place, you can make traditional breads (white, rye, whole wheat, etc.), rolls, biscuits, and even pancakes and waffles. To keep the starter going on through years, all you need to do is to "feed" it. This simply means to add a cup of warm water and a cup of flour every week to keep the yeast alive and well. Should you want *more* starter to bake a lot of different breads, *do not* add a lot more water and flour at one time. You may kill your starter. Instead, add a cup of flour and a cup of water one day, mix it, let it work outside the fridge at room temperature, then add more, and later on more, if you wish. When you get enough starter to suit you, you may then refrigerate or return to a cool location.

A good sourdough starter is bubbly, has a tangy, fermented odor, and continues to respond to feeding.

Grandma Eddy's sourdough starter

>   1 PKG. (2¼ TSP.) DRY YEAST
>   ½ TSP. SUGAR
>   2 CUPS FLOUR

Mix in crock or glass bowl, do not use metal. (I use a wide mouth, half-gallon canning jar.) To use, set out at room temperature for about 18 hours.

Sourdough starter II (without yeast)

Place 1 cup milk in crock or glass jar (no metal) and let stand at room temperature 24 hours. Stir in 1 cup flour. Leave uncovered in warm place for 2-5 days. If it starts to dry out, add tepid water. Each time you use starter, add equal amounts of milk and flour. Best used once a week.

Note: This starter depends on you "catching" wild yeast in the air. It often works, but is not infallible. You may catch "bad" yeast or mold. In that case, toss it, scald your container, and try again. Or use the yeast-started sourdough starter to be sure.

Sourdough bread

>1 cup sourdough starter
>2 cups warm water
>1 Tbsp. salt
>2 Tbsp. sugar
>1 tsp. baking soda
>6½ cups flour, divided
>cornmeal
>melted butter

Put starter, water, salt, sugar, soda, and 3 cups flour in large glass mixing bowl (no metal). Beat smooth. Cover loosely and let stand in warm place at least 18 hours. Stir down and add rest of flour to make a moderately stiff dough. Turn out on a floured surface and knead about 10 minutes. Divide into 2 balls and form loaves. Place in greased bread pans, which have been sprinkled with cornmeal. Brush tops with melted butter. Bake at 400° F for about 50 minutes. (Peek after 30 minutes and if tops are browning too quickly, cover with foil.) Remove from pans and cool on wire racks. *Don't forget to feed your starter for your next baking!*

Sourdough pancakes

>1 cup starter
>2½ cups flour
>2 cups warm water
>1 tsp. baking soda
>1 tsp. warm water
>2 egg yolks
>⅓ cup milk
>2 Tbsp. melted butter
>2 Tbsp. sugar
>2 egg whites, stiffly beaten

Add starter, flour, and warm water. Mix and let stand, loosely covered, overnight. In morning, add baking soda in warm water, egg yolks, milk, butter, and sugar. Beat well, then fold in stiffly beaten egg whites. Let stand 10 minutes. Bake on griddle.

Sourdough biscuits

If making for breakfast, start the night before; if for supper, start in the morning. Use a glass bowl — no metal!

>½ cup sourdough starter
>1 cup milk
>3½ cups flour, divided
>¾ tsp. salt
>½ tsp. baking soda
>1 tsp. baking powder
>1 Tbsp. sugar

Mix starter, milk, and 2½ cups flour. Let set in warm place several hours (or overnight), covered lightly. Stir down and turn out on 1 cup flour spread on bread board. Combine salt, baking soda, baking powder, and sugar with remaining ½ cup flour and sift over top of dough. Knead into a soft dough and roll out ½-inch thick. Cut and dip each biscuit in melted bacon grease or salad oil. Place close together in 9-inch square pan and let rise in warm place for about ½ hour. Bake at 375° F for 30-35 minutes.

English muffins

- 1 CUP SOURDOUGH STARTER
- 1 TSP. SUGAR
- ¾ CUP MILK, SCALDED THEN COOLED
- 3 CUPS FLOUR
- 1 TSP. SALT
- 2 TBSP. MELTED BUTTER OR SHORTENING
- CORNMEAL

In a large glass or crock bowl (no metal), mix starter, sugar, and lukewarm milk. Mix well, then mix in 3 cups flour and beat well. Lightly cover bowl and set it in a warm place. Let rise until it gets very light and bubbly. Beat in salt, then butter, then gradually add enough flour to make a medium stiff dough. Knead very well on a lightly-floured surface.

Form into a ball. Place in greased bowl, turning to grease the top. Cover with a warm, moist kitchen towel and let sit in warm place until doubled (about 2 hours). Turn dough out onto lightly-floured surface and punch down, then pat it out into a circle about ½-inch thick. Let it rest 10 minutes, covered. Sprinkle cornmeal on 2 cookie sheets.

Using a 4-inch cutter (I use a large mouth canning jar ring.), cut the dough into rounds and gently transfer to the cookie sheets. Place them about 1½ inches apart. You can gather up your scrap dough and reform it into another flattened ball and make more muffins with it. When all the muffins are on the sheets, gently pat down each one with your hand; just one press is plenty. This keeps the muffins flat, not dome shaped on top. Cover again with a kitchen towel and let rise about 20 minutes.

Heat an ungreased griddle or cast iron skillet (can use electric skillet set at 400° F). Transfer the muffins to the hot pan a few at a time, placing them at least an inch apart. Bake for 10 minutes or until undersides are lightly brown; do *not* scorch them. Keep watch carefully. Adjust heat, if needed. When bottom is done, gently turn the muffins, pressing them lightly with a spatula and bake the other side until golden.

Cool on wire rack and bake remaining muffins.

Rye sourdough starter

1 pkg. (2¼ tsp.) dry yeast
3 cups warm water, divided
3½ cups medium rye flour, divided
1 small onion, halved

Sourdough rye bread is made with a rye sourdough starter. Dissolve yeast in 2 cups warm water, then beat in 2 cups rye flour. Add onion, cover loosely, and let stand at room temperature for 24 hours. Remove the onion and beat in 1 cup warm water and 1½ cups rye flour. Cover with cloth and let stand for 24 hours longer. The starter should then be bubbly and pleasantly-fermented smelling. The starter is now ready to use; store in the refrigerator for up to 24 hours. If you wish to keep it longer, you have to add ½ cup warm water and ¾ cup rye flour and let stand at room temperature overnight.

As with regular sourdough starter, you can keep your starter going by feeding your starter every two weeks or so with additions of 2 parts water to 3 parts rye flour. Never add more flour than the amount of starter you have. Add a bit, let it ferment at room temperature, then add more if you want to increase the amount of starter you keep on hand. You can keep this starter in the refrigerator, then set it at room temperature to become active before use.

Pumpernickel rye bread

2 Tbsp. sugar
1¼ cups boiling water
½ cup cracked wheat
1½ tsp. salt
1 Tbsp. vegetable oil
¼ cup molasses
½ cup rye sourdough starter, stirred down before measuring, at room temperature
1½ cups pumpernickel flour (rye meal)

In small, heavy saucepan, melt sugar over medium heat. Let it become very deep brown. Standing well back because it'll sputter, add the boiling water, then stir until the caramel has dissolved. Remove from heat.

Put cracked wheat, salt, oil, and molasses in a mixing bowl (non-metal). Pour the hot caramel liquid in, stir, cover, and let stand until lukewarm. Stir in the sourdough starter, then mix in the pumpernickel flour, ½ cup at a time, to make a moderately stiff but workable dough. Cover the bowl with a moist, warm towel and set in a very warm place (90-100° F) for 8 hours. (I use my gas oven with only the pilot on.)

Turn the dough out onto a lightly-floured surface and knead just enough to shape it into a flat-topped loaf that will fit a greased bread pan. Place it in the pan and fit a piece of aluminum foil over the top, fastening it to the edges of the pan. Let the loaf rest in a warm place for 30 minutes. Put the pan in an unheated oven, then turn the heat to 275° F and bake the covered bread for 3 hours. If you want a crustier top, remove the foil for the last ½ hour. Remove the bread from pan and cool on a rack, covered with a towel to prevent it from drying out.

Bagels

1 PKG. (2¼ TSP.) DRY YEAST

1 CUP POTATO WATER, DIVIDED (WATER IN WHICH POTATOES HAVE BEEN BOILED IN FOR DINNER)

1 TBSP. HONEY, DIVIDED

4 CUPS UNBLEACHED FLOUR

1 TBSP. SALT

1 EGG

1 EGG WHITE, SEPARATED (RESERVE YOLK FOR GLAZE)

3 TBSP. VEGETABLE OIL

COARSE SALT, POPPY OR SESAME SEEDS (OPTIONAL)

Soften yeast in half of the potato water, warmed, and ½ tsp. honey. Sift flour into large bowl and add salt. Stir yeast mixture into flour and add the whole egg and remaining egg white (reserving yolk for glaze). Add the remaining potato water, honey, and oil. Mix to make a firm, not hard, dough. Add more flour, if necessary.

Turn out onto a floured board and knead 10 minutes. Place dough in a greased bowl and turn once to grease top. Cover with warm, moist kitchen towel and sit in warm place to rise until double. Preheat oven to 425° F.

Boil 3 quarts of water in a large pot. Punch the dough down and knead for about 2-3 minutes. Cut dough into about 14 pieces. Roll each piece between floured hands until it is about 7 inches long and ¾-inch thick. Coil each roll into a ring, moistening the ends so they stick together when pressed. Let rings stand about 10 minutes on an oiled pan. Using a slotted spoon, slip each bagel into the pot of boiling water. Don't put too many in at once. They will float. Boil 2 minutes on each side and remove with slotted spoon, placing them on an oiled cookie sheet.

Mix remaining egg yolk with 1 tsp. water and brush over each bagel. Sprinkle with coarse salt or sesame or poppy seed if you wish.

Bake at 425° F until golden brown. Place hot bagels on wire rack to cool.

Easy breadsticks

    1 PKG. (2¼ TSP.) DRY YEAST
    2 CUPS FLOUR
    1 TBSP. SUGAR
    ½ TSP. BASIL
    ½ TSP. OREGANO
    ½ TSP. SALT
    WARM WATER

In large bowl, combine yeast, flour, sugar, herbs, and salt. Add enough warm water to make a soft, not sticky, dough. Lightly knead right in the bowl until light and well blended. Cover with a warm, moist kitchen towel and let sit in warm place until double. Punch down and lightly knead. Turn out on lightly-floured surface and roll into a rectangle ½-inch thick and 6 inches wide. With a knife, cut into 1-inch strips 6 inches long and lay on lightly-greased cookie sheet. (You may brush with butter and sprinkle on sesame seeds, if you wish.) Cover and let rise for about 30 minutes. Bake at 375° F until lightly golden brown.

Serve hot with your favorite marinara sauce. A quick, easy one is made by mixing 1 pint of tomato sauce with 1 tsp. basil, 1 tsp. oregano, 1 tsp. garlic powder, and 1 tsp. onion powder. Heat and serve warm with your hot bread sticks.

Sweet breads and coffee cakes

Apple bread

    1 CUP SUGAR
    ½ CUP SHORTENING
    2 EGGS
    1 TSP. VANILLA
    2 CUPS FLOUR
    1 TSP. BAKING POWDER
    1 TSP. BAKING SODA
    ½ TSP. SALT
    2 CUPS CHOPPED, PEELED APPLES (ABOUT 4 MEDIUM)
    ½ CUP CHOPPED NUTS
    1 TBSP. SUGAR
    ¼ TSP. CINNAMON

Heat oven to 350° F. Grease and flour bread pan.

Mix sugar, shortening, eggs, and vanilla. Stir in flour, baking powder, baking soda, and salt until smooth. Stir in apples and nuts. Spread in pan. Mix 1 Tbsp. sugar and the cinnamon. Sprinkle over batter. Bake until wooden pick inserted in center comes out clean (about 1 hour). Immediately remove from pan. Serve hot or cool before slicing. Store tightly covered.

Peach-oat breakfast cake

When we lived in our little remote cabin in Montana, 1,000 feet above the Continental Divide, we took good eating seriously. This hot, stick-by-you breakfast cake would let you chop wood all morning without getting that hungry, hollow feeling. Every time I fix it, my son, David (all grown up now), is once again 2 years old and I can almost hear the elk bugling outside the cabin.

Cake:
- ¾ CUP MILK, SCALDED
- ½ CUP ROLLED OATS
- ¾ CUP PACKED BROWN SUGAR
- ½ CUP SHORTENING
- 1 EGG, BEATEN
- 1¼ CUPS FLOUR
- 2 TSP. BAKING POWDER
- ½ TSP. SALT
- ⅛ TSP. NUTMEG
- 1 PINT CANNED PEACH SLICES, DRAINED

Preheat oven to 375° F. Grease a bread pan. In a small bowl, mix milk and oats. In medium bowl, mix sugar and shortening. Add egg, mixing well. Stir in flour, baking powder, salt, nutmeg, and oat mixture until well moistened. Pour drained peaches into pan, then pour cake batter on top. Sprinkle topping evenly over cake mixture. Bake for 30-35 minutes or until done. Serve hot with sweetened milk or whipped cream if you want to be *really* fancy.

Topping:
- ½ CUP FLOUR
- ⅓ CUP PACKED BROWN SUGAR
- ¼ CUP ROLLED OATS
- 5 TBSP. BUTTER OR MARGARINE, SOFTENED
- ½ TSP. CINNAMON
- ½ CUP CHOPPED NUTS (OPTIONAL)

In a small bowl, combine flour, sugar, rolled oats, butter, and cinnamon. Add chopped nuts if you wish. Mix well and set aside.

Sally Lunn

There are two versions of this breakfast/dessert bread. One is leavened with yeast, but this one is a baking powder version that Mom made often. It's quick and easy.

Topping:
- ½ CUP BROWN SUGAR
- 1 TSP. CINNAMON
- 1 TBSP. BUTTER

Mix brown sugar, cinnamon, and butter together well and sprinkle over batter before baking.

Bread:
- ⅓ CUP SUGAR
- ⅓ CUP SHORTENING
- 1 BEATEN EGG
- ⅔ CUP MILK
- 2 CUPS FLOUR
- 3 TSP. BAKING POWDER
- ¾ TSP. SALT

Cream sugar and shortening together. Add egg, then milk. Add sifted dry ingredients. Stir just enough to moisten. Turn into greased 8x8x2-inch cake pan. Add topping and bake at 400° F for about 20 minutes. Serve this piping hot at breakfast or for a dessert. Butter melts quickly on this light, sweet bread.

Swedish tea ring

A dainty, tender, sweet, raisin-filled yeast bread from Sweden to you. As this takes considerable prep work, this yummy coffeecake isn't an everyday treat, but is usually reserved for holidays or "company" meals. It is well worth the extra fussing, though!

Bread:
- 1 PKG. (2¼ TSP.) DRY YEAST
- ½ CUP WARM WATER
- ¾ CUP MILK, SCALDED
- ⅓ CUP SUGAR
- 1 TSP. SALT
- ⅓ CUP SHORTENING
- 4 TO 4½ CUPS SIFTED FLOUR
- 2 EGGS, BEATEN

Soften yeast in warm water. Combine milk, sugar, salt, and shortening. Cool to lukewarm. Stir in about 2 cups flour. Add eggs. Beat well. Stir in softened yeast and mix. Add enough remaining flour to make a soft, yet not sticky, dough. Place in greased bowl, turning once to grease top. Cover and let rise in a warm place until double.

Punch down and let rise until double. Divide dough in half, making 2 balls. Cover and let dough rest 10 minutes. On lightly-floured surface, roll one ball into a 9x13-inch rectangle, ¼-inch thick.

Raisin filling:

½ cup sugar

2 tsp. cinnamon

½ cup raisins

2 Tbsp. melted butter or margarine, divided

Spread dough with 1 Tbsp. melted butter. Combine sugar, cinnamon, and raisins. Spread half on dough. Roll as for a jelly roll. Seal long edge. Shape into a ring, seam side down, on a greased baking sheet. Seal ends of ring. With scissors, snip 2/3 of the way to center at 1½-inch intervals. Turn each section slightly to one side. Repeat shaping and filling other half of dough.

Cover and let rise until double. Bake at 375° F for about 25 to 30 minutes. Remove from oven. Immediately brush with warm, light corn syrup and sprinkle inner edge of ring with about ¼ cups chopped walnuts or drizzle with confectioners' icing (1 cup confectioners' sugar, 1 tsp. vanilla, and enough milk to make a pourable icing) and circle with candied maraschino cherries or fruit peel and almond slices.

Mom's orange glory rolls

These were some of Mom's favorite rolls. Not only are they tasty, but they are very different and definitely not ho-hum!

Topping:

½ cup butter or margarine

2 cups sugar

1 cup orange juice and pulp

¼ cup grated orange rind

Combine butter, sugar, juice, pulp, and rind in saucepan. Boil 6 minutes, stirring to prevent sticking. Place 1 Tbsp. mixture in each greased muffin tin (3 dozen).

Rolls:

2 pkgs. (4½ tsp.) dry yeast

½ cup warm water

½ cup sugar

¼ cup shortening

2 tsp. salt

1 cup boiling water

¾ cup cold water

2 eggs

7½ cups flour

Soften yeast in ½ cup warm water. Combine sugar, shortening, salt, and boiling water to melt shortening. Then add ¾ cup cold water and cool to lukewarm. Add eggs and yeast. Mix well and add about 7½ cups flour and beat well. Turn out on floured board and knead well until no longer sticky. Add more flour if needed. Roll out ⅓ at a time, to make a 10x12-inch rectangle. Brush with melted butter and roll as for jellyroll. Cut in 1-inch slices and place in muffin cups, on top of orange sauce. Let rise until double in a warm place and bake at 375° F for about 20-25 minutes. Invert on cooling rack while still hot.

Mom's best-ever fruitcake

- 1 pound Brazil nuts, chopped
- 1 pound pitted dates, chopped coarsely
- ¾ cup candied cherries
- 1 pound candied pineapple
- ¾ cup sifted all-purpose flour
- ¾ cup white sugar
- ½ tsp. salt
- ½ tsp. baking powder
- 3 eggs
- 1 tsp. vanilla extract

Preheat oven to 300° F. Line two small loaf pans with parchment or wax paper.

In a large bowl combine Brazil nuts, dates, cherries, and pineapple. Sift the flour, sugar, salt, and baking powder over the fruit and nuts. Mix well.

In a small bowl combine eggs and vanilla; beat until foamy. Pour over fruit mixture and mix well. Spoon batter into prepared pans.

Bake in preheated oven for 1½ hours, or until a toothpick inserted into the cake comes out clean.

Cinnamon caramel pecan rolls

- ¾ cup scalded milk
- ¼ cup sugar
- 1 Tbsp. shortening
- 1 egg
- 1 pkg. (2¼ tsp.) dry yeast
- 3 cups flour
- ½ tsp. salt

Filling:
- ½ cup brown sugar
- 2 tsp. cinnamon

Topping:
- ¾ cup brown sugar
- 3 Tbsp. margarine or butter
- 2 Tbsp. corn syrup
- ½ tsp. vanilla
- chopped pecans

Mix hot scalded milk with sugar and shortening. Cool to lukewarm. Add beaten egg and yeast. Add flour and salt. Knead in enough flour to make a dough that you can handle, but not a stiff dough. Let rise in a covered bowl until doubled. Punch down and roll out into a rectangle about ¾-inch thick.

Make topping: Mix all ingredients and spread on the bottom of a 13x9x2-inch pan, sprinkling it with pecans.

Make filling: Mix filling ingredients. Rub softened butter onto the dough rectangle, and spread the filling on top.

Roll the rectangle up, jelly roll fashion, then pinch the ends shut. With a sharp knife, cut the roll into pieces about an inch thick and lay them on top of the topping in the pan (it's the bottom now!). Bake the rolls at 425° F for 15-20 minutes. Turn out onto cooling racks when hot, removing them from the pan. This sounds like a lot of prep work, but it actually goes very quickly and once you've done it, you'll make these gooey rolls often!

German Stollen

This is a sweet, glazed holiday bread, full of candied fruit peel, raisins, currants, and almonds.

- 1 PKG. (2¼ TSP.) DRY YEAST
- ¼ CUP WARM WATER
- 1 CUP MILK, SCALDED
- ¼ CUP SUGAR
- 1 TSP. SALT
- ½ CUP BUTTER OR MARGARINE
- 4-4½ CUPS FLOUR, DIVIDED
- 1 EGG, SLIGHTLY BEATEN
- 1 CUP RAISINS
- ¼ CUP CURRANTS (OR SUBSTITUTE RAISINS OR OTHER DRIED FRUIT)
- ¼ CUP CHOPPED MIXED CANDIED FRUITS
- 2 TBSP. GRATED ORANGE PEEL
- 1 TBSP. GRATED LEMON PEEL
- ¼ CUP CHOPPED, BLANCHED ALMONDS

Soften dry yeast in warm water. Mix hot milk, sugar, salt, and margarine. Cool to lukewarm. Stir in 2 cups flour. Beat well. Add softened yeast and egg. Beat again. Stir in fruits, peels, and nuts. Add enough of the remaining flour to make a soft, but not sticky, dough. Turn out on a lightly-floured surface. Knead about 10 minutes. Place in a greased bowl, turning once to grease top. Cover with warm, moist kitchen towel and let rise in warm place until doubled. Punch down; turn out on lightly-floured surface. Divide in 3 equal parts. Cover; let rest 10 minutes. Roll each of the 3 parts into a 10x6-inch rectangle, without stretching the dough. Fold the long side over to within 1 inch of the lower side. Seal edge. Place on greased cookie sheets. Cover and let rise in a warm place until almost double. Bake at 375° F for 15-20 minutes or until golden brown. While warm, but not hot out of the oven, brush with glaze.

Glaze:

- 1 CUP CONFECTIONERS' SUGAR
- 2 TBSP. HOT WATER
- ½ TSP. BUTTER)

You may add additional pieces of candied fruit or decorate on top of the glaze with peel to make holly leaves, berries, flowers, or leaves. Candied cherries, nuts, or citron make good material to cut decorations from and arrange artistically to suit the holiday or occasion.

Muffins and scones

Tip: To "fancy up" any of the following muffins, sprinkle fruit crisp mix on the tops of the muffins before baking.

Mom's muffins

    2 CUPS FLOUR
    2½ TSP. BAKING POWDER
    2 TBSP. SUGAR
    ¾ TSP. SALT
    ½ CUP SHORTENING
    ¾ CUP MILK
    1 EGG, BEATEN

Sift dry ingredients and cut in shortening until it resembles coarse meal. Stir in milk and egg until just moist. Fill greased muffin tins ⅔ full. Bake at 400° F about 25 minutes or until just golden brown on top.

Plain muffins

    2 CUPS FLOUR
    4 TBSP. SUGAR
    1 TBSP. BAKING POWDER
    ½ TSP. SALT
    1 EGG, WELL BEATEN
    3 TBSP. MELTED SHORTENING
    1 CUP MILK

Sift dry ingredients. Mix egg, shortening, and milk. Add dry ingredients. Mix only until moist; don't overbeat. Fill greased muffin tins ⅔ full and bake at 425° F for about 15-20 minutes.

Blueberry muffins

    2 CUPS FLOUR
    ½ CUP SUGAR
    2 TSP. BAKING POWDER
    ½ TSP. SALT
    1 EGG
    ¾ CUP MILK
    4 TBSP. MELTED SHORTENING
    ½ CUP BLUEBERRIES (FRESH, FROZEN, OR CANNED AND DRAINED)

Sift dry ingredients. Beat egg slightly and add milk. Add to dry ingredients. Stir in melted shortening. Fold blueberries into batter. Fill greased muffin tins ⅔ full and bake at 350° F.

Tip: You can substitute any berries in this recipe for the blueberries.

Cranberry muffins

- 2½ cups flour
- ½ cup sugar
- 2½ tsp. baking powder
- ½ tsp. salt
- 2 eggs, beaten
- 1 cup milk
- 4 Tbsp. melted butter
- ½ cup chopped cranberries

Sift dry ingredients. Mix eggs, milk, and melted butter. Add to dry ingredients. Fold in chopped cranberries. Bake at 425° F for about 25 minutes.

Nutty rhubarb muffins

This is one of my favorite recipes for using our plentiful rhubarb in the spring. The muffins are so moist and tangy-sweet, I never have leftovers. Serve them hot with sweet butter and I guarantee you won't be disappointed!

- ¾ cup packed brown sugar
- ½ cup buttermilk or sour milk
- ⅓ cup vegetable oil
- 1 egg, beaten
- 1 tsp. vanilla extract
- 2 cups flour
- ½ tsp. baking soda
- ½ tsp. salt
- 1 cup diced rhubarb
- ½ cup chopped nuts

Topping:
- ¼ cup packed brown sugar
- ¼ cup chopped nuts
- ½ tsp. cinnamon

In small mixing bowl, combine brown sugar, buttermilk (or sour milk), oil, egg, and vanilla. Mix well and set aside.

In another mixing bowl, sift dry ingredients, then add egg/milk mixture and stir just until moist. Fold in rhubarb and chopped nuts. Fill greased muffin tins ⅔ full.

Now mix topping ingredients and sprinkle over tops of muffins. Bake at 375° F for 20 minutes.

My favorite bran muffins

1⅓ cups bran
1 cup wheat germ
1 cup firmly packed brown sugar
2½ cups whole wheat flour
2½ tsp. baking soda
½ tsp. salt
1 Tbsp. grated orange peel (or orange juice, if you don't have peel)
2 eggs, slightly beaten
½ cup honey
¼ cup molasses
½ cup vegetable oil
2 cups buttermilk or sour milk
1 cup boiling water

In large bowl, mix first 7 ingredients. In another bowl, mix eggs, honey, molasses, oil, and buttermilk (or sour milk) and boiling water. Mix with dry ingredients until well moistened. Fill greased muffin tins ⅔ full and bake at 350° F for about 20 minutes. You can keep this mix in the fridge for 3-4 weeks and use what you wish, a little at a time, so you can have hot muffins in just a few minutes for breakfast or when friends show up.

Graham gems (whole wheat muffins)

1 cup whole wheat flour
1 cup flour
2 Tbsp. sugar
¾ tsp. salt
4 tsp. baking powder
1 cup milk
3 Tbsp. melted shortening or vegetable oil
1 egg, beaten

Sift dry ingredients together, then mix in the rest of the ingredients. Mix well. Fill well-greased muffin tins ⅔ full and bake at 400° F for about 25 minutes.

Scotch scones

1 cup sour cream
2 tsp. baking powder
4 cups flour
1 tsp. salt
1 cup sugar
¼ tsp. cream of tartar
1 cup butter
1 egg
1 cup raisins or other dried fruit, chopped if necessary (optional)

In a small bowl, mix sour cream and baking powder; set aside. In large bowl, mix dry ingredients well, cut in the butter, then add the sour cream mix and stir well. Add raisins. Turn out onto a lightly-floured surface and knead lightly. Roll or pat dough into a ¾-inch round. Cut into 12 wedges. Place 2 inches apart on greased cookie sheet. Bake at 350° F for about 12-15 minutes until golden brown on bottoms. I cut my own scones with a large mouth canning jar lid, then fold the scones with the top half just a little smaller than the bottom. It makes a nice-looking, easily-buttered scone. You can also use reconstituted dehydrated butter, sour cream, and egg powder in this recipe.

Poppyseed lemon scones

Lemon curd:
- 2 EGGS
- 1 CUP SUGAR
- 6 TBSP. BUTTER
- ¼ CUP LEMON JUICE
- 2 TBSP. GRATED LEMON PEEL (OR 1 TBSP. DEHYDRATED LEMON PEEL)

Beat eggs and sugar in a double boiler. Stir in butter and lemon juice and zest. Cook gently until thickened. Cover and chill.

Scones:
- 2 CUPS FLOUR
- ¼ CUP SUGAR
- 1 TBSP. BAKING POWDER
- 1 TBSP. POPPY SEEDS
- ¼ TSP. SALT
- ⅓ CUP COLD BUTTER
- ¾ CUP MILK
- 2 TBSP. LEMON JUICE
- ADDITIONAL SUGAR

Combine first 5 ingredients in bowl. Cut in butter until fine crumbs. Combine milk and lemon juice. Add to dry ingredients. Turn out soft dough onto lightly-floured surface. Knead gently and shape into a ball. Pat dough into an 8-inch circle. Using sharp knife, cut into 8 wedges. Separate and place on a greased cookie sheet. Sprinkle with sugar and bake at 425° F until lightly browned. Serve with chilled lemon curd.

Pancakes, waffles, and donuts

You can use the pancake and waffle mix from the "Basic pantry mixes" chapter, or use one of these recipes to make great homemade pancakes and waffles in a short time. Waffles have a reputation for being hard to make but it's not true, especially if you know a few tips. The stiffer the batter, the shorter the mixing period should be. If you use melted shortening, cool it slightly first. To prevent waffles from sticking, be sure to preheat your waffle iron sufficiently. It should be hot enough before you put your first batter in that a few drops of water sprinkled on the griddle dance, spitting hard. Use a brush to lightly grease grids with shortening, then add batter.

For even baking, close the lid quickly, and don't open it to peek. Wait until the steam stops. For crisper waffles, open the lid and let the waffle stay on the griddle for a few seconds. For extra crisp waffles, bake longer. Use a fork to remove the waffle. If it wants to stick, gently pick up one edge then work around the waffle until it pops free. It is generally necessary to lightly grease your waffle iron each time you bake a waffle on it to prevent sticking. Using a waffle iron on a wood-fired kitchen range works great, but you do need to preheat it well before the first use. When hot, add batter and bake. When steam stops around the edges, gently turn the iron over to bake the other side of the waffle. Most old waffle irons used on a wood range have a ring that sits around them, making turning the iron much easier, as it just swivels around on the knob at the top of the iron. It takes longer to bake waffles on a wood range, but they do turn out very nice.

Add blueberries, raspberries, wild strawberries, or other goodies to any of these recipes for an extra nice treat.

Note: You may use dehydrated, reconstituted shortening, buttermilk, milk, or eggs for most of these recipes. Any recipes that call for separating the eggs and beating the egg whites until they are stiff should use fresh eggs only.

My Grandma Eddy's pancakes

2 EGG YOLKS, BEATEN

2 CUPS SOUR MILK OR BUTTERMILK

¾ TSP. BAKING SODA

PINCH SALT

ENOUGH FLOUR TO MAKE A MEDIUM BATTER

2 EGG WHITES, BEATEN STIFF

1 TBSP. MELTED SHORTENING

Mix egg yolks, buttermilk, soda, and salt. Then add flour enough to make a medium batter. Fold in egg whites and melted shortening. Beat well and bake on hot, greased griddle. To give these more body and fill you up more (besides being tasty), substitute ¼ cup of cornmeal for ¼ cup flour in this recipe. It's very good!

Griddle cakes

1½ CUPS FLOUR

1 CUP MILK

3 TBSP. MELTED SHORTENING

3 TBSP. SUGAR

¾ TSP. SALT

3½ TSP. BAKING POWDER

1 EGG, BEATEN

Sift dry ingredients together. Then mix egg, milk, and shortening together and add to flour mix. Bake on greased hot griddle.

Yeast-leavened flapjacks

    1 PKG. (2¼ TSP.) DRY YEAST
    ¼ CUP WARM WATER
    1¾ CUPS MILK, SCALDED
    2 TBSP. SUGAR
    1 TSP. SALT
    ¼ CUP MELTED SHORTENING
    3 EGGS, BEATEN
    2 CUPS FLOUR

Mix yeast with warm water and let stand. To hot, scalded milk, add sugar, salt, and shortening. Let cool to lukewarm. Add beaten eggs and yeast mix. Add flour and beat well. Cover and let rise in a warm place at least 1 hour. Stir batter. Dip out with ¼ cup measuring cup and pour onto hot greased griddle. Turn and bake other side. These are very good and taste different than "regular" pancakes. Try them and see how your family reacts!

Baked peach pancake

    2 CUPS FRESH OR CANNED PEACH SLICES, DRAINED
    4 TSP. SUGAR
    1 TSP. LEMON JUICE
    3 EGGS
    ½ CUP FLOUR
    ½ CUP MILK
    ½ TSP. SALT
    2 TBSP. BUTTER OR MARGARINE
    GROUND CINNAMON AND NUTMEG

In a bowl, mix peaches, sugar, and lemon juice. Let stand. Beat eggs until light, then add flour, milk, and salt. Put butter in heavy skillet and put in oven at 400° F for 3-5 minutes (until melted, not browning). Immediately, pour batter into hot skillet and return to oven. Bake for 20-25 minutes (until pancake has puffed and is golden brown on top). Fill with peach slices and sprinkle with a pinch of cinnamon and nutmeg. Serve hot with whipped cream. (This pancake serves four.)

Tip: Besides syrup on your pancakes, try heated, melted homemade jams and jellies and a sprinkling of powdered sugar. You have instant gourmet pancakes! I also use any jellies that have not set up. Chokecherry is especially notorious for this, so I don't despair; I just rejoice that I have a batch of chokecherry pancake syrup!

Swedish pancakes

    2 EGGS
    1 CUP LIGHT CREAM
    ½ CUP FLOUR
    1½ TSP. SUGAR
    ¼ TSP. SALT

Beat eggs just enough to blend yolks and whites. Add cream. Sift flour, sugar, and salt into eggs and cream mixture. Beat until smooth. Let mixture stand in cool place for at least 2 hours so batter will thicken. Heat griddle to hot and lightly grease. Beat batter again and pour onto griddle. Brown pancakes on both sides. Tip: use a very thin spatula and roll edge of pancake up, then peel off griddle with fingers, as these are quite thin and tender.

Roll or fold pancakes on plate and keep hot in oven at 250° F while you finish the rest. To serve, unroll and fill with fresh sliced strawberries or other fresh berries or your favorite homemade jam. Top with whipped cream if you wish.

Best buttermilk pancakes

Mom used to make her own pancake syrup by boiling brown sugar and water together until nicely thickened, then adding a little vanilla. This was served hot with pancakes. When I was little, I was as horse-crazy as I am now. And I always sneaked to the syrup pitcher and picked off bits of cooled, crusty sugar. I'd stop on the way to school to feed them to the milkman's horse. I still can feel the horse's tickly soft whiskers and warm breath on my really sticky hands!

    2 CUPS FLOUR
    2 CUPS CULTURED BUTTERMILK
    2 EGGS, SLIGHTLY BEATEN
    2 TBSP. MELTED BUTTER OR BACON GREASE
    2 TBSP. SUGAR
    1 TSP. BAKING SODA
    1 TSP. SALT

Sift dry ingredients together into a bowl. Mix in other ingredients and stir. (There will be some lumps.) Bake on hot, lightly-greased griddle.

Buckwheat griddle cakes

    3½ CUPS STIRRED BUCKWHEAT FLOUR
    1 CUP FLOUR
    1 TSP. SALT
    1 PKG. (2¼ TSP.) DRY YEAST
    ¼ CUP WARM WATER
    1 TSP. SUGAR
    3¾ CUPS MILK OR LUKEWARM WATER

Combine flours and salt. (I grind hulls and all for my buckwheat flour as buckwheat is nearly impossible to hull at home; it tastes fine that way.) Soften yeast in ¼ cup warm water; set aside. Dissolve sugar in lukewarm water or milk; add yeast mixture and mix. Let stand overnight at room temperature. Bowl must not be more than ½ full as it rises. In the morning, stir batter and add 1 tsp. salt, 2 Tbsp. brown sugar, ¾ tsp. baking soda, and 1 Tbsp. melted shortening. Bake on hot, lightly-greased griddle.

Apple pancakes

- 2 cups flour
- 2 Tbsp. sugar
- 4 tsp. baking powder
- 1 tsp. salt
- 2 egg yolks, well beaten, whites reserved
- 2 cups milk
- 2 Tbsp. butter, melted
- 1 cup apples, finely chopped
- 2 egg whites, stiffly beaten

Sift dry ingredients together. Mix egg yolks and milk. Pour into dry ingredients; mix well. Stir in butter and apple. Fold in egg whites gently. Let mixture stand a few minutes to rise. Bake on hot, lightly-greased griddle. You may sprinkle with cinnamon sugar or confectioners' sugar and serve with whipped cream.

Iowa cornmeal pancakes

- 1½ cups flour
- 2 Tbsp. sugar
- 1 tsp. baking soda
- 1 tsp. salt
- ½ cup yellow cornmeal (may use white or homegrown colored cornmeal)
- 2 eggs, slightly beaten
- 2 cups cultured buttermilk
- 2 Tbsp. butter or bacon grease, melted

Sift dry ingredients together; stir in cornmeal. Add eggs, buttermilk, and melted butter, stirring gently; don't overmix. Bake on hot, lightly-greased griddle. (Bacon grease makes a nicely-flavored flapjack.) Turn pancake when topside has bubbles and edges are golden. Flip and bake other side.

Potato pancakes

- 3 large potatoes
- 1 Tbsp. grated onion
- 2 eggs, slightly beaten
- 2 Tbsp. flour
- 1 tsp. salt
- ½ tsp. baking powder
- vegetable oil for frying

Finely grate potatoes and onions. Drain any liquid. Add eggs, flour, salt, and baking powder. Mix well. In a frying pan, add ⅛-inch of oil and heat to about 375° F. Drop batter by heaping tablespoonsful into hot oil. Flatten to form patties. Fry until golden brown on first side, then turn to fry other side. Serve immediately with butter, syrup, or even applesauce. You can substitute dehydrated, reconstituted potatoes and onions in this recipe.

Everyday waffles

- 1¾ cups flour
- 1 tsp. sugar
- 3 tsp. baking powder
- ½ tsp. salt
- 2 egg yolks, beaten
- 1¼ cups milk
- ½ cup vegetable oil or melted shortening
- 2 egg whites, stiffly beaten

Sift dry ingredients together. Mix egg yolks and milk; stir into dry ingredients. Stir in melted shortening or oil. Fold in egg whites; don't overmix. Bake in lightly-greased, hot waffle iron.

Cornmeal waffles

Mom made waffle enchiladas, using these waffles, with an enchilada filling ladled over the tops of them and grated cheddar cheese melted on top. Add sour cream and salsa and they are very good, and filling too!

- 1 cup flour
- 1 tsp. sugar
- 1 tsp. baking soda
- ½ tsp. salt
- 1 cup cornmeal
- 2 cups buttermilk
- ¼ cup vegetable oil or melted shortening
- 2 eggs, beaten

Sift dry ingredients together. Stir in cornmeal. Mix in remaining ingredients until just moistened. Bake in a lightly-greased, hot waffle iron.

Dessert waffles

    1⅓ CUPS FLOUR
    3 TSP. BAKING POWDER
    ½ TSP. SALT
    2 EGGS, WELL BEATEN
    1 CUP LIGHT CREAM
    ¼ CUP MELTED BUTTER
    2 EGG WHITES, STIFFLY BEATEN

Sift dry ingredients together. Mix eggs and cream; stir into dry ingredients. Add butter. Fold in egg whites. Bake on lightly-greased, hot waffle iron. Serve with fresh fruit or fruit jam and ice cream or whipped cream.

Hoe cakes

Mom spent some of her childhood in Virginia, near her sister Iva's farm, and developed a taste for Southern cooking. One of her favorites was this recipe, eaten morning, noon, or night.

    2 CUPS BOILING WATER
    2 CUPS CORNMEAL
    1 TSP. SALT
    OIL FOR FRYING

Pour the boiling water over the cornmeal and salt and stir. The cornmeal will swell up, absorbing the water, making a very thick mash.

Heat some oil in a large skillet over medium high heat. You can use as little as 2 tablespoons of oil per batch, but it is a little easier to use 4 or 5 tablespoons of oil for each batch. Dip out tablespoonfuls of batter, and gently shape into patties. Then ease them into the hot oil. Turn when one side is done. Make some more, until you have a whole pan full. I usually cook about 4 or 5 at a time. When the underside is crispy brown, turn them and cook the other side. When both sides are crispy and brown, put them onto a plate to keep warm, and start another batch. These can be eaten hot with syrup or butter. The old-timers carried some out into the field to work, eating them cold for lunch, as a break from hoeing crops — thus the name.

Raised donuts

> 1 cup milk
> ½ cup sugar
> ½ cup cooking oil or lard
> 1 tsp. salt
> 2 eggs, well beaten
> 2 pkgs. (4½ tsp.) dry yeast
> 3⅔ cups flour

Scald milk and add sugar, oil, and salt. Cool to lukewarm and add eggs. Add yeast and mix to dissolve. Add flour and let rise, covered, about 1 hour. Punch dough down and let rise again. Roll out about ½-inch thick and cut with a donut cutter or a regular jar ring. Let rise and fry in a deep fryer (375° F). Keep grease hot between batches or the donuts will become grease-soaked and heavy.

Glaze with the following: Mix 1 cup confectioners' sugar with ½ tsp. vanilla and enough milk to make a thick glaze that will drizzle from a spoon. Wait until donuts are cooled before glazing or it'll run off. Or roll while hot in cinnamon sugar.

Potato donuts

> 3 eggs
> ⅔ cup sugar
> 2 Tbsp. melted shortening or vegetable oil
> 1 tsp. vanilla
> 3 cups flour
> 3 tsp. baking powder
> ½ tsp. nutmeg
> 1 cup cold mashed potatoes
> ¼ cup milk

Beat eggs, add sugar, shortening, and vanilla. Add dry ingredients, potatoes, and milk. Chill dough. Roll out, cut, and deep fry in oil at 375° F. Glaze or roll in sugar as desired.

Mom's chocolate nut donuts

¼ CUP SHORTENING

1¼ CUPS SUGAR

2 EGGS, WELL BEATEN

2 SQUARES SEMISWEET CHOCOLATE, MELTED

4 CUPS FLOUR

¾ TSP. SALT

1 TSP. BAKING SODA

1 TSP. CINNAMON

1 CUP SOUR MILK OR BUTTERMILK

1½ TSP. VANILLA

1½ CUPS FINELY CHOPPED NUTS

Cream shortening and sugar. Add eggs, then melted chocolate. Sift together flour, salt, baking soda, and cinnamon. Add to first mixture, alternately with buttermilk or sour milk. Add vanilla and nuts. Mix well. Chill. Roll out ⅜-inch thick on floured board. Cut and fry in deep fryer at 360° F. These are great iced with chocolate icing, and sprinkled with more chopped nuts.

Eggs

Nearly every homestead has a flock of chickens. There are times, especially in the spring and early summer, when the hens are laying so many eggs that we are practically inundated with them. It's a time of bounty and joy. During the winter, the chickens lay considerably fewer eggs, so our use of them declines, but when spring comes around again, creative country cooks everywhere put on their thinking caps, trying to discover delicious ways to use up these protein-rich treasures. Luckily, there are thousands of different ways to use these eggs. From quiche to meringue, eggs just can't be beat for both taste and nutrition. They are a nearly perfect food, all neatly wrapped in a smooth, shining shell.

Only use fresh, uncracked eggs. A cracked egg could be tainted with bacteria, such as salmonella. Refrigerate your eggs after you have collected them. Only wash them if they are stained or dirty, but don't immerse them, just scrub them off and wipe dry. Very fresh eggs are harder to peel after hard-boiling than those that have been in the refrigerator for a week or two.

To soft-boil eggs: Cover the eggs with water and bring the saucepan rapidly to a boil. Remove the pan from the heat, cover and let stand about 3 minutes. Cool under running water and serve.

To hard-boil eggs: Put eggs in a large saucepan and cover with an inch of cold water. Add 1 tsp. vinegar and 1 tsp. salt; it makes peeling a little easier. Bring rapidly to a boil and boil for 12-15 minutes. Take off heat and quickly pour off boiling water. Replace with cold. Drain when water warms. Lightly toss eggs up and down; this cracks the shells. Fill pan with cold water and let the eggs sit in the cold water for 20 minutes. Drain. Roll eggs on hard surface and peel shell off, including the membrane. The egg without the membrane feels slick and looks shiny. If it is rough and dull, you haven't gotten under the membrane and your egg will peel very badly and with great difficulty. Usually, if you start peeling at the large end, where the air pocket is, it peels easier because the membrane is more easily found and torn.

To poach eggs: Either poach in milk or water; the directions are the same. Fill a skillet about ⅔ full of water (or milk) and bring to the boiling point. Don't boil. Reduce the heat. Break egg into a cup before slipping one by one into the water. The water should cover the egg(s). Only cook as many eggs as the water will cover. When all eggs are in, cover and simmer to degree of firmness you desire. If you want firmer yolks, cook longer. Remove from water with a slotted spoon and serve immediately on hot buttered toast or English muffins.

To make scrambled eggs: To every 6 eggs, beaten, add half a cup of milk or cream and a little salt and pepper to taste. Beat well. Heat butter or bacon drippings in a skillet until moderately hot. Add egg mixture and cook over low heat, scraping the cooked eggs from the bottom of the pan and letting uncooked eggs coat pan bottom to cook. They should be fluffy, thick, creamy flakes.

To make fried eggs: Heat 2-3 tablespoons of butter or bacon drippings in a skillet until moderately hot. Remove pan from heat and carefully slip in eggs, one at a time. Return to heat. Cook to desired degree of firmness, basting occasionally with the butter or drippings to set top of egg and yolk. You may also cover the pan, letting the steam seal the yolk and cook the top of the white.

To fry on both sides, turn eggs quickly when whites are partially set on top, using a spatula. Cook until as done as you wish.

To bake eggs: Use individual baking dishes, such as custard cups or bake several in a shallow baking dish. Grease the baking dishes and carefully break eggs into them. Add a tablespoon of cream for each egg and sprinkle with salt and pepper. Dot with butter. You may also sprinkle with bread crumbs and paprika, if you wish. Bake at 350° F for about 15 minutes or until whites are set. Serve immediately.

Unscrambled eggs

2 Tbsp. butter or cooking oil
1 small onion, chopped finely
4 eggs, beaten well
¼ cup milk or cream
grated cheddar cheese
salt and pepper

In medium skillet, heat butter or cooking oil and sauté onion until tender. In mixing bowl, mix beaten eggs and milk. Pour into medium hot skillet; cook on one side until golden brown. Flip over and add grated cheese and salt and pepper, if you wish. Egg will puff up nicely. Serve hot in an egg sandwich or with hot buttered toast for breakfast or brunch.

Curried eggs

2 cups curry white sauce (recipe below)
8-9 eggs, hard-boiled, peeled, and sliced
3 cups hot cooked rice
1 green bell pepper, seeded
3 pimentos, canned

Curry white sauce:
4 Tbsp. butter or margarine
4 Tbsp. flour
1 tsp. curry powder
½ tsp. salt
2 cups milk

To make the curry sauce, melt butter in saucepan and stir in flour until smooth. Add curry powder and salt, then stir in milk slowly over heat until thickens. Reserve.

Mound hot rice in center of each serving plate. Arrange slices of hard-boiled eggs around each rice mound; pour hot curry sauce over each serving. Garnish with strips of green pepper and pimento.

Foolproof omelet

¼ CUP BUTTER OR MARGARINE

3½ TBSP. FLOUR

1 TSP. SALT

1 CUP MILK

4 EGGS, SEPARATED

2 TBSP. SHORTENING OR COOKING OIL

Melt butter in small saucepan. Blend in flour and salt; cook 1 minute, stirring constantly. Remove from heat; gradually stir in milk. Return to heat; cook until thickened. Cool. Beat egg whites until stiff enough to hold peaks. Then beat the yolks. Blend yolks into white sauce, then fold in beaten egg whites. Heat shortening over low heat in a 10-inch skillet. Pour in the omelet mixture and cover with a tight-fitting lid. Cook over low heat for 15 minutes or until the bottom is light brown and crusty. Fold omelet in half and slide onto a platter to serve. You may also add grated cheese to omelet just before folding and/or crumble bacon over it.

Deviled eggs

6 EGGS, HARD-BOILED

1 TSP. VINEGAR

1 TSP. PREPARED MUSTARD

4 TBSP. MAYONNAISE

½ TSP. SALT

PAPRIKA

Peel cold hard-boiled eggs. Cut into halves lengthwise. Remove yolks to small mixing bowl. Lay whites on plate. Mash yolks very well. Add vinegar, mustard, mayonnaise, and salt. Mix very well until smooth. Spoon egg yolk mixture into halves of egg white. Mound up nicely and sprinkle with paprika. You may also add one of the following to the mashed yolk: deviled ham, bacon bits, chopped chives, olives, pickles, grated onion, or ground cooked ham. I also often add a little chipotle pepper powder to mine, in place of the paprika, for a little more "kick."

Egg salad sandwich filling

6 EGGS, HARD-BOILED AND PEELED

4 TBSP. MAYONNAISE

1 TBSP. VINEGAR

1 TSP. PREPARED MUSTARD

½ TSP. SALT

1 MEDIUM ONION, CHOPPED FINELY

Mash hard-boiled eggs in mixing bowl with fork. Add mayonnaise, vinegar, mustard, and salt. Mix well. Add chopped onion. Refrigerate and serve between slices of nice homemade bread.

Quiche

    1 UNBAKED PASTRY FOR 10-INCH PIE
    3 EGGS, BEATEN OR RECONSTITUTED DEHYDRATED EGGS
    1½ CUPS GRATED CHEESE OF YOUR CHOICE
    ½ CUP SLICED MUSHROOMS OR 1 CAN (2½ OZ.) MUSHROOMS, DRAINED OR 2 TBSP. DEHYDRATED, RECONSTITUTED MUSHROOMS
    12 SLICES BACON, FRIED CRISP AND CRUMBLED (MAY USE BACON-FLAVORED TVPs)
    1 CUP CREAM
    1 MEDIUM ONION, CHOPPED FINELY
    MAY ALSO ADD CHOPPED BROCCOLI, GREEN PEPPER, SWEET RED PEPPER, OR CHILE PEPPER (MILD OR HOT)

Heat oven to 375° F. Flute edges of pie crust. Combine the rest of the ingredients and pour into shell. Bake for 45 minutes or until filling is lightly browned and set.

Eggs a la goldenrod

    6 HARD-BOILED EGGS, PEELED
    8 SLICES OF BUTTERED TOAST
    2 CUPS WHITE SAUCE
    SALT AND PEPPER

Thin white sauce:
    3 TBSP. BUTTER OR MARGARINE
    2 TBSP. FLOUR
    1 TSP. SALT
    2 CUPS MILK OR CREAM

Chop egg whites finely and add to white sauce. Add salt and pepper to taste. Arrange slices of toast on a serving dish and pour white sauce over them. Mash egg yolks through a sieve and sprinkle over top. Sprinkle with paprika, if you wish.

Egg casserole

    3 EGGS, SLIGHTLY BEATEN
    1 SMALL ONION, CHOPPED
    2 CUPS CHOPPED COOKED HAM OR 1 PINT CANNED, DRAINED
    1 CUP SHREDDED CHEESE
    ⅔ CUP CRUSHED CRACKER CRUMBS
    1 TBSP. BUTTER
    1½ CUP MILK

Mix all ingredients and pour into a buttered 9x9-inch pan. Bake for 45 minutes at 350° F until top is golden brown and set.

Asparagus quiche

I really like this recipe, because when the first asparagus is poking up through the mulch, I'm also getting a basketful of eggs every day from my hens. So the combination is perfect, using what's on hand and plentiful. And we really love this quiche! Tender, flaky crust mixed with tender, juicy asparagus, cheese, and fluffy eggs. Can't be beat!

1 UNBAKED PASTRY FOR 1 CRUST PIE
1 LB. FRESH ASPARAGUS, TRIMMED
3 TBSP. BUTTER OR MARGARINE
3 TBSP. FLOUR
½ TSP. SALT
1½ CUPS MILK
4 EGGS, BEATEN
½ CUP SHREDDED SWISS CHEESE
¼ CUP DRY BREAD CRUMBS

Cut eight asparagus spears into 4-inch pieces, including tips. Cut remaining spears into ½-inch pieces. Cook all of the asparagus in a small amount of water until tender; drain and set aside. Line pastry shell with foil and bake at 450° F for 5 minutes. Remove foil and bake for 5 minutes longer. Remove from oven and set aside. In a saucepan, melt butter. Stir in flour and salt until smooth. Gradually add milk, stirring until thickened. Stir a small amount into eggs, then return all to pan. Stir in cheese and short asparagus pieces. Pour into crust. Sprinkle with bread crumbs. Bake at 400° F for 30 minutes. Arrange the 4-inch asparagus pieces in a spoke pattern on top and return to oven for 5 minutes more. Serve immediately.

Skillet scrambled eggs and bacon

4 STRIPS BACON, FRIED CRISP AND CRUMBLED
1½ TBSP. BUTTER OR MARGARINE
4 EGGS
2 TBSP. CREAM OR MILK
SALT AND PEPPER TO TASTE

Fry bacon slices crisp; drain well. Crumble bacon. Heat butter in small skillet over low heat. Beat eggs and cream or milk. Pour into skillet and add bacon crumbles. As eggs start to set, lift bottom up and stir uncooked top eggs down to skillet. When eggs are cooked, remove from skillet and serve immediately.

Skillet strata

1 CUP CHOPPED, COOKED BROCCOLI
½ CUP CHOPPED ONION
½ CUP CHOPPED PIMENTO OR SWEET RED PEPPER
½ CUP SAUSAGE PIECES
6 EGGS, BEATEN

½ CUP MILK OR CREAM

3 DROPS HOT PEPPER SAUCE (LIKE TABASCO)

½ CUP SWISS CHEESE

2 TBSP. BUTTER OR MARGARINE

In a large mixing bowl, mix all ingredients except for butter. In a large skillet, heat butter to medium hot. Add mixture and turn down heat to low. When bottom of eggs begins to set, cut in half and lift bottom up and turn each half over to cook on the other side. Sprinkle with salt and pepper to taste. Serve immediately.

Sausage and egg breakfast

½ LB. SAUSAGE OR BACON

3 EGGS, BEATEN

1 CUP MILK

½ TSP. SALT

½ TSP. MUSTARD

1 SLICE BREAD, MADE INTO CRUMBS

½ CUP GRATED CHEESE

Brown your choice of meat in a skillet and drain off grease. Beat eggs in bowl and add milk, salt, and mustard. Then add bread crumbs and mix well. Add cheese and crumbled bacon or sausage. Pour into a small, greased baking dish. Bake at 350° F for 45 minutes until top is golden and middle is set. You can refrigerate overnight for a quick hot breakfast in the morning. Just put it into the oven for a few minutes at 300° F until thoroughly heated.

Egg Fu Yung

Egg Fu Yung sauce:

> 1 tsp. soy sauce
>
> 1 tsp. molasses
>
> 1 tsp. vinegar
>
> 2 tsp. cornstarch
>
> ½ cup canned chicken broth

In top of double boiler, mix soy sauce, molasses, vinegar, and cornstarch, stirring until smooth. Gradually stir in chicken broth and over direct heat, bring to boiling, stirring. Reduce heat and simmer 10 minutes. Sauce will be thickened and translucent. Keep warm over hot water.

Egg Fu Yung:

> 1 cup finely chopped cooked ham or ½-pint canned, drained
>
> 1 cup canned bean sprouts, drained
>
> 1 cup finely chopped onion
>
> 6 eggs, slightly beaten
>
> 1 tsp. salt
>
> 1 Tbsp. soy sauce
>
> cooking oil

In large bowl, combine ham, bean sprouts, and onion. Add eggs, salt, and soy sauce, stirring until combined. Slowly heat a little oil in a small skillet. Add egg mixture about 2 Tbsp. at a time. Cook on one side and then turn over and repeat on the other side. Remove and keep warm while others are cooking. Serve hot with hot Egg Fu Yung sauce poured over them. Very good with fried rice!

Snacks

Saltines

    1½ cups flour, divided
    1 pkg. (2¼ tsp.) dry yeast
    ½ tsp. salt, plus extra for sprinkling
    ¼ tsp. baking soda
    ¼ tsp. cream of tartar
    ⅔ cup hot water
    2 Tbsp. solid vegetable shortening
    2 Tbsp. butter, melted, to brush

Into a bowl, measure 1 cup flour and the dry ingredients. In a small bowl, combine the hot water and shortening. Stir to blend and pour the liquid into the dry ingredients; stir vigorously to blend with a wooden spoon. Add the balance of flour to make a ball that can be worked with your hands. If the dough is sticky, add more flour. Turn out onto lightly-floured surface to knead. Knead with a rhythmic push-turn-fold motion until the dough is soft and elastic. Add sprinkles of flour to control stickiness. Knead only until smooth, about 4 minutes.

Drop the dough into buttered bowl, cover, and place in the refrigerator to chill — from 1 hour to overnight. The longer the better, up to 18 hours.

Turn dough out onto a lightly-floured surface and with a heavy rolling pin, roll the dough into a rectangle about 18x6 inches and no thicker than ⅛ inch. Fold the dough from the short ends, brushing off the excess flour, to make 3 layers.

Roll again with the rolling pin or through a pasta machine.

Prick the dough with the tines of a fork. Cut the dough along the edge of a ruler or yardstick with a pizza or knife into desired shapes.

Place the crackers close together on a lightly-greased (or lined with parchment paper) baking sheet. Sprinkle lightly with salt from 12 inches above the crackers to distribute salt evenly.

Bake at 425° F for 10-20 minutes. Bake on the middle shelf of the oven until lightly browned and crisp, depending on the thickness of the crackers. Inspect the crackers several times during the bake period to make certain those on the outer edge of the baking sheet are not getting too brown. If so, move them around — out to in.

Brush the crackers with melted butter before removing them from the baking sheet to cool on a metal rack.

Crackers

½ CUP LARD OR SHORTENING
7 CUPS FLOUR
1 TSP. SALT
1 TBSP. BAKING POWDER
WATER

Mix dry ingredients well; cut in lard or shortening. Add enough water to make a stiff dough, a little at a time so you don't get it sticky. Knead lightly on a floured board, then roll thin. Cut into squares and prick with a fork. Place on lightly-greased cookie sheet and bake at 350° F for 10-12 minutes. You may use a pasta machine or noodle maker to roll your cracker dough out thinly.

Cheese cornmeal crackers

2 CUPS SHARP CHEDDAR CHEESE, GRATED (AT ROOM TEMPERATURE)
½ CUP GRATED PARMESAN CHEESE, ROOM TEMPERATURE
½ CUP SOFT BUTTER OR MARGARINE
¼ CUP MILK
1 TSP. GARLIC POWDER
1 TSP. ONION POWDER
1 TSP. PAPRIKA
1 CUP ROLLED OATS
½ CUP FLOUR
½ CUP CORNMEAL
2 TBSP. SESAME SEEDS

Combine cheeses, butter, milk, garlic and onion powder, and paprika in mixing bowl. Stir in rolled oats, flour, cornmeal, and sesame seeds. Shape dough into a 12-inch roll; wrap tightly in a piece of plastic wrap, and refrigerate for 4 hours or overnight. (You can also place the roll in a covered bowl.) Slice the dough roll into about ⅛-inch slices and arrange on a lightly-greased cookie sheet. Bake in preheated oven at 400° F for 8-10 minutes or until nice and crisp. Remove immediately and place on wire rack. To make these snack crackers hot and spicy, you can also add ⅛ tsp. hot chili or cayenne powder to the dough as you mix it.

Whole wheat thin crackers

1¾ CUPS WHOLE WHEAT FLOUR
1½ CUPS ALL-PURPOSE FLOUR
¾ TSP. SALT
⅓ CUP VEGETABLE OIL
1 CUP WATER
SALT FOR SPRINKLING

In a medium bowl, stir together the whole wheat flour, all-purpose flour, and salt. Pour in the vegetable oil and water; mix just until blended.

On a lightly-floured surface, roll out the dough as thin as possible — no thicker than ⅛ inch. Place dough on an ungreased baking sheet, and mark squares out with a knife, but don't cut through. Prick each cracker with a fork a few times, and sprinkle with salt.

Bake at 350° F for 15 to 20 minutes, or until crisp and light brown. When cool, remove from baking sheet, and separate into individual crackers.

Cheddar cheese crackers

½ CUP BUTTER, SOFTENED
2 CUPS GRATED CHEDDAR CHEESE
1½ CUPS FLOUR
½ TSP. SALT
1 TBSP. DRIED CHIVES

In medium bowl, combine butter and cheese. Mix together until well blended. Add flour, salt, and chives to butter mixture and mix until blended. Form dough into 1-inch balls and place on ungreased cookie sheets. Flatten balls using the bottom of a drinking glass. If they start to stick, use a piece of plastic between the glass and dough ball. Make them as thin as possible. Prick each cracker several times with a fork. Bake crackers at 350° F for 12-15 minutes until very lightly browned around the edges. Remove to a wire rack and cool.

Graham crackers

4 CUPS WHOLE WHEAT FLOUR (GRAHAM FLOUR)
2 CUPS FLOUR
1 TSP. BAKING POWDER
1 TSP. BAKING SODA
2 CUPS BROWN SUGAR
1 CUP LARD OR SHORTENING
1 CUP MILK
1 TSP. VANILLA

Mix dry ingredients well, then cut in lard or shortening. Add milk and vanilla and mix into firm dough. Turn out onto lightly-floured surface and roll out thin with rolling pin. Cut into squares (you can use a ruler or yardstick for a guide to get really straight squares). Prick each square with a fork several times. Place on a lightly-greased cookie sheet and bake at 375° F until brown and crisp.

Honey graham crackers

> 3 CUPS WHOLE WHEAT FLOUR
> ½ TSP. SALT
> ½ TSP. BAKING POWDER
> ½ TSP. BAKING SODA
> ½ TSP. CINNAMON
> 6 TBSP. BUTTER
> ½ CUP HONEY
> WHITE FLOUR FOR HANDLING

Sift together flour, salt, baking powder, baking soda, and cinnamon into a bowl.

Melt together the butter and honey. Pour into dry ingredients. Mix with a fork, then push the dough together with your hands. If the dough is too sticky, add white flour to get a workable dough. Don't knead or overmix. Place the dough on a well-floured surface, and roll it with a well-floured rolling pin to ⅛-inch thick. Cut rectangles (approximately 1¼ x 3 inches) with a knife, and prick them with a fork.

Place on a lightly-greased baking sheet, and bake for 10 minutes in a 375° F oven. Cool on a rack.

Corn chips

These homemade snacks are like Fritos only with more corn taste.

> 1 EGG YOLK
> 1 CUP WARM WATER
> 1 TSP. SALT
> ¾ CUP MASA HARINA (CORN FLOUR — DON'T SUBSTITUTE CORNMEAL)
> CORN OIL FOR FRYING

In a mixing bowl, beat egg yolk and water. Add salt and mix again. Gradually add enough masa harina to make a soft dough that is stiff enough that it doesn't stick to your fingers. Fill a cookie press with the dough, attaching the plate to make a flat ribbon shape. Heat oil in deep fryer to 375° F. (Important! If the oil is not hot enough, your corn chips will be grease-soaked and heavy.) Press out a few short lengths of dough into the hot oil. As they emerge, cut them off with a knife, if necessary. Don't overfill the deep fryer; do one layer at a time. Turn the chips once as they fry, until they are just golden brown. Skim off chips and drain on a cookie sheet covered with paper towels. While they are hot, sprinkle with salt or your favorite dry taco seasoning, if you wish.

Nacho chips

Bake up some corn tortillas. Stack them up, several high, then cut in half with sharp knife, then in quarters, then eighths, until you have nice chip-size triangles. Heat corn oil in deep fryer to 375° F and gently slide a few at a time into the hot oil to fry. Turn once with fork, then as they get golden brown, lift out of oil onto a cookie sheet covered with paper towels to drain. Add salt or your favorite dry taco seasoning, if you wish. Serve with salsa, black olives, and sour cream.

Salted, baked pumpkin seeds (pepitas)

ONE MEDIUM-SIZED PUMPKIN

SALT

OLIVE OIL

Preheat oven to 350° F. Cut open the pumpkin and use a strong metal spoon to scoop out the insides. Separate the seeds from the stringy core. Rinse the seeds. Don't throw away the pumpkin! You can use it for pumpkin pie or pumpkin bars.

In a small saucepan, add the seeds to water, about 2 cups of water to every ½ cup of seeds. Add a 1½ tsp. of salt for every cup of water (more if you like your seeds saltier). Bring to a boil. Let simmer for 10 minutes. Remove from heat and drain.

Spread about a tablespoon of olive oil over the bottom of a roasting pan. Spread the seeds out over the roasting pan, all in one layer. Bake on the top rack just until the seeds begin to brown (10-20 minutes). When browned to your satisfaction, remove from the oven, and let the pan cool on a rack. Let the seeds cool all the way down before eating.

Potato chips

3 LARGE POTATOES, PEELED

SHORTENING OR VEGETABLE OIL TO DEEP FRY

SALT

After peeling, slice potatoes very thin. Put slices in a large bowl of ice water for one hour. You may sit bowl in refrigerator. Dry the slices by tossing them lightly in a clean towel. Heat frying grease to 390° F and slip a few slices at a time in the fryer. Do only one layer at a time or the grease will cool too much and the chips will get limp and soggy. When chips are light golden brown, remove them and place on a layer of paper towels to soak off any clinging grease. Lightly salt and store in a plastic bag after cooled.

Desserts

Pies

There is nothing like a homemade pie to finish up a meal. You can use such a wide variety of fillings from your orchard, berry patch, or pantry that you and your family will never tire of freshly-made pies. They're so much better than store-bought pies with their tender crusts and fresh fillings — *boy* can you taste the difference! If you grow your own fruit, your pies will cost only pennies to make, too. Pies take just a few minutes to put together and your family will rave for days!

But aren't pie crusts really difficult to make? Hardly. They do require a little practice to get perfect, but I guarantee you'll make a very delectable crust your very first time with these hints.

Tip #1: Don't handle your pie dough any more than necessary. While bread dough loves to be handled and kneaded, pie dough doesn't. The more you handle it, the tougher it will become. But, of course, you do have to handle it in order to get the dough ball to hang together and to roll out the dough. The reason the dough gets tough is that the lard or shortening you use in the dough gets too thoroughly mixed with the flour.

Tip #2: Add very cold water to your flour, slowly, and add just enough that the dough ball holds together nicely for rolling out, yet is *not* sticky in the least. When I started baking, Mom had told me this and I *never* added enough water, so when I tried to roll out my crusts, they always broke up. How discouraged I was at my ugly patched-together pie crusts! One day one of my kids said "Mom, why don't you add more water?" So I did, to humor him. It worked! Soon I had a beautiful crust rolled out. No patches, no rips, no bumpy edges!

Tip #3: Keep your pie crusts cold. Chill the dough after you divide your dough balls in half for a two-crust pie, keeping it covered so it won't dry out. This makes a flakier crust as the shortening or lard hardens.

Tip #4: When rolling out your bottom crust, make that dough ball slightly larger than the top crust. Roll out the dough lightly on a floured surface, rolling in all directions to maintain a round shape. Make the crust slightly larger than the pan and allow for the depth, as well. This leaves you with enough overhang to trim off so your edges are neat.

Tip #5: When you finish rolling your crusts, simply roll them up on your rolling pin to pick them up to transfer them to your pie pan. Then unroll them right in place — no rips, no tears from handling the tender crusts.

Tip #6: When you make your top crust, cut steam vents in the top to allow steam to escape. If you don't, juices will run out of the edges of the pan all over your oven. Or a rip will rupture in the top of the crust and make a very ugly pie. I make two semi-circular cuts in the center of the top crust, then with the end of my fork, I create parallel dots up and down the cuts to resemble ears of wheat on a stalk. Mom did this and her pies always looked so pretty. Mine do too.

Tip #7: To seal the top crust to the bottom crust, before you lay the top crust in place, first moisten the top edge of the bottom crust with cold water from your fingertips. Then lay on your top crust. I seal the two crusts together by laying my thumb and first finger on the top of the edge, then pushing between them with the end of a knife, making an indentation. By moving my fingers around the pie and making indentations each time, the edge is soon sealed and fluted nicely. This prevents juices from leaking and helps the pie bake well.

Tip #8: When making a single crust pie, such as lemon meringue or pumpkin, take a fork and poke the bottom crust a few times all over the surface before baking. This eliminates bubbles in the bottom. Crimp the edges as for a double crust pie.

Tip #9: To make a very crunchy, sugary, bubbled top crust, rub butter on it, then sprinkle sugar or cinnamon sugar over the butter before baking. This makes almost a cinnamon-sugar pie crust "cookie" like we kids used to love, when Mom had leftover pie dough.

Okay, let's make some pies!

Basic two-crust pie pastry

When my oldest son, Bill, was dating his wife, Kelly Jo, he called me from Minnesota to talk him through his first pie crust. He's quite the cook, but he'd never attempted a pie crust from scratch. So, from Montana, I helped him put together the pie, step by step. "Oh, it's falling apart when I'm trying to roll it out." "Add a little more water to it." "Okay, it's a ball now. It's rolling out. Now what…?" He got the pie made and it must have worked magic because he and Kelly Jo have just celebrated ten years of marriage. And he still bakes pies!

> 2 CUPS SIFTED FLOUR
> 1 TSP. SALT
> ¾ CUP LARD OR SHORTENING
> 4-5 TBSP. ICE WATER

Sift flour and salt into medium mixing bowl. With pastry blender or fork, cut in shortening until mixture resembles coarse cornmeal. Sprinkle in ice water, tossing lightly until dough holds together in a ball that can be handled without breaking apart, yet is not sticky. Divide in halves, with one half a little larger for the bottom crust. Flatten each ball somewhat with your hands. Cover and refrigerate if you have the time. Remove from refrigerator and take out larger ball and place on a lightly-floured surface. Sprinkle flour on your rolling pin and lightly begin rolling out dough from center to outside edges, working in alternate directions to keep a rounded shape. You can lay the pie tin, upside down, on your crust-in-progress to check the size you need. Remember to allow for the depth of the pan and the edges when making your decision. When the crust is the right size, gently roll it up on your rolling pin and unroll it over your pan. Trim crust at edge of pan with a knife and fill.

Flaky pastry for a one-crust pie

>1 CUP SIFTED FLOUR
>½ TSP. SALT
>⅓ CUP LARD OR SHORTENING
>2-2½ TBSP. ICE WATER

Sift flour with salt into medium mixing bowl. Cut in lard or shortening until mixture resembles coarse cornmeal. Sprinkle in ice water, tossing lightly until dough holds together in a ball that can be handled without breaking apart, yet is not sticky. Shape into a ball, flatten with your hand, and cover well. Refrigerate until ready to use or at least one hour (if you can wait!). Roll out as above. Lay pastry in pie tin. Cut off excess dough at edge of pan. With a fork, prick the bottom of the crust several times to prevent large bubbles from forming during baking. Flute edge of crust nicely. For a baked pie shell, bake at 400° F until golden brown but not dark. Cool completely before filling. Or for an unbaked crust, fill unbaked pie shell, then bake as directed.

Graham cracker pie crust

>1¼ CUPS GRAHAM CRACKER CRUMBS (ABOUT 18 CRACKERS)
>¼ CUP SOFT BUTTER OR MARGARINE
>¼ CUP SUGAR
>¼ TSP. CINNAMON

Combine all ingredients in medium mixing bowl; blend well with fork. Press evenly on bottom and sides of a 9-inch pie plate, not on rim. Refrigerate until ready to fill. Or if you want a baked graham crust, bake pie crust at 375° F for about 8 minutes or until crust is golden brown.

Jackie's famous apple pie

>PASTRY FOR TWO-CRUST PIE
>5 MEDIUM, FIRM, TART PIE APPLES, PEELED AND SLICED
>1 CUP BROWN SUGAR
>1 TSP. CINNAMON
>3 TBSP. FLOUR
>2 TBSP. BUTTER OR MARGARINE

On a lightly-floured surface, roll out half of the pastry to make the bottom crust. Line a 9-inch pie pan, trimming off the edges of the pastry, just over the edges of the pan. Refrigerate with the rest of the pastry until ready to use.

In mixing bowl, slice apples and add sugar, cinnamon, and flour, mixed together. Stir well, coating all apple slices. Pour into pie shell. Dot with butter in several places. Moisten edges of the crust. On a lightly-floured surface, roll out top crust. Cut vents into the center of the crust. Roll crust up with rolling pin and gently unroll over apples. Trim off excess, just past the pan edges. Flute edges of crust to seal well. Brush top with softened butter and sprinkle with brown sugar and cinnamon. Bake on a cookie sheet at 375° F for about 50 minutes or until crust is golden brown.

Dried apple pie

>PASTRY FOR TWO-CRUST PIE
>
>1 LB. DRIED, SLICED TART APPLES
>
>1 QUART COLD WATER
>
>1 TBSP. CINNAMON
>
>1½ CUPS SUGAR
>
>4 TSP. GRATED ORANGE RIND
>
>½ CUP ORANGE JUICE

Put apples and water into a covered saucepan and gently cook until softened. Add cinnamon, sugar, grated orange rind, and juice. Line a pie pan with pastry. Fill with apple mixture. Dot with butter. Cover with vented top crust and flute edges. Bake at 400° F for 10 minutes, then reduce heat to 350° F and continue baking until crust is golden brown.

Apple dumplings

While not a "pie," apple dumplings taste like a pie, wrapped up in a tender crust, each apple to its own little shell, smothered in sweet, spicy juice. They're great when apples are plentiful and although very easy to make, they taste like you've spent hours!

Sauce:

>2 CUPS SUGAR
>
>2 CUPS WATER
>
>¼ TSP. CINNAMON
>
>¼ TSP. NUTMEG
>
>¼ CUP BUTTER

Cook sauce in a saucepan, simmering 5 minutes; set aside.

Crust:

>2 CUPS FLOUR
>
>1 TSP. SALT
>
>2 TSP. BAKING POWDER
>
>¾ CUP SHORTENING
>
>½ CUP MILK

Mix flour, salt, and baking powder. Cut in shortening until resembles coarse meal. Add milk and mix. Form into a ball and turn out onto a lightly-floured surface. Roll dough out ¼-inch thick and cut six 5-inch squares.

>6 MEDIUM FIRM APPLES, PEELED AND CORED, KEPT WHOLE

Place an apple on each square, sprinkle with cinnamon, nutmeg, sugar, and dot with butter. Fold corners toward top and pinch edges together. Place in deep buttered baking dish. Pour the sauce over the dumplings and bake at 375° F for 35 minutes. Cool slightly and serve hot. Ladle extra sauce back over dumplings just before serving. Serve with vanilla ice cream or whipped cream, if you wish.

Apple pecan pie

  PASTRY FOR A ONE-CRUST PIE
  ¼ CUP PECANS, CHOPPED
  6 CUPS PEELED APPLES, SLICED
  1 CUP SUGAR
  2 TBSP. FLOUR
  ½ TSP. CINNAMON
  ¼ TSP. NUTMEG

 Sprinkle chopped pecans in bottom of pie shell. Mix apples, sugar, flour, cinnamon, and nutmeg in bowl. Pour into pie shell and spread out.

Topping:
  ¼ CUP BUTTER OR MARGARINE
  ½ CUP BROWN SUGAR
  ⅓ CUP FLOUR
  ½ TSP. CINNAMON
  ¼ CUP CHOPPED PECANS

 Mix butter, brown sugar, flour, and cinnamon together well. Stir in pecans. Spread well over apple mixture. Bake at 400° F until apples are tender and pie topping is brown.

Sour cream apple pie

  PASTRY FOR A ONE-CRUST PIE
  2 EGGS
  1 CUP SOUR CREAM
  1 CUP SUGAR
  6 TBSP. FLOUR, DIVIDED
  1 TSP. VANILLA EXTRACT
  ¼ TSP. SALT
  3 CUPS APPLES, PEELED AND CHOPPED
  3 TBSP. BUTTER OR MARGARINE, MELTED
  ¼ CUP FIRMLY PACKED BROWN SUGAR

 In a mixing bowl, beat eggs. Add sour cream. Mix in sugar, 2 Tbsp. flour, vanilla, and salt; mix well until blended. Stir in apples. Pour into pie shell. Bake at 375° F for 15 minutes.
 Meanwhile, combine remaining flour, brown sugar, and butter. Sprinkle over pie after 15 minutes baking, then return to oven until filling is set. Cool and serve.

Apple blackberry pie

  PASTRY FOR TWO-CRUST PIE
  1 CUP GREEN SUMMER APPLES, PEELED AND SLICED
  3 CUPS FRESH BLACKBERRIES
  1 CUP SUGAR

½ tsp. cinnamon

3 Tbsp. quick cooking tapioca or 3 Tbsp. cornstarch

2 Tbsp. butter or margarine

In large bowl, combine apples, berries, sugar, cinnamon, and tapioca or cornstarch. Mix well. Turn into pastry-lined 9-inch pie pan. Dot with butter in several places. Place top crust with vents cut into it on pie and seal edges. Bake at 400° F until crust is golden brown (about 45 minutes).

Cherry pie

Dad used to own a small orchard near Grand Junction, Michigan. We would drive over from Minnesota in the fall to pick apples from his trees to bring home for the winter. Next door was an abandoned cherry orchard with sadly neglected, broken down trees. But they were full of pie cherries! Dad called the neighbor, who owned the orchard, and got permission to pick as many as we wanted. Wow! Traipsing through the long grass and weeds with buckets in one hand and a ladder in the other, I felt like a fruit thief...even though we had received permission to pick. And pick we did! That was more than 30 years ago and I still have four pints of those wonderful cherries in our pantry...plus so many great memories. (It was the first time my oldest son, now 39, had ridden a bike by himself. And he also drove Grandpa's riding lawnmower like a champ...in first gear. Except Grandpa forgot to teach him how to STOP it. Grandpa told him to park it into the apple barn. So in he went. BANG! Right into the wall. After the dust and pigeons had settled, and we found out that Billy was okay, we all had a good laugh. And Grandpa showed him how to use the brake!)

pastry for two-crust pie

5 cups fresh pie cherries or 1 quart canned cherries, drained and juice reserved or 2 cans (15-oz.) cherries packed in water, juice reserved

1½ cups sugar

⅓ cup flour

⅛ tsp. salt

2 Tbsp. butter or margarine

¼ tsp. almond extract (optional but nice!)

1 egg yolk, beaten slightly

Drain cherries, reserving 1 cup liquid. If using fresh cherries, pit and place in mixing bowl. In another bowl, combine sugar, flour, and salt. Stir well, then stir into cherry liquid or into fresh cherries. If stirring into canned cherry juice, mix in saucepan, then bring to boiling, stirring as it thickens. Stir in butter. Add almond extract and cherries and remove from heat. If using fresh cherries, just stir sugar mix into cherries and pour into pie shell. Add dots of butter in several places and sprinkle almond extract over cherries. When using canned cherries, pour cooled cherry mixture into pie shell. Top with pie crust with vents cut into it over the top *or* cut the top crust into ½-inch strips and arrange a lattice top over the pie, sealing edges and fluting them to keep juice in pie as it bakes. Paint with egg yolk to make a shiny crust. Bake at 400° F on a cookie sheet until top is nicely browned.

Banana cream pie

- 1 BAKED PASTRY SHELL
- ¾ CUP SUGAR
- ⅓ CUP FLOUR
- ¼ TSP. SALT
- 2 CUPS MILK, DIVIDED
- 3 EGG YOLKS, WHITES RESERVED
- 1 TBSP. BUTTER OR MARGARINE
- 1 TSP. VANILLA
- 2-3 LARGE RIPE BANANAS, SLICED

In saucepan, mix together sugar, flour, and salt. Add 1 cup of milk; mix smooth. Bring to a boil over medium heat, stirring constantly to avoid scorching. Continue until smoothly thickened; about 2 minutes. Remove from heat. Mix egg yolks with remaining 1 cup milk and gradually stir into hot mixture. Put back over heat and slowly bring to a boil, stirring constantly until mixture thickens. Remove from heat; stir in butter and vanilla. Add sliced bananas to bottom of pie shell. Add warm filling.

Meringue:
- 3 EGG WHITES
- ¼ TSP. CREAM OF TARTAR
- ⅓ CUP SUGAR

Make meringue: Beat room temperature egg whites with cream of tartar until soft peaks form. Gradually add sugar and continue beating until stiff peaks form. Spoon over pie, sealing to edge of crust. Bake at 400° F until meringue is golden. Cool away from drafts until serving.

Northwoods blueberry pie

- PASTRY FOR TWO-CRUST PIE
- 5 CUPS FRESH BLUEBERRIES OR 1 QUART CANNED BLUEBERRIES, DRAINED, JUICE RESERVED
- 1½ CUPS SUGAR
- 3 TBSP. CORNSTARCH
- 2 TBSP. BUTTER OR MARGARINE

Mix blueberries or drained blueberries with sugar and cornstarch in mixing bowl. Toss gently so as not to damage berries. Add ½ cup juice. Mix again. Pour into unbaked pie shell. Dot with butter in several places. Top with top crust with vents cut into it. Seal edges and flute if desired. Rub softened butter on top and sprinkle with sugar. Bake at 400° F on a cookie sheet until top is golden brown (about 45 minutes).

Grandma Eddy's butterscotch pie

- 1 BAKED PASTRY SHELL
- 1 CUP FIRMLY PACKED BROWN SUGAR

½ cup flour
2 egg yolks, beaten (whites reserved)
1¼ cups milk
½ tsp. salt
1 Tbsp. butter or margarine
1 tsp. vanilla

Mix brown sugar, flour, and salt. In another bowl, mix egg yolks with milk. Slowly add to flour mix. In saucepan over low heat, slowly cook until stirring. Stir constantly as it will scorch easily; if you have a double boiler, use that, instead. When thickened, add butter and vanilla and pour into baked pie shell.

Meringue:
2 egg whites, at room temperature
¼ tsp. cream of tartar
2 Tbsp. sugar

In medium bowl, beat egg whites and cream of tartar until soft peaks form. Gradually beat in sugar and continue to beat until stiff peaks form. Spread meringue over warm filling, sealing to edge of crust. Bake at 400° F until meringue is golden. Cool well before serving.

Cranberry cream cheese pie

1 baked pie shell
1 package (3 oz.) cream cheese or ½ cup fresh cream cheese
¼ cup sugar
1 Tbsp. milk
1 tsp. vanilla
½ cup whipped cream

Topping:
1 can (8 oz.) jellied cranberry sauce
⅓ cup sugar
1 small box raspberry flavored gelatin

In mixing bowl, mix gelatin and sugar; set aside. Heat 1¼ cups water to boiling and pour over gelatin mixture. Stir very well until dissolved. Stir in cranberry sauce. Chill until slightly thickened.

Meanwhile, in another mixing bowl, beat cream cheese, sugar, milk, and vanilla until fluffy. Fold in whipped cream. Spread evenly in baked pie shell. Beat cranberry topping until light, then pour over filling. Chill overnight.

Chocolate pie

    1 BAKED PIE SHELL
    3 CUPS MILK
    ⅓ CUP CORNSTARCH
    3 TBSP. COCOA
    3 EGG YOLKS
    ⅛ TSP. SALT
    1¼ CUPS SUGAR
    1 TSP. VANILLA

Mix a little milk with the cornstarch to make a thick paste. Gradually add more milk until all cornstarch has been added. Mix in cocoa. Over medium heat, bring to a boil, stirring until thickened. Make sure it doesn't scorch. Cool a little, then add beaten egg yolks, salt, and sugar. Again, cook, stirring until thickened. Add vanilla and mix well. Pour out into baked pie shell. Cool and serve topped with whipped cream.

Cranberry raisin pie

    PASTRY FOR TWO-CRUST PIE
    3 CUPS FRESH CRANBERRIES
    2 TBSP. FLOUR
    2 CUPS SUGAR
    ¼ TSP. SALT
    ⅔ CUP BOILING WATER
    1 CUP RAISINS
    2 TBSP. BUTTER OR MARGARINE
    1 EGG, BEATEN OR 1 EGG YOLK, BEATEN

Line a 9-inch pie pan with the bottom pie crust. Trim and refrigerate. Wash cranberries, removing stems and drain. Combine flour, sugar, and salt in medium saucepan. Stir in cranberries, water, and raisins. Cook, covered, over medium heat until cranberries start to pop open; about 10 minutes. Add butter; cool a few minutes. Meanwhile, roll out top crust and cut into ½-inch strips. Turn cranberry-raisin filling into pie shell. Moisten edge of shell with cold water. Make a lattice cover for pie and press edges down to seal. Flute edges to keep juice in pie. Paint with egg to make a shiny crust. Bake at 400° F on a cookie sheet for 45 minutes or until top is golden brown.

Custard pie

    PASTRY FOR A ONE-CRUST PIE
    2½ CUPS MILK
    ½ CUP SUGAR
    1 TSP. VANILLA
    ½ TSP. ALMOND EXTRACT (OPTIONAL BUT GOOD!)
    ¼ TSP. SALT
    4 EGGS, SLIGHTLY BEATEN

Scald milk; add sugar, flavorings, and salt. Mix well. Slowly stir into beaten eggs. Pour into unbaked pie shell; bake at 400° F for 20-35 minutes or until custard is set.

Pioneer's elderberry pie

    PASTRY FOR TWO-CRUST PIE
    1 CUP SUGAR
    ⅓ CUP FLOUR
    ¼ TSP. SALT
    3½ CUPS WASHED, STEMMED ELDERBERRIES
    1 TBSP. VINEGAR OR LEMON JUICE
    1 TBSP. BUTTER OR MARGARINE

In medium mixing bowl, combine sugar, flour, and salt. Mix in elderberries. Sprinkle on vinegar or lemon juice. Spread elderberries in pastry-lined 9-inch pie pan. Dot with butter. Lay on top crust with vents cut in and flute edges. Bake at 400° F for 35-40 minutes or until juices show in vents and crust is golden brown.

Key lime pie

    1 BAKED PIE SHELL
    3 EGG YOLKS, WHITES RESERVED
    1¼ CUPS GRANULATED SUGAR
    ¼ TSP. SALT
    ⅓ CUP CORNSTARCH
    2 CUPS WATER
    2 TBSP. BUTTER
    ⅓ CUP LIME JUICE
    1 TBSP. GRATED LIME PEEL
    FEW DROPS GREEN FOOD COLORING

Beat egg yolks and set aside. Combine sugar, salt, and cornstarch in a medium saucepan. Gradually add water and stir well with a whisk. Bring to a boil, stirring constantly, and boil 2 minutes. Remove from heat. Add a quarter of the mixture to the egg yolks and stir to prevent eggs from cooking. Return to hot mixture, add butter and lime juice; stir well. Return saucepan to stove and boil 2 minutes. Remove from heat and add grated lime peel and food coloring. Pour into pie shell.

Meringue:

    3 EGG WHITES, AT ROOM TEMPERATURE
    PINCH OF SALT
    4 TBSP. GRANULATED SUGAR

Place egg whites, cream of tartar, and salt in a medium bowl and beat until foamy; beat in sugar and continue to beat until the sugar dissolves and meringue is stiff. Cover pie filling with meringue, spreading it to the crust. Bake at 350° F for about 12 minutes or until very lightly browned. Serve cool.

Best-ever lemon pie (and it is!)

    PASTRY FOR TWO-CRUST PIE
    1¼ CUPS SUGAR
    2 TBSP. FLOUR
    ⅛ TSP. SALT
    ¼ CUP BUTTER OR MARGARINE
    3 EGGS, WELL BEATEN
    1 TSP. GRATED LEMON PEEL
    1 MEDIUM LEMON, PEELED AND THINLY SLICED
    ½ CUP WATER
    1 TBSP. MELTED BUTTER
    2 TBSP. SUGAR

Combine sugar, flour, and salt. Cream butter into sugar mixture. Add eggs. Grate lemon peel, then peel lemon, discarding the white membrane and seeds. Cut lemon into paper thin slices. (There should be ⅓ cup.) Add lemon peel, slices, and water to sugar mixture. Stir well and pour into bottom crust. Add vented top crust and flute edges. Brush top with melted butter, then sprinkle with 2 Tbsp. sugar. Bake at 400° F for 30-35 minutes or until top is golden brown.

Lemon meringue pie

    1 BAKED PIE SHELL
    ⅓ CUP CORNSTARCH
    1½ CUPS SUGAR
    1½ CUPS WATER
    4 EGG YOLKS, SLIGHTLY BEATEN, WHITES RESERVED
    ¼ CUP LEMON JUICE
    2 TBSP. GRATED LEMON PEEL (OPTIONAL BUT GOOD)
    3 TBSP. BUTTER OR MARGARINE

In a small saucepan, mix cornstarch, sugar, and salt. Gradually add water, stirring until smooth. Over medium heat, bring to a boil and stir constantly about 1 minute. Remove from heat; quickly stir in half of hot mixture into egg yolks, mixing well. Return to saucepan, blending well. Return to heat, stirring, for 1 minute. Remove from heat and stir in lemon juice, lemon peel, and butter. Pour immediately into pie shell. Preheat oven to 400° F.

Meringue:

    4 EGG WHITES AT ROOM TEMPERATURE
    ¼ TSP. CREAM OF TARTAR
    ½ CUP SUGAR

Beat egg whites and cream of tartar to make soft peaks, then slowly beat in sugar and continue beating until stiff peaks form when beater is raised. Spread meringue over hot filling, carefully sealing to edge of crust all around. Bake at 400° F until meringue is golden brown. Let cool on wire rack, away from drafts, and serve cold.

Old-fashioned peach pie

  PASTRY FOR TWO-CRUST PIE
  6 CUPS SLICED, PEELED RIPE PEACHES OR 1 QUART CANNED, DRAINED PEACHES
  ¾ CUP SUGAR
  2 TBSP. FLOUR

Line bottom pie pan with pastry; trim edges. In a medium bowl, combine peaches, sugar, and flour. Stir to mix well. Pour into pie shell. Moisten edges of bottom crust and lay vented top crust in place; seal and flute to keep juices in pie. If you wish, rub softened butter or margarine on top crust and sprinkle sugar on for an extra flaky fancy crust. Bake on a cookie sheet at 400° F until crust is golden.

Great-Grandma Jones' lemon raisin pie

(Great-Grandma Jones was Mom's mother's mother, so it's an old family recipe.)

  1 BAKED PIE SHELL
  1 LEMON
  1 CUP SUGAR
  3 TBSP. CORNSTARCH
  2 CUPS COLD WATER
  1 TBSP. BUTTER
  2 EGG YOLKS, BEATEN, WHITES RESERVED
  GRATED PEEL OF ½ LEMON
  PULP AND JUICE FROM 1 LEMON
  1 CUP GROUND RAISINS

Mix sugar and cornstarch. Add cold water, stirring well as you add. Add butter. Bring to a boil and add egg yolks, grated lemon peel, and juice and pulp of lemon. Stir as it thickens over a medium heat. Add raisins, stir well, and pour into baked pie shell.

Meringue:

  4 EGG WHITES AT ROOM TEMPERATURE
  ¼ TSP. CREAM OF TARTAR
  ½ CUP SUGAR

Beat egg whites and cream of tartar to make soft peaks, then slowly beat in sugar and continue beating until stiff peaks form when beater is raised. Spread meringue over hot filling, carefully sealing to edge of crust all around. Bake at 400° F until meringue is golden brown. Let cool on wire rack, away from drafts, and serve cold.

Oatmeal pie

PASTRY FOR ONE-CRUST PIE
⅔ CUP SUGAR
1 CUP FIRMLY PACKED BROWN SUGAR
⅔ CUP ROLLED OATS
2 TBSP. BUTTER OR MARGARINE
3 EGGS, WELL BEATEN
½ CUP MILK
1 TSP. VANILLA
⅔ CUP COCONUT

Mix sugars and rolled oats. Cut in butter or margarine. Add eggs, milk, and vanilla; stir well. Fold in coconut. Pour into unbaked pie shell and bake at 375° F for 30 minutes.

Mincemeat pie

PASTRY FOR TWO-CRUST PIE
4 CUPS CANNED MINCEMEAT (MAY USE STORE-BOUGHT, HOMEMADE MINCEMEAT, OR GREEN TOMATO MINCEMEAT)

Fill bottom crust with mincemeat. Dampen edges of crust with a little water and lay on vented top crust. Seal and flute. Bake at 400° F until crust is golden. Serve warm or cold.

New Mexico peach pie

PASTRY FOR ONE-CRUST PIE
1 EGG WHITE
6 CUPS PEACHES, FRESH, SLICED OR 1 QUART SLICED CANNED PEACHES, DRAINED
¾ CUP FLOUR
½ CUP FIRMLY PACKED BROWN SUGAR
½ CUP WHITE SUGAR
¼ CUP CHILLED BUTTER OR MARGARINE

Beat egg white and brush over the bottom and sides of the pastry shell. In a small bowl, combine flour and sugars; cut in butter until mixture resembles fine crumbs. Sprinkle ⅔ of mixture into bottom of the pastry; top with peaches. Sprinkle with remaining crumb mixture. Bake at 375° F for 40-45 minutes or until filling is bubbly and peaches are tender.

Old Virginia pecan pie

PASTRY FOR ONE-CRUST PIE
3 EGGS
½ CUP FIRMLY PACKED LIGHT BROWN SUGAR
1 CUP CORN SYRUP (DARK IF YOU HAVE IT)
½ TSP. SALT
1 TSP. VANILLA

¼ CUP BUTTER OR MARGARINE, MELTED

1 CUP PECAN HALVES OR PIECES

Beat eggs well in mixing bowl. Add sugar, corn syrup, salt, and vanilla. Beat well. Stir in butter and pecans, mixing well. Turn into unbaked pie shell; bake at 375° F for 45-50 minutes or until filling is set in center when pie is gently shaken. Cool and serve with whipped cream, if desired.

Plum pie

PASTRY FOR TWO-CRUST PIE

4 CUPS PITTED, UNPEELED, SLICED SWEET PLUMS, SUCH AS PRUNE PLUMS

2 TBSP. LEMON JUICE

1 CUP SUGAR

2 TBSP. CORNSTARCH OR FLOUR

½ TSP. CINNAMON

½ TSP. NUTMEG

2 TBSP. BUTTER OR MARGARINE

Sprinkle lemon juice over sliced plums in large bowl. Combine sugar, cornstarch, cinnamon, and nutmeg. Stir in plums until coated well. Let stand 15 minutes. Roll out bottom crust and lay in pie pan. Trim off edges. Turn plum mixture into pastry-lined pie pan, mounding the plums up in the center. Dot with butter in several places. Lay vented top crust on pie and seal edges. Flute to keep in juices. Bake at 400° F for 45 to 50 minutes or until top crust is golden brown. Cool; serve partly warm if you wish with whipped cream or ice cream.

Pumpkin pie

PASTRY FOR ONE-CRUST PIE, CHILLED

2 TBSP. BUTTER OR MARGARINE

1½ CUPS PUMPKIN (MAY BE FRESHLY BAKED AND PUREED, CANNED AND DRAINED CHUNKS, OR STORE-BOUGHT PUMPKIN)

1 TSP. CINNAMON

¼ TSP. NUTMEG

¼ TSP. CLOVES

½ TSP. SALT

2 EGGS, BEATEN

½ CUP SUGAR

½ CUP FIRMLY PACKED BROWN SUGAR

2 TBSP. FLOUR

1 CUP MILK (HOME CANNED WORKS VERY NICELY)

Melt butter and stir into pumpkin. Add spices and salt. Beat eggs and stir into sugars which have been mixed with flour. Add to pumpkin mixture and stir well. Add 1 cup milk and stir again. Pour into unbaked pie shell and bake at 375° F until a knife comes out clean when inserted in the center of the pie, about 1 hour. Cool and serve with whipped cream.

Tip: Some of the best pumpkin pies are made with squash.

Grandma Eddy's rhubarb pie

> PASTRY FOR ONE-CRUST PIE
> 2 Tbsp. flour
> ½ tsp. salt
> 1½ cups sugar
> 1 Tbsp. butter or margarine
> 3 egg yolks, slightly beaten, whites reserved
> water or reserved rhubarb juice
> 6 cups cut rhubarb pieces or enough to fill a 9-inch pie tin, heaped in center a bit or may use 1 quart + 1 pint canned rhubarb, drained, saving 1 cup of juice

In a mixing bowl, mix flour, salt, and sugar. Mix in melted butter. Add egg yolks and just enough water to make a batter which will pour from a spoon. Put rhubarb in unbaked pie shell and pour on batter. If using canned rhubarb, add 1 cup of reserved juice to batter instead of water, then pour over drained rhubarb in pie shell. Bake at 375° F until edges are golden brown and rhubarb is tender.

Meringue:

> 3 egg whites
> pinch of salt
> 3 Tbsp. sugar

While pie bakes, beat egg whites with salt until soft peaks form. Gradually add sugar and continue beating until stiff peaks hold when beater is held up from meringue. Spoon meringue on pie, completely sealing to edges of crust. Lift up peaks with spoon. Bake in oven at 375° F until meringue is golden brown.

Shoofly pie

> PASTRY FOR ONE-CRUST PIE
> 1 cup flour
> ½ cup firmly packed light brown sugar
> ½ tsp. salt
> ½ tsp. cinnamon
> ⅛ tsp. nutmeg
> ⅛ tsp. cloves
> 2 Tbsp. butter or margarine
> ¾ cup hot water
> ½ tsp. baking soda
> ½ cup light molasses
> 1 egg, well beaten

Refrigerate unbaked pie shell. In medium bowl, mix flour, sugar, salt, and spices, mixing well. Add butter and cut into flour mix. Pour hot water over baking soda in small bowl; stir to dissolve. Beat in molasses and egg, mixing well. Sprinkle ¼ crumb mixture in bottom of pie shell. Top with

⅓ molasses mixture. Continue layering, ending with crumb mixture. Bake at 375° F or until filling is set. Serve with vanilla ice cream or sweetened whipped cream if you wish.

Strawberry chiffon pie

    1 graham cracker crust
    3 egg yolks, whites reserved
    1 tsp. lemon juice
    ½ tsp. salt
    ½ cup plus 2 Tbsp. sugar
    1 envelope unflavored gelatin
    ½ cup cold water
    1 pint fresh strawberries
    red food coloring (optional)
    3 egg whites at room temperature

In top of double boiler, beat egg yolks until frothy. Add lemon juice, salt, and ½ cup sugar. Place over hot water and cook, stirring, until thickened (about 8 minutes). Remove from heat. Meanwhile, sprinkle gelatin over ½ cup cold water in small bowl; let stand 5 minutes to soften. Then stir into egg mixture to dissolve. Hull strawberries; reserve ½ cup, then put the rest in medium mixing bowl and mash them with a potato masher. Stir in egg-gelatin mixture and red food coloring, if desired. Refrigerate until consistency of unbeaten egg white (about 1 hour). In a large bowl, beat egg whites until stiff peaks form when beater is slowly raised. Gradually beat in 2 Tbsp. of sugar. Gently fold in strawberry mixture, just until combined. If too thin to mound, refrigerate 10 minutes or until slightly set. Turn into graham cracker crust and refrigerate 2 hours. Before serving, garnish with reserved strawberries, cut in half, with cut side down. Sprinkle with powdered sugar, if you wish.

Strawberry rhubarb pie

    pastry for two-crust pie, chilled
    2½ cups chopped red rhubarb, fresh or 1 pint canned rhubarb, drained
    2½ cups hulled, washed, and cut strawberries (in larger pieces)
    1½ cups sugar
    2 Tbsp. tapioca or 2 Tbsp. cornstarch
    1 Tbsp. all-purpose flour
    1 tsp. vanilla
    3 Tbsp. butter, cubed small

Mix the rhubarb, strawberries, sugar, tapioca, flour, and vanilla. Mix well in a large bowl and pour out into chilled crust. Dot the top of the filling with the butter. Moisten edges with water and lay on top crust. Seal and flute edges. Rub top with soft butter and sprinkle with sugar. Bake at 400° F for 15 minutes. Decrease temperature to 375° F and bake for an additional 45 to 50 minutes, or until the filling starts bubbling and top is golden brown.

Super good fresh strawberry pie

1 BAKED PIE SHELL

Glaze:

1 PINT FRESH STRAWBERRIES
1 CUP SUGAR
2½ TBSP. CORNSTARCH
1 TBSP. BUTTER OR MARGARINE
½ CUP WATER

Hull strawberries and crush with a potato masher in medium saucepan. Mix sugar and cornstarch, then stir into strawberries. Add water. Bring to a boil over low heat, stirring constantly. When thickened and translucent, strain and add butter. Cool.

Lining:

1 PKG. (3 OZ.) CREAM CHEESE, SOFTENED OR ½ CUP SOFT FRESH CREAM CHEESE
1 TBSP. LIGHT CREAM
2 TBSP. POWDERED SUGAR

Mix softened cream cheese, cream, and powdered sugar until smooth and fluffy. Add lining to cooled, baked pie shell.

Filling:

2 PINTS FRESH STRAWBERRIES, HULLED AND SLICED

Add filling and top with cooled glaze. Just before serving, top with sweetened whipped cream.

Sugar pie

This is one of Grandma Eddy's inventions from back in the Great Depression era. Food was scarce, and sometimes the family cow was dry. So Grandma substituted water for the milk or cream in the recipe and still turned out a very respectable pie. It's a quick and easy pie to make, requiring very few ingredients. Mom made it often, no doubt remembering home as a child and savoring this dessert back then. And we also have it quite often...probably for the very same reasons.

PASTRY FOR ONE-CRUST PIE
¾ CUP SUGAR
3 TBSP. FLOUR
1 TBSP. BUTTER OR MARGARINE
2 EGGS, BEATEN
¾ CUP MILK, LIGHT CREAM, OR WATER
1 TSP. VANILLA
NUTMEG TO SPRINKLE TOP

Mix sugar and flour in mixing bowl. Work in butter or margarine. Stir in eggs and milk. Add vanilla. Pour into unbaked pie shell. Sprinkle top with nutmeg. Bake at 375° F until set. For a larger pie or deeper filling, double recipe.

Sweet potato pie

    PASTRY FOR ONE-CRUST PIE
    2 CUPS MASHED SWEET POTATOES
    2 EGGS, SLIGHTLY BEATEN
    1⅔ CUPS EVAPORATED MILK (OR HOME-CANNED MILK)
    ¾ CUP SUGAR
    ½ TSP. SALT
    ½ TSP. GINGER
    ½ TSP. NUTMEG
    1 TSP. VANILLA
    ½ CUP BUTTER OR MARGARINE, MELTED

Combine sweet potatoes, beaten eggs, and milk. Add sugar and spices. Blend in melted butter or margarine. Pour into unbaked pie shell and bake at 400° F until firm and set. Serve with whipped cream or ice cream if you wish.

Vinegar pie

This is another recipe from before the Great Depression. When times were hard and fruits for pie fillings were scarce, the milk cow was dry, and everyone really wanted a nice pie, wives put together this delicious pie and the family was treated to a surprise dessert. And it's just as good today!

    1 BAKED PIE SHELL
    3 EGG YOLKS, WHITES RESERVED FOR MERINGUE
    1 CUP SUGAR
    3 TBSP. FLOUR
    ⅓ TSP. SALT
    2 CUPS BOILING WATER
    ¼ CUP VINEGAR
    1 TSP. LEMON FLAVORING OR JUICE

Beat egg yolks until thick in medium saucepan. Add sugar, flour, and salt. Mix well. Add boiling water slowly, stirring constantly. Add vinegar. Heat slowly, stirring constantly, until thickened. Add lemon flavoring. Pour into baked pastry shell.

Meringue:
    3 EGG WHITES
    PINCH OF SALT
    3 TBSP. SUGAR

Make meringue by beating egg whites and a pinch of salt until soft peaks stand. Gradually add in the 3 Tbsp. sugar and continue beating until stiff peaks stand when beater is slowly lifted. Spoon meringue over pie and seal to edges completely. Raise some peaks to make the meringue pretty. Bake at 350° F until meringue is golden and set.

Black walnut pie

    1 BAKED PIE SHELL
    1 CUP FIRMLY PACKED BROWN SUGAR
    1 TBSP. MELTED BUTTER OR MARGARINE
    3 TBSP. CORNSTARCH
    ⅛ TSP. SALT
    1½ CUPS MILK
    2 EGG YOLKS, BEATEN; WHITES RESERVED
    ½ CUP BLACK WALNUT PIECES
    1 TSP. VANILLA
    2 EGG WHITES

Combine sugar, butter, cornstarch, and salt. Add milk slowly stirring constantly until smooth. In a saucepan, heat gently, stirring constantly, until thick and smooth. Add beaten egg yolks. Cook 1 minute, stirring constantly to avoid scorching. Add black walnuts and vanilla. Beat egg whites until stiff then fold into mixture. Pour into baked pastry shell. Bake at 400° F until filling is set.

Green tomato pie/mock apple pie

This is one of our very favorite too-early-for-apples apple pie recipes. You can not tell it from apple pie; I promise! Just don't tell the family what they're eating until their second piece! Like apple pie, it's great with a wedge of cheddar cheese or a dip of vanilla ice cream or whipped cream on top. Dad was a picky eater and I knew that no way was I going to get him to try it. Apple pie was his favorite pie, so when I asked him if he'd like a piece of the warm pie I'd just taken out of the oven, he was quick to answer "Yes!" After he'd eaten his second piece, I told him it was green tomato pie. His eyebrows furrowed as he looked at the last piece on his plate and quickly scooped that up. "Pretty good. Got any more?" That tells the whole story!

    PASTRY FOR TWO-CRUST PIE
    5 CUPS SLICED SMALL, HARD, GREEN TOMATOES
    1 CUP SUGAR
    1 TSP. CINNAMON
    2 TBSP. FLOUR
    ½ TSP. SALT
    2 TBSP. BUTTER OR MARGARINE
    BROWN SUGAR AND CINNAMON FOR SPRINKLING ON TOP

Roll bottom crust out and lay over pie pan. Trim off rough edges. In a medium mixing bowl, combine green tomatoes, sugar, cinnamon, flour, and salt. Mix well. Pour into pie shell. Dot top with butter in several spots. Moisten edges of bottom crust with water and lay on vented top crust. Seal and flute to keep juices in pie. Rub top of crust with softened butter and sprinkle brown sugar and cinnamon on top. Bake on a cookie sheet at 375° F until top is golden brown.

Mom's butter tarts

Tarts are simply little pies — tartlets are even littler! They both use a basic pie crust pastry for the crust. To form the tart crust, you can just invert a muffin tin and form a circle of pie crust pastry over that, fluting the edges for a pretty tart. Of course, if you have a tart pan, it's even easier. A recipe for a double-crust pie pastry will make many tarts or tartlets.

To cut tart pastry shells, find a plain, round cookie cutter that cuts a 4½-inch circle. Lacking that, just find a can, mug, or bowl that is about the right diameter and use it as a cookie cutter. For tartlets, a 3-inch round cookie cutter is about the right size.

Use care to get as many circles as you can from each pastry ball. While it's best to *not* reroll your dough pieces to make more tart shells, I confess that I do that and no one seems to notice that they were, perhaps, a little tougher than the best tart shells.

Once you have the tart shells formed on the muffin tins or in the tart tins, prick the bottoms of each one several times to prevent large bubbles from forming during baking. These bubbles prevent you from filling the baked shells evenly.

Bake the tart shells at 375° F until golden; about 20 minutes. Cool partially in the pans, then gently remove to wire racks to finish cooling so they stay crisp and don't get soggy. Fill them as desired.

You can use any of the fruit pie fillings in this chapter, or try jams, preserves, mincemeat, creamed chicken, creamed asparagus, creamed tuna and fresh peas, softened cream cheese topped with a dab of hot pepper jelly, smoked salmon or trout, a ham dice, green olive, half of a cherry tomato, ground nuts, a mandarin orange slice, bacon bits or bacon-flavored TVPs, or even a scoop of ice cream for a quick, very easy, beautiful dessert.

Here's one of Mom's tart recipes that I use frequently. I vary the filling ingredients of currants and/or coconut to fit what I have on hand. Instead of currants, I might substitute ground raisins; instead of coconut, I might substitute ground nuts; you get the picture.

> PASTRY FOR TWO-CRUST PIE
>
> 1 CUP FIRMLY PACKED BROWN SUGAR
>
> ⅓ CUP BUTTER OR MARGARINE
>
> 1 EGG, BEATEN
>
> 2 TBSP. MILK
>
> 1 TSP. VANILLA
>
> ADDITIONS: ½ CUP DRIED CURRANTS OR ¼ CUP EACH, DRIED CURRANTS AND COCONUT.

Cream brown sugar and butter together until smooth. Add egg, milk, and vanilla. Beat well until smooth. In a saucepan, heat while stirring, until slightly thickened. Add dried currants or other additions such as ground raisins, chopped pecans or hazelnuts, ground sweet cherries, etc. Spoon into each tart shell. Cool and serve.

Cheesecakes

Although cheesecakes are neither cakes nor pies, I figure they must lie somewhere in between. Most have a graham cracker crust, like some pies. Some are baked, where some are not. Most have cream cheese as an ingredient, thus the "cheese" in cheesecake. There are a few that take a while to put together, but some take less than fifteen minutes between thought and sitting on the table. And all of them gather huge "*wows*" at the table!

Quick strawberry cheesecake

    1 GRAHAM CRACKER CRUST, BAKED

Filling:

    2 PKGS. (8 OZ. EACH) CREAM CHEESE, SOFTENED OR 1½ CUPS FRESH CREAM CHEESE

    1 CUP SOUR CREAM

    1 CUP POWDERED SUGAR

    1 TBSP. LEMON JUICE

    1 TSP. VANILLA

Beat cream cheese, sugar, lemon juice, and vanilla together until smooth. Spoon into crust.

Topping:

    1 CUP SOUR CREAM

    ¼ CUP SUGAR

    1 TSP. VANILLA

Prepare topping by combining sour cream, sugar, and vanilla. Spread over filling. Refrigerate.

Strawberry glaze:

    ¼ CUP WATER

    2 TBSP. CORNSTARCH

    1 JAR (12 OZ.) STRAWBERRY JELLY OR 1 PINT STRAWBERRY JELLY

    2 TBSP. LEMON JUICE

    1 PINT FRESH STRAWBERRIES

In a saucepan, combine a small amount of water with cornstarch to make a smooth paste. Mix in the rest of the water. Add jelly and cook over medium heat, stirring constantly until jelly melts and the mixture thickens. Remove from heat and stir in lemon juice. Cool to room temperature. Arrange whole, hulled strawberries on top of the cheesecake, points up, then spoon glaze over berries, allowing some to drip down sides. Serve immediately.

Will's blackberry cheesecake

    1 GRAHAM CRACKER CRUST, UNBAKED

    2 PKGS. (8 OZ. EACH) CREAM CHEESE, SOFTENED OR 2 CUPS FRESH CREAM CHEESE

    1 CUP SOUR CREAM

    1 TSP. VANILLA

    1 TBSP. LEMON JUICE

1 CUP POWDERED SUGAR

½ CUP BLACKBERRY JELLY, PRESERVES, OR JAM

1 PINT FRESH BLACKBERRIES, IN SEASON (OPTIONAL, BUT VERY GOOD!)

In a large mixing bowl, beat cream cheese and sour cream together until smooth and light. Add vanilla and lemon juice. Mix in powdered sugar until very smooth. Spoon into graham crust. Refrigerate for about 2 hours or as long as you can stand to wait! Top with blackberry jelly, preserves, or jam. In season, I also top this with fresh blackberries, dusted with powdered sugar. Your family will *beg* for this, and it only takes a short time to put together.

Best baked cheesecake

Crust:

¾ CUP GRAHAM CRACKER CRUMBS

1 TBSP. SUGAR

1 TBSP. MELTED BUTTER OR MARGARINE

In medium bowl, combine crumbs, sugar, and butter, mixing well. Spread evenly over bottom of a 9-inch springform pan, pressing lightly with fingertips. Refrigerate while filling is made.

Filling:

1 PKG. (8 OZ.) CREAM CHEESE, ROOM TEMPERATURE OR 1 CUP FRESH CREAM CHEESE

4 EGGS

1 TSP. VANILLA

1 CUP SUGAR

In large bowl, beat cream cheese until light. Add eggs, vanilla, and sugar. Continue beating until creamy and light. Pour into crust. Bake at 375° F for 35 minutes.

Topping:

2 CUPS SOUR CREAM

1 TBSP. SUGAR

1 TSP. VANILLA

In mixing bowl, beat sour cream, sugar, and vanilla. Set aside. Remove cheesecake from oven. Spread topping evenly over surface; bake 5 minutes longer. Cool in pan, on wire rack. Refrigerate 5 hours or overnight. Remove side of springform pan and serve.

Jam cheesecake glaze

Use 1 pint of any flavored fruit jam or preserves: strawberry, cherry, blueberry, blackberry, raspberry, peach, chokecherry, or black raspberry. Spoon into a saucepan and gently heat while stirring. Add 2 Tbsp. lemon juice and continue stirring. When melted, remove from heat and allow to cool but not re-set. Spoon over cheesecake just before serving; it's easy, quick, and very good.

Blueberry cheesecake glaze

1 pint fresh blueberries or 1 pint canned blueberries, drained, reserving ½ cup liquid
2 Tbsp. sugar
2 Tbsp. cornstarch
1 Tbsp. lemon juice

Place blueberries in medium saucepan or ½ cup blueberry liquid from canned berries, with sugar, cornstarch, and lemon juice. Slowly heat until fresh blueberries soften and the mixture thickens. (If using canned blueberries, add berries now.) Remove from heat and cool well. Spread over refrigerated cheesecake. Or use 1 pint home-canned or store-bought blueberry pie filling.

Cherry cheesecake glaze

1 pint fresh pie cherries, pitted or 1 pint canned pie cherries, drained, reserving ½ cup liquid
½ cup sugar
2 Tbsp. cornstarch

Place cherries in medium saucepan with just a bit of water. Simmer until juice flows. Spoon about 3 Tbsp. juice into small bowl and mix with cornstarch to make a smooth paste. Add more juice, then pour into cherries. (If using canned cherries, instead pour ½ cup reserved cherry liquid into saucepan and slowly stir in cornstarch while heating.) When cornstarch is well mixed, add sugar and slowly heat until simmering, stirring constantly. When mixture thickens, add canned, drained cherries, or remove from heat if using fresh cherries. Cool well. Spread over refrigerated cheesecake. *Or* use 1 pint home-canned or store-bought cherry pie filling.

Cakes

Like pies, cakes come in all different shapes, forms, textures, and flavors. Some are basic sweet desserts, taking only a few minutes to put together, where others are works of art, having many ingredients and taking much longer to assemble. These, of course, are not "every day" cakes, but rather ones you would serve for special occasions or holiday meals.

Cakes are a good way to use many ingredients in your pantry to very good use. Everyone in the family enjoys a good cake for dessert, then leftovers to snack on until there's just an empty pan on the counter.

One thing I love about cakes is that anyone can bake one. It's so easy that I doubt anyone could make a bad cake, unless it was on purpose or you forgot to check the oven! Even very young children can bake their own cakes, with a little supervision from an adult in the kitchen, of course. Most have only a few common ingredients and don't have any "fancy" baking techniques needed, such as kneading, rolling, etc.

And even a simple cake can quickly become "fancy" with just the addition of fruit, nuts, or a great icing or decorations on top. No, you do *not* have to buy canned icing from the store. It only takes a few minutes to make your own, which is so much better than canned icing, and homemade has *no* preservatives, either.

With many cakes, the "sparkle" is the frosting or icing that finishes off the kitchen work of art. There are as many frostings as there are cakes, from minimal spiced sugar sprinkled on top of a warm cake to fancy, yet easy to make, cream cheese and butter cream icings. You can quickly change the personality of a cake by simply changing the icing you use.

You can serve a cake chilled, at room temperature, or warm from the oven. Each lends its own special flavor to the same basic cake. There are so many choices. And they are all great. Talk about a win-win situation!

Texas sheet cake

    1 CUP BUTTER OR MARGARINE

    1 CUP WATER

    2 CUPS FLOUR

    2 CUPS SUGAR

    2 EGGS, BEATEN (MAY USE RECONSTITUTED POWDERED WHOLE EGGS)

    ½ CUP SOUR CREAM

    1 TSP. ALMOND EXTRACT

    1 TSP. SALT

    1 TSP. BAKING SODA

In a large saucepan, bring butter and water to a boil. Remove from heat. Stir in flour, sugar, eggs, sour cream, almond extract, salt, and baking soda until smooth. Pour into a greased 13x9x2-inch cake pan and bake at 375° F for 20-22 minutes or until cake is golden brown and a toothpick inserted into the center of the cake comes out clean. Cool for 20 minutes. Frost with Nutty white frosting.

No-fuss coconut cake

    1 PKG. YELLOW CAKE MIX

    1 PKG. (3½ OZ.) INSTANT VANILLA PUDDING MIX

    1⅓ CUPS WATER

    4 EGGS, ROOM TEMPERATURE (MAY USE RECONSTITUTED POWDERED WHOLE EGGS)

    ¼ CUP VEGETABLE OIL

    2 CUPS COCONUT

    1 CUP CHOPPED PECANS

In a large bowl, mix cake mix with pudding, water, eggs, and oil. Beat well. Stir in coconut and nuts. Pour into three lightly-greased 8-inch cake pans. Bake at 350° F for about 25 minutes or until cake is golden brown and springs back when you lightly push a finger down in the center. Cool in cake pans for 10 minutes, then turn out onto wire racks to complete cooling.

Try it with Coconut frosting and California fruit filling.

Great-Grandma Jones' layer cake

- 1 cup sugar
- 3 Tbsp. butter or margarine
- 2 eggs (may use reconstituted powdered whole eggs)
- 1 cup milk
- 2½ cups flour
- 2 tsp. baking powder
- 1 tsp. vanilla

Cream sugar and butter together until fluffy. Add eggs. Beat again. Add milk. Mix flour and baking powder together, then mix into milk/sugar mixture. Add vanilla. Pour into three or four 8-inch lightly-greased cake pans. Bake at 350° F until done (about 15 minutes). Cool on wire racks. Fill with this or another filling of your choice:

Filling:

- ¼ cup cornstarch
- 1 cup milk
- 2 cups milk
- ⅓ cup butter or margarine
- 1 cup sugar
- 2 eggs, slightly beaten

Slowly mix cornstarch with 1 cup milk until smooth. Set aside. In large saucepan, stir 2 cups milk with butter and sugar, heating slowly. Pour in cornstarch mixture. Heat slowly, stirring constantly. When thickened, stir in eggs. Cook until mixture thickens. Cool well and use as a filling for above cake.

Sparkling citrus cake

- ¼ cup vegetable shortening
- 1 cup butter or margarine, softened
- 2 cups sugar
- 5 eggs (may use reconstituted powdered whole eggs)
- 3 cups flour
- 1 tsp. baking powder
- ½ tsp. baking soda
- 1 cup buttermilk (may use reconstituted powdered buttermilk)
- 1 tsp. vanilla
- ½ tsp. lemon extract

In a medium mixing bowl, cream shortening, butter, and sugar together until light and fluffy. Add eggs, beating well. Combine dry ingredients; add to creamed mixture alternately with buttermilk. Stir in extracts. Pour into three lightly-greased and floured 9-inch cake pans. Bake at 350° F for 25-30 minutes or until cake springs back quickly after you press a finger in the center. Cool for 10 minutes in pans before turning out onto wire cooling racks to cool completely. When cool, frost. This cake is great with Citrus frosting and Lemon filling or Fresh orange filling.

Hot milk cake

    2 EGGS (MAY USE RECONSTITUTED POWDERED WHOLE EGG)
    1 CUP SUGAR
    1 CUP FLOUR
    ⅛ TSP. SALT
    1½ TSP. BAKING POWDER
    1 TBSP. BUTTER OR MARGARINE
    ½ CUP HOT MILK (MAY USE RECONSTITUTED POWDERED MILK)
    ½ TSP. VANILLA
    ½ TSP. LEMON EXTRACT

Beat eggs and slowly add sugar. Beat 5 minutes. Sift flour, salt, and baking powder. Fold into egg mix. Melt butter in ½ cup hot milk and add. Add vanilla and lemon extract. Mix well to blend. Turn into greased and floured 8-inch pan. Bake at 350° F for about 30 minutes or until top is golden. Remove from oven and invert pan over wire cooling rack for 1 hour. This cake is good served with a pudding sauce, such as Lemon pudding or Lemon filling. You can also turn it into a Boston cream pie by cutting this cake in half and filling with Rich Vanilla cream filling, then putting Quick fudge frosting on top.

Chiffon cake (like an angel food cake)

    2¼ CUPS FLOUR
    1½ CUPS SUGAR
    1 TBSP. BAKING POWDER
    1 TSP. SALT
    ½ CUP VEGETABLE OIL
    5 EGG YOLKS, RESERVE WHITES
    ¾ CUP COLD WATER
    2 TSP. VANILLA
    GRATED RIND OF 1 LEMON
    5 EGG WHITES
    ½ TSP. CREAM OF TARTAR

Sift together flour, sugar, baking powder, and salt into large mixing bowl. Make a well in the center and add vegetable oil, egg yolks, cold water, vanilla, and grated lemon rind. Mix well until blended. In another mixing bowl, put egg whites and cream of tartar. Beat very stiff. Slowly pour batter over egg whites, folding in very gently until just blended. Do *not* stir. Pour into an ungreased angel food 10-inch cake pan. Bake at 325° F for 55 minutes. Invert pan and let hang free. I use 3 canning jars. When cake is totally cool, loosen with knife and turn out onto a plate. You may use this cake, served with a fruit pudding or sweetened fresh fruit over it, as you would for a shortcake, drizzle chocolate over it before serving, or serve with ice cream. It is a very versatile cake.

Grandma Rhead's spice layer cake

Grandma Rhead was my grandmother, my Dad's mother. She lived with us when I was a child, and I still remember her and Mom making this plain, easy, but totally great cake in the little galley kitchen. It was there I developed my love of gardening, canning, and cooking. I'm sure I was a pest, but no child ever had a better childhood, bouncing around the huge yard, peeking at the goldfish in the pond, sheltered by huge blooming wisteria vines, snacking on fresh peaches and grapes, "helping" can in the cool basement, and getting to lick the bowl when this spicy cake was baking.

- ½ cup sugar
- ½ cup shortening
- ½ cup molasses
- 1 egg + 1 egg yolk
- ½ cup sour milk or buttermilk (To quickly sour milk, just add 1 tsp. lemon juice or vinegar to fresh milk. You may also use reconstituted powdered buttermilk.)
- 2 cups flour
- ¼ tsp. salt
- 1 tsp. cinnamon
- 1 tsp. ground cloves
- 1 tsp. baking soda
- 1 tsp. allspice

Cream sugar and shortening together until fluffy and smooth. Add molasses, then beat in egg and egg yolk. Slowly add sour milk or buttermilk. Mix well, then slowly beat in flour. Add salt and spices, mixing until well blended. Pour into two lightly-greased and floured 9-inch cake pans. Bake at 350° F for 20-25 minutes or until cake springs back quickly when your finger is pressed into the center. Cool for 10 minutes in pans before turning out onto wire cooling racks. Let cool completely, then frost and/or fill, as you wish. Grandma Rhead used the Basic buttercream frosting, but I like to use Cream cheese frosting. You could also choose a plain frosting and use a fruity filling for the center.

Wacky cake

- 1½ cups flour
- 1 cup sugar
- 5 Tbsp. cocoa
- 1 tsp. baking soda
- ½ tsp. salt
- 1 Tbsp. vinegar
- 6 Tbsp. vegetable oil
- 1 tsp. vanilla
- 1 cup cold water

In an 8x8-inch lightly-greased and floured cake pan, sift the flour, sugar, cocoa, baking soda, and salt. Level off and make three holes with the back of a spoon. In one hole, put the vinegar, in one, the vegetable oil, and in one put the vanilla. Spill 1 cup of cold water all over and stir with a fork. Bake at 350° F for 25 minutes or until top of cake is golden. Frost as you wish.

Florence Bates' white cake

- ½ cup shortening
- 1⅓ cups sugar
- 2¼ cups flour
- ½ tsp. salt
- 1 Tbsp. baking powder
- 1 cup low-fat milk (may use reconstituted powdered milk)
- 1 tsp. vanilla or almond extract
- 3 egg whites

Cream shortening and sugar together until light and fluffy. Sift flour, salt, and baking powder three times. Add alternately with milk, mixing well. Add vanilla or almond extract. Beat egg whites until stiff and fold into cake. Turn out into greased, floured 8-inch cake pans. Bake at 350° F for 25-30 minutes or until cake springs back quickly when a finger has been pressed in the center. You might like this cake frosted with one of the Buttercream frostings, Fluffy white frosting, or even Coconut frosting.

Debbie's carrot cake

- 1 cup butter or margarine
- 2 cups sugar
- 4 eggs (may use reconstituted whole powdered eggs), beaten
- 1½ cup grated carrots
- ¼ cup buttermilk (may use reconstituted powdered buttermilk)
- 2½ cups flour
- 1½ tsp. baking soda
- 1½ tsp. cinnamon
- ½ tsp. mace or nutmeg
- 1 tsp. vanilla
- ¾ cup chopped walnuts

Cream butter and sugar together until light and fluffy. Add eggs and blend well. Mix carrots and buttermilk. Sift dry ingredients together and add alternately with carrot mixture. Add vanilla and nuts. Blend gently. Turn out into a greased, floured 13x9x2-inch pan and bake at 350° F for about an hour or until cake tests done by inserting a toothpick into the center. When it comes out clean, the cake is done. Frost with cream cheese frosting.

Frosty snowberry cake

2¼ cups flour
1 Tbsp. baking powder
1 tsp. salt
⅔ cup shortening
1½ cups sugar, divided
1 tsp. grated lemon peel
¾ cup milk (may use reconstituted powdered milk)
4 egg whites
1 cup jellied cranberry sauce, cut into ¼-inch cubes

Sift together flour, baking powder, and salt. Cream together shortening, sugar, and lemon peel. Add dry ingredients alternately with milk to creamed ingredients. Beat well. In another bowl, beat egg whites until soft peaks form, then gradually beat in ½ cup sugar. Beat until stiff peaks form. Fold into batter. Fold in cubed cranberry sauce. Turn into two 8-inch well-greased and floured cake pans. Bake at 375° F for 30-35 minutes or until top is golden. Cool in pans for 10 minutes, then turn out onto cooling racks. Cool completely.

Add 2 Tbsp. jellied cranberry sauce to Fluffy white frosting for a fluffy, pink frosting to go with the cake. (Or you could just add a couple of drops of red food coloring to the frosting, but I like the cranberry version best.)

Meringue cradle cake (self-iced)

4 egg whites, yolks reserved
1½ cups sugar, divided
1 cup finely chopped pecans
1 square unsweetened chocolate, grated
2 cups flour
2½ tsp. baking powder
1 tsp. salt
½ cup butter
4 egg yolks
1 cup milk (may use reconstituted powdered milk)
1 tsp. vanilla

Beat egg whites until soft peaks form, then gradually beat in 1 cup sugar. Beat until stiff peaks form. Fold in pecans and grated chocolate. Line a well-greased and floured 10-inch tube angel food cake pan with waxed paper on the bottom. Spread egg white meringue mix evenly over bottom and ¾ the way up the sides. Sift flour, baking powder, and salt. Cream butter and ½ cup sugar until light and fluffy in another bowl. Add egg yolks and beat well. Mix milk and vanilla and add alternately to butter mixture with dry ingredients. Beat well. Turn into the meringue-lined pan. Bake at 325° F for 1¼ to 1½ hours. Do not underbake! Cool 20 minutes in pan. Loosen with a knife or spatula. Cool 30 minutes more. Remove from pan. Decorate with pecan halves dipped in melted semisweet chocolate. (I just melt some chocolate chips.) This cake does not need further icing or frosting.

Igloo cake

    ½ CUP FLOUR
    1 CUP SUGAR
    1 TSP. BAKING POWDER
    ¼ TSP. SALT
    2 TSP. VANILLA
    4 EGGS YOLKS, WHITES RESERVED
    1 LB. CHOPPED DATES
    1 CUP WALNUTS
    4 EGG WHITES

Combine dry ingredients in mixing bowl. Add vanilla, egg yolks, dates, and nuts. Mix well. In another mixing bowl, beat egg whites until stiff. Fold into dry mixture. Pour into a greased, floured 13x9x2-inch pan and bake at 350° F for 30 minutes. Cool cake. Cut cake in half. Break half of cake into pieces and arrange on a serving plate, in a circle (the base for the "igloo").

Topping:
    2 ORANGES, PEELED, SEEDED, AND CUT UP
    3 BANANAS, SLICED
    1 CAN (15 OZ.) CRUSHED PINEAPPLE, DRAINED
    3 Tbsp. SUGAR
    1 PINT CREAM, SWEETENED WITH ABOVE SUGAR, WHIPPED

Make topping of oranges, bananas, sugar, and pineapple. Place fruit on broken cake, adding the other half of the cake, broken, to add on top, making an igloo shape. Frost with whipped cream and serve immediately.

Color vision cake

    1 PKG. WHITE CAKE MIX
    3 Tbsp. DRY FLAVORED GELATIN, ANY FLAVOR

Bake cake as directed on package with flavored gelatin mixed in it. Cool cake well and frost with Fluffy white frosting, to which remaining flavored gelatin has been added during cooking. Frost when frosting has cooled. Not only do you get colors with this cake, but it is a little denser and moister than usual. Kids love it!

Mrs. Troxler's cake

Mrs. Troxler was a neighbor of Grandma and Grandpa Eddy, Mom, and Uncle Hubert when they lived on a farm in Battleford, Saskatchewan, Canada. Mom says Mrs. Troxler was a German lady and a very fine cook. It was also during the Great Depression and money was tight. This cake cost little to bake and was a great treat.

¼ CUP BUTTER OR MARGARINE
⅔ CUP SUGAR
1 EGG (MAY USE RECONSTITUTED POWDERED WHOLE EGG)
½ CUP MILK (MAY USE RECONSTITUTED POWDERED MILK)
1½ CUPS FLOUR
2½ TSP. BAKING POWDER
½ TSP. SALT
1 TSP. VANILLA

Cream butter and sugar together until light and fluffy. Add egg and milk, mixing well. Mix dry ingredients and add to creamed mixture. Beat well. Add vanilla. Blend well. Pour into a lightly-greased 8x8-inch pan. Bake at 350° F for 25-30 minutes or until the top is golden brown. Cool slightly, but while top is still hot, brush with melted butter and sprinkle with cinnamon and sugar (¼ cup sugar with 1 tsp. cinnamon). This hardens to make a delectable crust when it cools. But this cake is also excellent when served warm from the oven.

Orange kiss-me cake

1 LARGE ORANGE
1 CUP RAISINS
⅓ CUP WALNUTS
2 CUPS FLOUR
1 CUP SUGAR
1 TSP. BAKING SODA
½ TSP. SALT
½ CUP SHORTENING
1 CUP MILK (MAY USE RECONSTITUTED POWDERED MILK), DIVIDED
2 EGGS (MAY USE RECONSTITUTED WHOLE EGG)

Squeeze large orange and reserve juice. After removing seeds, grind pulp and rind together with raisins and walnuts, using coarse blade on food grinder.

Sift together dry ingredients. Add shortening and ¾ cup milk. Beat two minutes. Add eggs and remaining ¼ cup of milk. Beat well again. Fold orange/walnut/raisin mixture into batter. Turn into a greased and floured 13x9x2-inch pan. Bake at 350° F for 40 to 50 minutes. Drizzle ⅓ cup orange juice over warm cake. Sprinkle with a mixture of ⅓ cup sugar and 1 tsp. cinnamon and ¼ cup or more of chopped walnuts. This cake is excellent and is an old family favorite.

Anna's favorite applesauce cake

- 1 CUP BUTTER, ROOM TEMPERATURE
- 1 CUP SUGAR
- 2 EGGS (MAY USE RECONSTITUTED WHOLE POWDERED EGG)
- 3½ CUPS FLOUR
- 1 TSP. BAKING SODA
- 1 TSP. CINNAMON
- ½ TSP. CLOVES
- 2 TSP. NUTMEG
- PINCH OF SALT
- 2 CUPS UNSWEETENED APPLESAUCE (YOU CAN USE SWEETENED AND JUST REDUCE THE SUGAR BY ¼ CUP)
- 1 CUP CHOPPED WALNUTS
- 2 CUPS RAISINS

Cream butter and sugar together until light and fluffy. Add eggs; beat well. Set aside. Sift dry ingredients, salt, and spices together. Take ½ cup dry ingredients out and mix with nuts and raisins. Set both aside. Alternately stir flour mixture and applesauce into creamed mixture. Mix well. Add nuts and raisins; stir well to blend. Pour into greased and floured bundt cake pan or 10-inch tube (angel food) pan. Bake at 350° F for 65-75 minutes or until cake tests done by inserting a toothpick into the center of the cake; if it pulls out clean, the cake is done. Cool in pan 10 minutes; turn out on rack to complete cooling. This cake is served with simple cinnamon sugar sprinkled on top of the hot cake. Whipped cream or ice cream is always welcome with it, too.

Peach pound cake

- 1 CUP BUTTER OR MARGARINE
- 3 CUPS SUGAR
- 6 EGGS, BEATEN (MAY USE RECONSTITUTED WHOLE EGG)
- ½ CUP SOUR CREAM (MAY USE RECONSTITUTED POWDERED SOUR CREAM)
- 1 TSP. VANILLA
- 1 TSP. ALMOND EXTRACT
- 3 CUPS FLOUR (OR MORE TO MAKE MEDIUM BATTER)
- ¼ TSP. BAKING SODA
- ¼ TSP. SALT
- 2 CUPS FINELY CHOPPED PEACHES (MAY USE FRESH, FROZEN OR CANNED, DRAINED)

Cream butter and sugar together. Add eggs and sour cream. Mix well until light and fluffy. Add vanilla and almond extract. Mix dry ingredients together and add alternately to creamed mixture, along with chopped peaches. Mix lightly but well. Pour into a greased, floured 10-inch tube or bundt pan and bake at 325° F for about 70 minutes.

Hummingbird cake

I made a lot of this cake in New Mexico. My late husband, Bob, operated a small general store in Gladstone, out on the Santa Fe Trail, on the high plains, way away from anything. Tourists, cowboys, and ranchers often stopped just for a piece of Hummingbird, which at that time, sold for 85 cents a slice. There were 10 slices. I sometimes baked three or four cakes a day, with some travelers calling in advance to reserve a whole cake to take to family doings. This cake was a legend! And it's well deserved, too! (I never told anyone how easy it was to bake.)

- 3 CUPS FLOUR
- 2 CUPS SUGAR
- 1 TSP. SALT
- 1 TSP. BAKING SODA
- 3 EGGS, BEATEN (MAY USE RECONSTITUTED WHOLE POWDERED EGG)
- 1½ CUPS VEGETABLE OIL
- 1 CAN (8 OZ.) CRUSHED PINEAPPLE, UNDRAINED
- 1 CUP CHOPPED PECANS (CAN SUBSTITUTE WALNUTS)
- 2 CUPS CHOPPED BANANAS
- ½ CUP CHOPPED DATES (OPTIONAL)

Combine dry ingredients. Add eggs and oil; stir until just moistened. Stir in remaining ingredients. Pour into a greased, well-floured 10-inch tube (angel food) pan or bundt pan. Bake at 350° F for 60-75 minutes or until cake tests done by inserting a toothpick into the center of the cake; if it pulls out clean, the cake is done. Cool in pan 10 minutes; turn out on rack to complete cooling. This is a dense, very moist, chewy cake and needs no icing.

Devil's food cake

- 2 CUPS SIFTED FLOUR
- ½ CUP SUGAR
- 1 TSP. BAKING SODA
- ¾ TSP. SALT
- ½ CUP VEGETABLE SHORTENING
- ½ CUP BROWN SUGAR, FIRMLY PACKED
- ⅔ CUP BUTTERMILK OR THICK SOUR MILK (MAY USE RECONSTITUTED POWDERED BUTTERMILK)
- 1 TSP. VANILLA
- 2 EGGS, UNBEATEN (MAY USE RECONSTITUTED WHOLE POWDERED EGG)
- ½ CUP BOILING WATER
- 3 SQUARES UNSWEETENED CHOCOLATE

Sift dry ingredients together into a mixing bowl. Cream shortening and brown sugar together, then add buttermilk, vanilla, and eggs. Beat for 2 minutes, then add to dry ingredients. Beat again. Combine boiling water and chocolate; stir until smooth. Add to batter and stir very well. Turn batter into two greased, floured 9-inch layer pans. Bake at 350° F for about 25 minutes or until cake springs quickly back when a finger is pressed in the center. Let stand in pans for 5 minutes, then turn out onto wire cooling racks to completely cool. Try this with EZ fudge frosting.

Hickory nut cake

½ CUP BUTTER OR MARGARINE

1½ CUPS SUGAR

1 TSP. VANILLA

2 CUPS FLOUR

2 TSP. BAKING POWDER

¼ TSP. SALT

¾ CUP MILK (MAY USE RECONSTITUTED POWDERED MILK)

4 EGG WHITES

1 CUP FINELY CHOPPED HICKORY NUTS

Cream butter, sugar, and vanilla together until fluffy. Sift dry ingredients together; add alternately with milk to creamed mixture. Beat until smooth. With a clean mixer, beat egg whites until stiff peaks hold when the beaters are lifted. Fold into batter with nuts. Pour into two greased 8x8x2-inch pans. Bake at 350° F for 35 minutes. Cool in pans for 5 minutes then turn out onto wire racks to cool completely. Put layers together with sweet whipped cream with chopped hickory nuts sprinkled on it, then frost with the same. This cake is best if you make it one day (except for whipped cream), cover it well, and serve the second day. This is a great use for all those hickory nuts you gather in the fall.

Black walnut cake

1¼ CUPS SHORTENING

1 TSP. ALMOND EXTRACT

1 TSP. VANILLA

1¾ CUPS SUGAR, DIVIDED

4 EGG YOLKS, WHITES RESERVED

3½ CUPS FLOUR

5 TSP. BAKING POWDER

1 TSP. SALT

1½ CUPS MILK (MAY USE RECONSTITUTED POWDERED MILK)

4 EGG WHITES

1¼ CUPS CHOPPED BLACK WALNUTS

Cream shortening; add flavorings. Gradually add 1½ cups sugar and beat well until light and fluffy. Add egg yolks; beat. Mix dry ingredients together. Alternately add flour mixture and milk, beating until smooth after each addition. With a clean beater, beat egg whites until frothy; add remaining ¼ cup sugar; beat until meringue is glossy but not dry. Lightly fold meringue and walnuts into batter. Pour into two well-greased 9-inch layer pans. Bake at 350° F for 45 minutes. Cool pans 15 minutes. Turn out onto wire racks to finish cooling. This cake is very good with Cream cheese frosting.

Easy rhubarb upside-down cake

 1 WHITE CAKE MIX, MIXED ACCORDING TO PACKAGE DIRECTIONS
 3 TBSP. BUTTER, MELTED
 ½ CUP SUGAR
 2 CUPS DICED RHUBARB

Combine butter, sugar, and rhubarb. Lightly spread in greased 9x9-inch cake pan. Pour white cake batter on rhubarb mixture. Bake at 375° F for 35 minutes. As soon as it is done, invert on platter and let syrup drain down for about 5 minutes before removing pan. Serve hot or cold, topped with whipped cream or vanilla ice cream.

Pineapple upside-down cake

 BUTTER FOR BUTTERING PAN
 ½ CUP FIRMLY PACKED BROWN SUGAR
 1¾ CUPS FLOUR
 1 CUP SUGAR
 2 TSP. BAKING POWDER
 ½ TSP. SALT
 ⅓ CUP SHORTENING
 ¾ CUP MILK (MAY USE RECONSTITUTED POWDERED MILK)
 1 TSP. VANILLA
 1 EGG (MAY USE RECONSTITUTED WHOLE POWDERED EGG)
 1 LARGE CAN (ABOUT 20 OZ., DEPENDING ON BRAND) PINEAPPLE RINGS
 MARASCHINO CHERRIES
 ENGLISH WALNUTS

Liberally butter the bottom of a 13x9x2-inch cake pan. Sprinkle with brown sugar. Sift dry ingredients together. Add shortening, milk, and vanilla. Beat very well until smooth and light. Add egg and beat 1½ minutes. Set aside.

In sugared pan, arrange round pineapple slices so they touch. Put a maraschino cherry in the center of each pineapple slice. Sprinkle English walnuts over all and gently pour batter over fruit.

Bake at 350° F until top is golden brown and cake tests done. Cool in pan. Loosen edges with knife and invert over large serving dish. The beautiful pineapple/fruit is on top, with a nice brown sugar glaze. Serve with whipped cream, if you wish.

Tip: Instead of pineapple and maraschino cherries, you may substitute sliced apples, sprinkled liberally with cinnamon and sugar or drained pie cherries, sprinkled liberally with sugar.

Apple cake with lemon sauce

 3 EGGS
 1¾ CUPS SUGAR
 1 CUP VEGETABLE OIL
 1 TSP. VANILLA
 2 CUPS FLOUR

 1 tsp. baking soda
 1 tsp. cinnamon
 1 tsp. salt
 2 cups peeled, sliced apples
 1 cup raisins
 1 cup pecans

Beat eggs, sugar, oil, and vanilla. In another bowl, mix dry ingredients. Add to egg mixture. Mix well. Add apples, raisins, and nuts to this mixture. Mix well again. Pour into well-greased, floured 13x9x2-inch pan. Bake at 350° F for about 45 minutes or until cake tests done by inserting a toothpick into the center; if it comes out clean, the cake is done.

Lemon sauce:
 1 lemon
 2 egg yolks
 2½ Tbsp. cornstarch
 1 cup sugar
 1½ cups water
 4 tsp. butter or margarine

Grate peel of lemon and measure 1½ tsp. grated rind. Squeeze lemon and measure 3 Tbsp. juice. Set aside. Beat egg yolks lightly in small bowl; set aside. In another bowl, mix cornstarch, and sugar together. Measure water into saucepan and gradually stir in sugar/cornstarch mixture, while heating. Cook stirring, until mixture thickens and becomes translucent. Remove from heat. Add small amount into egg yolks and mix. Then pour all egg yolk and mix into saucepan. Cook, stirring, for about 2 minutes. Remove from heat; add grated lemon peel, lemon juice, and butter. Blend well.

To serve, cut cake into serving-sized pieces and place on a dessert plate. Spoon hot sauce over cake and serve.

Apple cake with warm sauce

>1 cup firmly packed brown sugar
>1 cup sugar
>2 Tbsp. butter or margarine
>2 eggs (may use reconstituted whole powdered egg)
>2 cups flour
>1 tsp. baking powder
>1 tsp. baking soda
>1 tsp. cinnamon
>1 tsp. vanilla
>4 cups peeled, sliced apples or 1 quart canned apples, drained
>1 cup chopped pecans (optional)

Cream sugars and butter. Add eggs and beat until smooth. Sift dry ingredients together and stir into egg mixture. Add vanilla, apples, and pecans. Beat well. Pour into greased 13x9x2-inch pan. Bake at 350° F for about 30 minutes or until top is golden and cake tests done. Serve with warm sauce or other topping of your choice.

Sauce:
>½ cup butter or margarine
>1 cup sugar
>½ cup cream or condensed milk (you may use home-canned milk for this sauce)

Cream butter and sugar together, then slowly mix in cream. Simmer on low heat for 3-4 minutes. Pour the hot sauce on warm cake and serve. (I often add 1 tsp. cinnamon to this sauce and sprinkle the sauce with chopped, toasted pecans. It's very good.)

Lane cake

I don't very often make fussy or fancy cakes; I just don't have the time or inclination. *But* once in a while, I do make a Lane cake. It's so rich and full of goodies, it's well worth the extra time and work assembling it. For a special occasion, give it a try!

Cake:
>1 cup butter
>2 cups sugar
>1 tsp. vanilla
>3¼ cups flour
>3½ tsp. baking powder
>½ tsp. salt
>1 cup milk (may use reconstituted powdered milk)
>8 egg whites, beaten; reserve yolks

Cream butter with sugar. Add vanilla. Sift flour, baking powder, and salt together. Add alternately with milk. Beat until smooth. Beat egg whites with clean, dry egg beater blades until stiff.

Fold in with batter. Pour into 4 greased, floured 9-inch round cake pans. Bake at 375° F for 15 minutes. Let cool in pans for 5 minutes, then turn layers out onto wire racks to cool completely.

Filling:
- 8 EGG YOLKS
- 1¼ CUP SUGAR
- ½ CUP BUTTER
- 1 CUP CHOPPED PECANS
- 1 CUP CHOPPED RAISINS
- 1 CUP SHREDDED COCONUT
- 1 CUP FINELY CUT CANDIED CHERRIES
- ¼ TSP. SALT
- ⅓ CUP BOURBON (OPTIONAL)

Beat egg yolks well, then add sugar, and butter. Stir and cook on low heat for 5 minutes. Don't let yolks become scrambled in appearance; they should be almost translucent. Remove from heat and add chopped pecans, raisins, coconut, cherries, and salt. I don't use alcohol, but if desired, you may add ⅓ cup bourbon or rye for flavoring. I substitute the juice from maraschino cherries and this cake turns out scrumptious anyway. Cool cake well and serve.

Frostings and fillings

In addition to frostings, many cakes boast a scrumptious filling as well, giving even more dimension to our cakes. This filling may be a pudding type filling, cream filling, fruity filling full of ground fruits and nuts, a jam or preserve filling, a citrus or custard filling, to name a few. These are also quick and easy to put together and really put a bang in your dessert. Double any of these recipes to fill between more than two layers.

Basic buttercream frosting

- ⅓ CUP SOFT BUTTER OR MARGARINE
- 1 TSP. VANILLA
- ⅛ TSP. SALT
- 1 LB. POWDERED SUGAR
- 3-4 TBSP. MILK TO MAKE PROPER THICKNESS

Cream butter with vanilla. Add salt. Mix in powdered sugar, adding just enough milk to make the proper thickness. Beat well until fluffy. This makes enough icing for a two-layer cake.

Buttercream frosting II

- ⅓ cup flour
- ⅔ cup sugar
- 2 Tbsp. cornstarch
- 2¼ cups cold milk
- 3 egg yolks, slightly beaten
- 2 tsp. vanilla
- ¾ cup butter or margarine, well whipped

Combine flour, sugar, and cornstarch in medium saucepan. Blend in cold milk, stirring until smooth. Heat, stirring constantly, until thick. Add small amount to egg yolks and then add the rest to remaining mix. Cook, stirring constantly for 2 minutes. Stir in vanilla. Cover and cool to lukewarm. Add creamed butter or margarine and beat well. Cool completely. This will frost an 8-inch two-layer cake.

Mrs. Lucas' buttercream frosting

- 1 stick (¼ lb.) butter or margarine
- ½ cup vegetable shortening
- 1 lb. powdered sugar
- 1 tsp. vanilla
- ¼ cup powdered cocoa (if you want chocolate butter cream frosting)
- ¼ cup milk (or less)

Cream together butter and shortening. Add powdered sugar and vanilla. Add cocoa if you want chocolate icing. Slowly add in milk until you get the right consistency. This will frost the top of a 13x9x2-inch cake or an 8-inch round or square two-layer cake.

Cream cheese frosting

- 6 Tbsp. butter or margarine, softened
- 2 pkgs. (3 oz. each) cream cheese or 1¼ cup of fresh cream cheese, softened
- 3 cups powdered sugar
- 1 tsp. vanilla

Cream butter and cream cheese with powdered sugar very well. Beat in vanilla until frosting is very light and fluffy. This will frost a 13x9x2-inch cake top or top and center only of an 8-inch round or square cake.

Chocolate cream cheese frosting

- 2 pkgs. (3 oz. each) cream cheese or 1¼ cups fresh cream cheese
- 6 Tbsp. milk
- ⅛ tsp. salt
- 5 cups sifted powdered sugar
- 2 squares semisweet chocolate, melted or ¼ cup powdered cocoa
- 1 tsp. vanilla

Blend cream cheese, milk, salt, then slowly mix in powdered sugar. Blend in melted chocolate or cocoa. Add vanilla and more milk, if necessary, to get the correct consistency. Beat well until light and fluffy. Will frost an 8-inch round or square cake or the top and sides of a 13x9x2-inch cake.

Fluffy white frosting

¾ CUP SUGAR

¼ CUP LIGHT CORN SYRUP

2 EGG WHITES, BEATEN

2 TBSP. WATER

¼ TSP. SALT

¼ TSP. CREAM OF TARTAR

1 TSP. VANILLA

Combine sugar, corn syrup, egg whites, water, salt, and cream of tartar in top of double boiler. Cook over boiling water, beating with mixer until it stands in peaks. Remove from heat and add vanilla. Beat until frosting reaches spreading consistency.

Tip: For orange frosting, substitute 2 Tbsp. orange juice and 1 tsp. grated orange rind for water. Omit vanilla. For marshmallow frosting, add 6 large marshmallows, cut into pieces into hot frosting and beat until dissolved.

Citrus frosting

½ CUP BUTTER OR MARGARINE, SOFTENED

2 TBSP. ORANGE JUICE

3 TBSP. LEMON JUICE

1-2 TBSP. GRATED ORANGE PEEL

1-2 TBSP. GRATED LEMON PEEL

1 TSP. LEMON EXTRACT

6 CUPS POWDERED SUGAR

Cream butter, juices, peels, and extract together until smooth. Beat in powdered sugar until frosting reaches spreading consistency. Beat well. Will frost center, sides, and top of 9-inch round or square cake.

Nutty white frosting

½ CUP BUTTER OR MARGARINE

¼ CUP MILK

4½ CUPS POWDERED SUGAR

½ TSP. ALMOND EXTRACT

1 CUP CHOPPED WALNUTS

Combine butter and milk in a saucepan. Bring to a boil. Remove from the heat; add sugar and extract. Mix well. Stir in walnuts; spread warm over warm cake for a nice, thick glaze. Frosts a 13x9x2-inch cake.

Coconut frosting

4 Tbsp. butter, divided
2 cups coconut
1 pkg. (8 oz.) cream cheese or 1 cup fresh cream cheese
2 tsp. milk
½ tsp. vanilla
3½ cups powdered sugar

Melt 2 Tbsp. butter in skillet; add coconut and stir, browning to golden. Remove from pan and drain on paper towel. Cream remaining butter with cream cheese, milk, and vanilla. Add sugar, beating well. Stir in 1½ cups toasted coconut. Frosts top, middle, and sides of 8-inch two-layer cake. Sprinkle remaining coconut over cake.

Quick fudge frosting

2 squares unsweetened chocolate
¼ cup butter or margarine, softened
3 cups sifted powdered sugar
½ tsp. salt
¼ cup hot cream
1 tsp. vanilla

Melt chocolate slowly to avoid scorching. Combine butter, sugar, salt, and hot cream with chocolate. Beat well until mixture is smooth and light. Add vanilla and beat again. If mixture is too thick, add a bit more cream until just right. Makes enough to fill and frost an 8- or 9-inch two-layer cake.

Easy caramel frosting

½ cup butter or margarine
1 cup light brown sugar, firmly packed
⅓ cup light cream
2½ cups sifted powdered sugar
1 tsp. vanilla

Melt butter in small saucepan over low heat. Remove from heat. Add brown sugar, stirring until smooth. Over low heat, bring to boiling (while stirring). Boil for one minute, stirring constantly. Remove from heat. Add cream. Over low heat, return just to boiling. Remove from heat; let cool until bottom of saucepan feels lukewarm. Beat in 2 cups powdered sugar until frosting is thick and light. If it is too thin, add more powdered sugar. Add vanilla. Set in bowl of ice water; beat until frosting is thick enough to spread and barely holds its shape. Frosts top, middle, and sides of 8-inch two-layer cake or top of a 13x9x2-inch cake.

EZ fudge frosting

¼ cup butter or margarine
¼ cup milk

> 1 CUP SUGAR
>
> ½ CUP CHOCOLATE CHIPS

Put butter, milk, and sugar in a large saucepan and bring to a boil. Boil 1 minute, stirring constantly to avoid scorching. Remove from heat and stir in chocolate chips. Stir until chips dissolve. Cool a little and spread on cooled cake. Frosts top and sides of an 8-inch double-layer cake or the top of a 13x9x2-inch cake.

Wedding frosting

> ½ CUP VEGETABLE SHORTENING
>
> 1½ CUPS POWDERED SUGAR
>
> 1 TSP. VANILLA
>
> 1 EGG WHITE, BEATEN
>
> PINCH OF SALT

Cream shortening together with powdered sugar and vanilla. Beat well. With a clean egg beater, beat egg white with pinch of salt until stiff peaks form. Gently fold into sugar/shortening mixture. Mix lightly.

Wedding cake filling

> 3 EGG WHITES, BEATEN
>
> PINCH OF SALT
>
> 1¼ CUPS VEGETABLE SHORTENING
>
> 3 CUPS POWDERED SUGAR
>
> 3 TBSP. FLOUR
>
> 1 TBSP. VANILLA
>
> 5 TBSP. MILK (AS NEEDED)

Beat egg whites with pinch of salt until stiff peaks form. In another bowl, cream shortening with powdered sugar and flour until well mixed. Add vanilla and enough milk to make a filling. Fold in egg whites and mix lightly. Add more milk, if needed. This filling goes with the above wedding frosting, and combined, will frost an 8-inch two-layer cake.

Rich vanilla cream filling

> ½ CUP SUGAR
>
> ¼ CUP CORNSTARCH
>
> ¼ TSP. SALT
>
> 2 CUPS MILK
>
> 4 EGG YOLKS, SLIGHTLY BEATEN
>
> 1 TSP. VANILLA EXTRACT

In medium saucepan, mix sugar with cornstarch and salt. Gradually add milk over medium heat, bringing to a boil, stirring. Remove from heat. Add half of hot mixture to egg yolks; mix well. Gradually return to saucepan, stirring. Over medium heat, bring to boiling, stirring. Remove from heat. Add vanilla. Cool completely and fill cake. Fills one 8 or 9-inch cake.

Lemon filling

    4 EGG YOLKS
    ½ CUP SUGAR
    ¼ CUP LEMON JUICE
    2 TSP. GRATED LEMON PEEL
    1 TBSP. HEAVY CREAM

In top of double boiler, beat egg yolks with sugar until smooth. Stir in lemon juice and peel; cook over boiling water, stirring, 5-8 minutes or until mixture thickens. Remove from heat. Stir in cream. Cool. Makes filling for an 8-inch two-layer cake.

Fresh orange filling

    ¾ CUP SUGAR
    2½ TBSP. CORNSTARCH
    ½ TSP. SALT
    ½ CUP ORANGE JUICE
    ½ CUP WATER
    2 TBSP. GRATED ORANGE PEEL
    2 TBSP. LEMON JUICE
    2 TBSP. BUTTER OR MARGARINE

In small saucepan, combine sugar with cornstarch and salt. Gradually stir in orange juice and water; over medium heat, bring to boiling, stirring; boil 1 minute. Remove from heat. Stir in remaining ingredients. Cool. Makes filling for an 8-inch two-layer cake.

Chocolate custard filling

    1 PKG. (6 OZ.) SEMISWEET CHOCOLATE CHIPS
    ½ CUP BUTTER OR MARGARINE, SOFTENED
    ⅔ CUP SIFTED POWDERED SUGAR
    2 EGG YOLKS, WHITES RESERVED
    1 TSP. VANILLA
    2 EGG WHITES

Melt chocolate in top of double boiler, over hot water. Remove from heat; let cool. In small bowl, beat butter until light; add sugar, beating until very light and fluffy. Add egg yolks, one at a time, beating after each addition. Gradually beat in chocolate. Add vanilla. With a clean egg beater, beat egg whites just until peaks form. Fold into chocolate mixture. Fills one 8- or 9-inch double-layer cake.

California fruit filling

    1 TBSP. CORNSTARCH
    2 TBSP. COLD WATER
    ¼ CUP SUGAR

3 Tbsp. dried apricots, chopped
¼ cup dates, chopped
½ cup raisins
⅔ cup boiling water
1 tsp. lemon juice

Dissolve cornstarch in cold water; add sugar and fruits. Add boiling water gradually, stirring constantly. Cook in saucepan, over moderate heat, until thickened, stirring constantly; cool, then add lemon juice. Makes enough filling for a 9-inch two-layer cake.

Cherry filling

½ cup sugar
1½ Tbsp. cornstarch
½ cup cherry juice
¾ cup sour red pie cherries, well drained

Combine sugar and cornstarch; stir in cherry juice drained from cherries. Cook until clear and thickened, stirring constantly. Remove from heat; add cherries and cool. Makes enough filling for a two-layer cake.

Honey almond filling

⅓ cup butter or margarine
½ cup honey
½ cup sugar
½ tsp. salt
½ tsp. cinnamon
½ cup almonds, chopped and toasted

Combine butter, honey, sugar, salt, and cinnamon in a saucepan; bring to a boil over low heat, stirring constantly; boil 2 minutes. Remove from heat. Beat about 10 minutes or until very thick and taffy-like; fold in almonds. Makes enough filling for a two-layer cake.

You may also use your imagination to use powdered sugar mixed with softened cream cheese, coupled with your choice of preserves or jams; peach preserves, cherry jam, raspberry jam, apricot preserves, or pineapple jam are all good choices. Don't forget other easy no-cook fillings from your pantry: mincemeat, green tomato mincemeat, rhubarb conserve, plum conserve, wild plum sauce, or orange marmalade, for example. Get creative! It's so much fun and oh-so-tasty.

Pineapple filling

- ½ CUP SUGAR
- 2 TBSP. CORNSTARCH
- ⅔ CUP PINEAPPLE JUICE
- 1 TBSP. LEMON JUICE
- ½ CUP PINEAPPLE CHUNKS (SMALL BITS)

Mix sugar and cornstarch in saucepan. Slowly mix in juices. Over medium heat, stir while heating. Cook until clear and thickened, stirring constantly. Remove from heat and add pineapple. Cool. Makes enough filling for a two-layer cake.

Cobblers, crisps, and shortcakes

These are not cakes, puddings, or bars, but something in between. They are fruity, cake-like, and scrumptious. Luckily, they are also very easy to make.

Cherry cobbler

When I was growing up, we camped a lot. Mom always made great campfire meals, including a wonderful cherry cobbler in her covered Dutch oven over the coals. One evening, we had the cobbler for dinner. The evening was cool and Mom set the Dutch oven, with the top on, on the table so we could have the leftovers for breakfast. All night I kept hearing this clang-clang-clang noise, but was too sleepy to pay much attention to it. I should have. When we got up, the Dutch oven was still on the table, covered, but when we gathered for breakfast, there were little cherry raccoon tracks all over the table. The handle on the lid was cherry-sticky, and the Dutch oven was empty! A hungry raccoon had spent the night lifting the lid, scooping out a handful of cherry cobbler, then putting the lid back down to eat. Clang! Clang! Clang! It was funny how he set the lid right down each time, yet still ate all the cobbler. But we sure wished he hadn't! When you set your sights on cherry cobbler, oatmeal just doesn't cut it.

- 2 CUPS SUGAR
- 2 TBSP. BUTTER OR MARGARINE
- 1 EGG, BEATEN (MAY USE RECONSTITUTED WHOLE POWDERED EGG)
- 3 CUPS FLOUR
- ½ TSP. SALT
- MILK ENOUGH TO MAKE A MEDIUM BATTER (MAY USE RECONSTITUTED POWDERED MILK)
- 1 QUART SOUR CHERRIES, DRAINED OR 2 CANS (21 OZ. EACH) STORE-BOUGHT PIE FILLING

Mix sugar, butter, and egg together until well mixed. Add flour and salt. Mix in enough milk to make a medium batter. Pour batter into greased 13x9x2-inch cake pan, then pour drained cherries over the top. Bake at 375° F until top is golden and cake-like. This cobbler may also be baked in a greased Dutch oven.

Peach cobbler

> 1 QUART CANNED PEACH SLICES OR 2 CANS (14-OZ. EACH) SLICED, UNDRAINED PEACHES
> ⅓ CUP SUGAR
> ⅛ TSP. NUTMEG
> 1 TBSP. BUTTER OR MARGARINE

In a medium saucepan, combine peaches with sugar, nutmeg, and butter. Cook, stirring, over low heat until mixture boils; set aside.

Topping:
> ¼ CUP SUGAR
> ½ TSP. SALT
> ½ CUP BUTTER OR MARGARINE
> 1 EGG (MAY USE RECONSTITUTED WHOLE POWDERED EGG)
> 2 CUPS FLOUR
> ¾ CUP MILK (MAY USE RECONSTITUTED POWDERED MILK)

Mix sugar, salt, and butter together and cream well until fluffy. Add egg. Beat again. Alternately mix in flour and milk. Beat until smooth.

Pour hot fruit into 2-quart baking dish. Drop topping by large spoonfuls onto hot fruit. Bake at 400° F for 15-20 minutes or until topping is firm and golden brown. Serve warm, with sweetened milk or cream, if desired.

Fresh blueberry cobbler

Filling:
> ½ CUP SUGAR
> 1 TBSP. CORNSTARCH
> 4 CUPS FRESH OR FROZEN BLUEBERRIES
> 1 TSP. LEMON JUICE

Blend ½ cup sugar and cornstarch in saucepan. Stir in blueberries and lemon juice. Cook, stirring constantly until thickens and boils. Boil one minute, stirring. Pour into ungreased 2-quart baking dish. Set aside.

Topping:
> 1 CUP FLOUR
> 1 TBSP. SUGAR
> 1½ TSP. BAKING POWDER
> ½ TSP. SALT
> 3 TBSP. SHORTENING
> ½ CUP MILK (MAY USE RECONSTITUTED POWDERED MILK)

Sift flour, sugar, baking powder, and salt into a medium mixing bowl. Add shortening, mixing well into dry ingredients. Add milk. Mix well. Drop dough into 6 portions, onto hot fruit. Bake uncovered at 400° F for 25 to 30 minutes or until topping is golden brown and set.

Peach crumb

- 5 cups sliced fresh peaches or 1 quart canned sliced peaches, drained
- ½ cup firmly packed brown sugar
- 3 Tbsp. flour
- 1 tsp. cinnamon

Topping:

- 1 cup flour
- 1 cup sugar
- 1 tsp. baking powder
- ¼ tsp. salt
- ½ tsp. nutmeg
- 1 egg, beaten
- ½ cup melted butter or margarine

Toss peaches together with brown sugar, flour, and cinnamon. Lay out in a 13x9x2-inch cake pan.

Make topping: Mix flour, sugar, baking powder, salt, and nutmeg. Mix thoroughly, then add egg and mix with fork until crumbly. Sprinkle over peach filling. Drizzle with melted butter. Bake at 350° F until peaches are soft and top is golden.

Fresh rhubarb crisp

Rhubarb filling:

- 4 cups cut rhubarb in ½-inch pieces or 1 quart canned rhubarb, lightly drained
- 1 cup sugar
- ¼ cup flour
- ½ tsp. cinnamon
- ½ cup water

Topping:

- 1 cup flour
- ½ cup raw rolled oats
- 1 cup light brown sugar, firmly packed
- ½ cup butter or margarine

In lightly-greased 8x8x2-inch cake pan, combine rhubarb, sugar, flour, cinnamon, and water. Stir to mix well.

Make topping: In a large bowl, mix flour, oats, and brown sugar; stir in butter well to make a crumbly mixture.

Sprinkle topping mixture evenly over filling. Bake at 375° F, uncovered, for 35 minutes or until topping is golden brown and rhubarb is tender. Serve warm with ice cream or sweetened cream or whipped cream, if desired.

Apple cobbler

> 5 CUPS TART APPLES, PEELED AND SLICED OR 1 QUART LIGHTLY-DRAINED, CANNED APPLE SLICES
> ¾ CUP SUGAR
> 2 TBSP. FLOUR
> ½ TSP. CINNAMON
> ¼ TSP. SALT
> 1 TSP. VANILLA
> ¼ CUP WATER
> 1 TBSP. BUTTER OR MARGARINE, SOFTENED

Topping:
> ½ CUP FLOUR
> ½ CUP SUGAR
> ½ TSP. BAKING POWDER
> ¼ TSP. SALT
> 2 TBSP. BUTTER OR MARGARINE, SOFTENED
> 1 EGG, SLIGHTLY BEATEN (MAY USE RECONSTITUTED WHOLE POWDERED EGG)

In medium bowl, mix apples, sugar, flour, cinnamon, salt, vanilla, and ¼ cup of water. (If using canned apples, substitute liquid drained from canned apples for water.) Turn into a 9x9x2-inch cake pan. Dot apples with butter.

Make topping: In a medium bowl, combine all topping ingredients and beat until smooth. Drop batter on apples in 9 portions, spacing evenly. The batter will spread during baking to cover apples. Bake at 375° F for 35 to 40 minutes or until apples are tender and topping is golden brown.

Skillet fruit cobbler

> ¼ LB. BUTTER OR MARGARINE
> 1 CUP FLOUR
> 2 TSP. BAKING POWDER
> ¼ TSP. SALT
> 1¼ CUP SUGAR
> 1 CUP MILK (MAY USE RECONSTITUTED POWDERED MILK)
> 2 CUPS DRAINED, CANNED FRUIT OF YOUR CHOICE (PEACHES, APPLES, CHERRIES, ETC.)

Melt butter in heavy skillet. Sift flour, baking powder, salt, and sugar together in mixing bowl. Stir in milk. Pour into buttered skillet. Add about 2 cups of any desired canned fruit in the middle. Do not stir. Bake at 400° F until top is golden brown. Serve with whipped cream or sweetened milk, if desired.

Lemon custard pudding cake

6 Tbsp. flour
6 Tbsp. butter or margarine, melted
2 cups sugar, divided
4 eggs yolks, reserve whites
1½ cups milk
grated peel of 1 lemon
2 Tbsp. fresh lemon juice
4 egg whites
powdered sugar

In a large mixing bowl, combine flour, butter, and 1½ cups sugar. Beat egg yolks. Add with milk and lemon peel to above mix. Mix well; add lemon juice. In another bowl with clean beaters, beat egg whites until stiff, slowly adding remaining ½ cup sugar while beating. Fold into batter. Pour into a greased baking dish and place in a shallow pan of hot water half way up the baking dish and bake at 350° F for 55-60 minutes or until top is golden brown. Serve warm or cool with powdered sugar dusting on top.

Strawberry shortcake (with biscuit)

2 pints fresh strawberries
1 cup sugar

Shortcake:

2⅓ cups flour
4 tsp. baking powder
2 Tbsp. sugar
½ tsp. salt
⅓ cup shortening
⅔ cup milk, possibly a little more (May use reconstituted powdered milk)

Sift dry ingredients into medium bowl. Cut in shortening. Mix in just enough milk to make a medium dough that sticks together but is not sticky to handle. Lightly knead in bowl, then turn out onto lightly-floured surface. Knead lightly, then roll out ½-inch thick. Cut with biscuit cutter (I use a regular-sized canning jar ring.) Place on greased 8-inch pan and bake at 400° F for 15 minutes or until golden.

Meanwhile, slice strawberries into medium bowl. Add sugar and stir well. Set aside; juice will form. Take hot biscuits out of oven and split in halves. Put the bottom half in bowl, cut side up, spread with butter and spoon on berries and juice. Top with other half of biscuit, cut side down, and spoon on more sliced berries and juice. Serve with whipped cream for an old-fashioned treat.

Old-fashioned berry shortcake (for raspberries, blackberries, etc.)

    1½ QUARTS BERRIES OF YOUR CHOICE
    ¾ CUPS SUGAR

Shortcake:
    2 CUPS FLOUR
    ¼ CUP SUGAR
    1 TBSP. BAKING POWDER
    ½ TSP. SALT
    ½ CUP BUTTER OR MARGARINE
    ¾ CUP MILK (MAY USE RECONSTITUTED POWDERED MILK)

Sift dry ingredients together into a medium mixing bowl. Cut in butter until mixture resembles coarse meal. Make a well in the center and pour in milk. Mix with fork just until all flour is moistened. Dough will be lumpy. Pour into lightly-greased 8x8x2-inch pan. Press with fingers to fit pan evenly. Bake at 425° F for 12-15 minutes or until golden. Cool partially. Cut into 9 squares.

Meanwhile, place berries in bowl and combine with sugar. Mash a little with a potato masher.

To serve, split shortcake squares (either warm or cold) in half, crosswise. Place bottom half in serving bowl, cut side up. Spoon berry mixture on it, then top with other half, cut side down. Top with more berries and serve with whipped cream or ice cream.

Aunt Hannah's gingerbread

(Aunt Hannah was my grandmother's aunt.)

    ¾ CUP SHORTENING
    1 CUP BROWN SUGAR, FIRMLY PACKED
    1 EGG, BEATEN (MAY USE RECONSTITUTED WHOLE POWDERED EGG)
    1 CUP MOLASSES
    3 CUPS FLOUR
    1 TBSP. GINGER
    1 TSP. CINNAMON
    ½ TSP. CLOVES
    2 TSP. BAKING SODA
    1 CUP BOILING WATER

Cream shortening and sugar together. Add egg and molasses. Mix well. Sift and add flour and spices. Mix in baking soda, dissolved in the boiling water. Pour into a greased and floured 13x9x2-inch cake pan and bake at 350° F until a toothpick inserted in the center comes out clean (about 30 minutes).

Puddings

Not only are puddings inexpensive and quick to make, but they taste so much better than the boxed, store-bought variety. You can serve them plain or use them warm on top of cakes or bars or cooled between cookies as a filling. Some are fruity and others are chocolate heaven; others are hearty and nearly a meal in themselves.

Floating island

Pudding:
- 2 CUPS MILK (MAY USE RECONSTITUTED POWDERED MILK)
- 4 EGG YOLKS, WHITES RESERVED
- ⅓ CUP SUGAR
- DASH SALT
- 1 TSP. VANILLA

Several hours before serving, make pudding. In top of double boiler over direct heat, heat milk until bubbles form around the edge. In medium bowl, beat egg yolks with sugar and salt until well blended. Gradually pour hot milk into egg mixture, beating constantly with a wire whisk. Return mixture to top of double boiler; place over hot, not boiling water. Cook, stirring constantly, until pudding coats a metal spoon; about 10 minutes. Pour into a bowl; press waxed paper right on the surface to prevent a skin from forming on it. When cool, stir in vanilla. Refrigerate, covered, until well chilled.

Meringue (the islands):
- 4 EGG WHITES
- DASH SALT
- ½ CUP SUGAR
- ½ TSP. VANILLA

Three hours before serving, make meringue: In large bowl, let egg whites warm to room temperature (about an hour). Lightly butter a 13x9x2-inch cake pan and coat it with sugar. Beat egg whites and a dash of salt at high speed until soft peaks form. Beat while adding sugar slowly. Continue beating until stiff peaks form. Add vanilla and beat 1 minute longer. Spoon meringue onto cake pan in small dollops. Bake at 350° F for 15 minutes or until meringue is lightly browned. Place on wire rack to cool. Refrigerate until serving. To serve, spoon pudding into serving dishes and top with meringue "cloud."

Just-right baked custard

- 2 EGGS
- 2 CUPS MILK (MAY USE RECONSTITUTED POWDERED MILK)
- ¼ CUP SUGAR
- DASH SALT
- ½ TSP. VANILLA
- ½ TSP. LEMON EXTRACT
- NUTMEG

Preheat oven to 350° F. Beat eggs and milk together. Add sugar, salt, and extracts. Spoon into a small baking dish. Sprinkle top with nutmeg. Place in a shallow pan and fill ½ inch deep with water. Bake for 35 minutes or until a knife inserted ½ inch into the center of the custard comes out clean. Do not over-bake.

Lemon pudding

1½ CUPS SUGAR
7 TBSP. CORNSTARCH
¼ TSP. SALT
2 CUPS WATER
3 EGG YOLKS
2 TBSP. BUTTER OR MARGARINE
⅓ CUP LEMON JUICE

Combine sugar, cornstarch, and salt in saucepan. Stir in water. Cook, stirring, until thickened. Cool slightly, then add slightly beaten egg yolks to hot mixture, stirring vigorously. Cook for 2 minutes, stirring constantly. Add butter. Cool. Add lemon juice and stir well. Refrigerate after cooling with waxed paper pressed on top of pudding to prevent a skin from forming on it.

Baked lemon pudding

½ CUP FLOUR
½ TSP. BAKING POWDER
¼ TSP. SALT
1½ CUPS SUGAR, DIVIDED
3 EGGS YOLKS, RESERVE WHITES
2 TSP. GRATED LEMON RIND
2 TBSP. MELTED BUTTER
1½ CUPS MILK
3 EGG WHITES

Sift flour, baking powder, salt, and 1 cup sugar together. Separate eggs into two mixing bowls. Beat egg yolks and add lemon rind, melted butter, and milk. Stir into the flour mixture. Beat smooth. Beat egg whites until soft peaks form, then gradually beat in ½ cup sugar. Beat until stiff peaks form. Fold egg whites into flour mixture. Pour into greased baking dish. Set in a pan that has ½ inch of hot water in it. Bake at 350° F for 45 minutes. Chill. Serve with whipped cream, if desired.

Caramel custard

    1½ CUPS SUGAR, DIVIDED
    6 EGGS, BEATEN
    2 TSP. VANILLA
    3 CUPS MILK (MAY USE RECONSTITUTED POWDERED MILK)

In a heavy saucepan, cook while stirring ¾ cup sugar until melted and caramel in color. Pour into 8 custard cups (6 oz.) or plain coffee cups (oven safe). Tilt to cover entire bottom of cups. Let stand for 10 minutes. Meanwhile, mix eggs, vanilla, and milk together in large bowl. Pour over caramelized sugar. Place cups in a large, shallow pan. Pour boiling water in pans to a depth of 1 inch and bake at 350° F for 40-45 minutes or until a knife inserted in the center of a custard comes out clean. Remove from pan and cool on wire rack. Run a knife around the rim of each cup and invert onto a serving plate.

Apple snow

When I was a little girl, every time I would get really sick with a cold or the flu, Mom would make Apple snow for me. It was a "special" dessert, and one that was very easy to eat and tempting, as well. I'll confess, sometimes I'd get "sick," just to see if I could weasel Apple snow out of Mom. It didn't work; she figured if I didn't have a temperature and still was up and about, I wasn't really sick. Now that I've been a Mom, I can see that mothers really CAN tell when their children are sick, just by looking at them. I thought Mom could read minds!

    2 EGGS WHITES, YOLKS RESERVED
    1 CUP SUGAR
    2 TART APPLES, PEELED AND FINELY GRATED

Beat egg whites until very stiff. Gradually add sugar and grated tart apples. Chill.

Sauce:
    2 EGG YOLKS
    1⅓ CUP MILK
    2 TBSP. SUGAR
    2 TSP. CORNSTARCH
    1 TSP. VANILLA

Beat egg yolks, milk, sugar, and cornstarch. Cook over medium heat, stirring constantly, until thickened. Add vanilla. Chill.

To serve, put a spoonful of apple mixture in each serving bowl and cover with the sauce.

Devil's float

    1 CUP FLOUR
    2 TSP. BAKING POWDER
    ¼ TSP. SALT
    1½ TBSP. POWDERED COCOA

¾ cup sugar

½ cup milk (may use reconstituted powdered milk)

2 Tbsp. melted butter or margarine

1 tsp. vanilla

Mix flour, baking powder, salt, cocoa, and sugar together. Add milk, melted butter, and vanilla. Pour into a buttered 9-inch square pan.

Topping:

½ cup sugar

½ cup brown sugar, firmly packed

4 Tbsp. powdered cocoa

1 cup hot water

Mix sugar, brown sugar, and cocoa together. Pour hot water over all of it in pan. Do not stir. Bake at 350° F for about 50 minutes.

Old-fashioned rice pudding

4 cups milk (may use reconstituted powdered milk)

⅔ cup sugar

¼ cup rice

½ tsp. salt

1 tsp. vanilla

nutmeg

½ cup raisins

Into a 2-quart baking dish, mix milk, sugar, rice, salt, and vanilla. Sprinkle with nutmeg. Bake, uncovered, for 3 hours at 300° F, stirring often. After 2 hours of baking, add raisins, stirring them in well. I often do not stir for the last ½ hour so a little crust forms on the pudding. It adds a nice flavor and texture to this easy pudding.

Tapioca pudding

4 Tbsp. tapioca

⅓ cup sugar

⅛ tsp. salt

3 cups milk (may use reconstituted powdered milk)

3 eggs, separated

1 tsp. vanilla

Combine tapioca, sugar, salt, milk, and egg yolks (beaten) in saucepan. Cook over low heat, stirring, until thickened and tapioca is clear; about 12 minutes. Stir constantly to prevent scorching or use double boiler. Remove from heat. Beat egg whites until stiff; fold hot mixture slowly into them. Add vanilla and cool with a waxed paper or plastic on the top to prevent a skin from forming.

Daffodil pudding

This is a two-part, white and yellow pudding — daffodil colors!

White part:
- 3 Tbsp. sugar
- 2 Tbsp. cornstarch
- ¼ tsp. salt
- ¼ cup cold milk (may use reconstituted powdered milk)
- 3 egg whites, beaten

Mix sugar, cornstarch, and salt. Dissolve in milk. Cook in saucepan over low heat until thickened. Fold in stiffly beaten egg whites and remove from heat. Rinse tea cups or other molds in cold water; drain but don't dry. Pour in mixture and chill. Turn out of cups onto dessert dishes.

Yellow part:
- 2 cups milk (may use reconstituted powdered milk)
- 3 Tbsp. sugar
- 3 egg yolks, beaten
- 2 tsp. vanilla

Heat in saucepan, stirring, over low heat. Cook until thickened and smooth, stirring constantly. Remove from heat and add vanilla. Chill and serve spooned over the white part.

Cottage pudding

- 1¾ cups flour
- ¾ cup sugar
- 2 tsp. baking powder
- ½ tsp. salt
- 1 egg (may use reconstituted whole powdered egg)
- ⅔ cup milk (may use reconstituted powdered milk)
- ¼ cup soft shortening
- 1 tsp. vanilla

Sift dry ingredients together. Mix in the rest of ingredients until well blended. Pour into a lightly buttered, floured 9-inch square baking pan and bake at 350° F for 25-30 minutes. Serve with hard sauce (recipe follows).

Hard sauce (without alcohol)

- ½ cup butter or margarine
- 1½ cups powdered sugar
- 1 lemon, juiced or 2 Tbsp. lemon juice
- salt to taste

Cream softened butter and powdered sugar together until smooth. Beat in lemon juice. Add a sprinkle of salt to taste, if desired.

Tip: To make a fruit hard sauce, simply make as above, then add in 1 cup crushed strawberries, peaches, raspberries, blackberries, etc.

Brown betty

Put a layer of bread crumbs in bottom of well-buttered, rather deep baking dish. Add a layer of peeled, chopped apples. Sprinkle with sugar, cinnamon, and salt. Dot with butter or margarine. Repeat layers until pan is full, with buttered, cinnamon sugar sprinkled bread crumbs on top. Bake at 350° F about 1 hour. Serve warm with sweetened milk or other sauce or ice cream.

Bread pudding

3 CUPS MILK (MAY USE RECONSTITUTED POWDERED MILK)
¼ CUP MELTED BUTTER OR MARGARINE
½ CUP SUGAR
4 CUPS BREAD CUBES
3 EGGS (MAY USE RECONSTITUTED WHOLE POWDERED EGG)
¼ TSP. SALT
1 TSP. VANILLA
¼ TSP. NUTMEG
½ CUP RAISINS

Heat milk, add butter, sugar, and bread cubes. Beat eggs, salt, vanilla, and nutmeg together. Mix with bread cube mixture. Stir in raisins. Pour into greased, 2-quart baking dish and bake at 350° F for about 55 minutes or until set. Serve with sweetened milk, whipped cream, or a sauce of your choosing.

Carrot pudding

½ CUP SHORTENING
½ CUP BROWN SUGAR, FIRMLY PACKED
1 EGG (MAY USE RECONSTITUTED WHOLE POWDERED EGG)
1 CUP GRATED RAW CARROT
1 TBSP. CHOPPED, CANDIED LEMON PEEL
½ CUP RAISINS
½ CUP DRIED CURRANTS
1¼ CUPS FLOUR
1 TSP. BAKING POWDER
½ TSP. SALT
½ TSP. NUTMEG
½ TSP. CINNAMON
½ TSP. BAKING SODA

Mix shortening, brown sugar, beaten egg, carrots, and fruits together. Sift flour, baking powder, salt, nutmeg, cinnamon, and baking soda together. Stir into first mixture. Pour in a buttered, 2-quart baking dish and bake, uncovered, at 350° F until firm; about 1 to 1¼ hours. Serve with desired sauce.

Graham pudding

¼ cup butter or margarine
⅔ cup brown sugar, firmly packed
1 egg, beaten (may use reconstituted whole powdered egg)
¼ cup molasses
½ cup milk (may use reconstituted powdered milk)
1½ cups whole wheat flour
½ tsp. baking soda
½ tsp. nutmeg
½ tsp. salt
1 cup raisins

Cream butter and sugar; add egg, molasses, and milk. Beat well. Sift dry ingredients together and add to creamed mixture. Add raisins. Pour into a greased, 2-quart pan and set pan onto a wire rack, into a large roasting pan with a tight-fitting cover, adding 1 inch of boiling water to the bottom of the roasting pan. Cover roasting pan and steam over low heat on the stovetop for 2 hours.

Serve with warm sauce:

1 cup sugar
1 Tbsp. flour (heaping)
½ cup butter
boiling water
1 tsp. vanilla

Mix sugar, flour, and butter. Add boiling water to desired thickness, cooking over medium heat for 2-3 minutes, until thickened. Add 1 tsp. vanilla and serve immediately over warm pudding.

Steamed apple pudding

1½ cups flour
1 tsp. baking soda
½ tsp. salt
½ tsp. cinnamon
½ tsp. nutmeg
¼ tsp. cloves
¼ cup butter or margarine, softened
1 cup sugar
2 eggs, well beaten
4 apples, peeled and shredded (2⅓ cups)
½ cup raisins
light cream

Generously butter a 1½ quart, oven-proof bowl. In a small bowl, mix flour with baking soda, salt, and spices; set aside. In a large bowl, mix butter, sugar, and eggs until smooth and fluffy. Stir in flour mixture. Add apples and raisins. Turn into prepared bowl. Cover surface of pudding with double thickness of waxed paper. Cover top of bowl completely, using fitted, heat-proof top or foil, secured with twine around the edges of the bowl. Place bowl on wire rack or trivet in large kettle. Pour boiling water around bowl to come halfway up side. Cover kettle, bring to a boil, then reduce heat. Boil gently for 2 hours. Remove bowl to cooling rack. Let stand 5 minutes, then with knife, loosen edge of pudding from sides of bowl and turn out onto serving dish. Serve warm with cream or hard sauce.

Old English plum pudding (has no plums!)

- 5½ CUPS FINE, DRY BREAD CRUMBS
- 2 TSP. SALT
- 1½ CUPS BROWN SUGAR, FIRMLY PACKED
- ½ TSP. CLOVES
- 1 TSP. NUTMEG
- 1 TSP. CINNAMON
- 1½ CUPS MILK, SCALDED (MAY USE RECONSTITUTED POWDERED MILK)
- 12 (YES 12!) EGGS, WELL BEATEN (MAY USE RECONSTITUTED WHOLE POWDERED EGGS)
- 1 LB. BEEF SUET, FINELY GROUND
- 2 CUPS RAISINS
- 2 CUPS DRY CURRANTS
- ½ CUP CANDIED LEMON PEEL, CHOPPED
- ½ CUP CANDIED ORANGE PEEL, CHOPPED
- ½ CUP CANDIED CITRON, CHOPPED
- 1 CUP CANDIED CHERRIES, CHOPPED
- 2 TBSP. GRATED ORANGE RIND
- 1½ CUPS APPLES, PEELED AND CHOPPED
- ½ CUP CIDER

Combine bread crumbs, salt, brown sugar, and spices. Stir in hot milk; cool. Add eggs, suet, fruits, and cider. Mix well. Turn into two buttered 2-quart baking dishes that will fit inside a large roasting pan (or use two covered roasting pans, if necessary). Add 1 inch of boiling water to the bottom of the roasting pans, then place puddings on wire racks, in roasting pans, and cover. Steam 6 hours, maintaining adequate water in the bottoms of the roasting pans to keep steam flowing. Use a low heat under the pans to just keep steam flowing, but not vigorously. You may use the oven, at 300° F, and keep the roasting pans covered as well.

Note: As you can easily see, this huge pudding is full of richness and expensive candied fruit peels (you may also make your own!). And because it takes so long to steam, it is usually only served at special holiday meals.

Baked Indian pudding

    4½ cups milk, divided (may use reconstituted powdered milk)
    ⅓ cup yellow cornmeal
    1 Tbsp. butter or margarine
    ¼ cup light brown sugar, firmly packed
    ¼ cup dark molasses
    ½ tsp. salt
    1 tsp. cinnamon
    ½ tsp. ginger
    ⅛ tsp. cloves
    ⅓ cup cream

In a small mixing bowl, combine 1 cup of milk and cornmeal; let stand. In medium saucepan, slowly heat 2 cups milk until bubbles form around edge of pan. Gradually stir cornmeal mixture into hot milk; cook over medium heat 10 minutes, stirring. Add rest of milk, butter, sugar, molasses, salt, and spices. Stir just until butter is melted. Turn into ungreased 1½ quart baking dish; add cream and mix in well; bake at 300° F for 30 minutes, uncovered. Let cool on wire rack 1 hour before serving; serve slightly warm with ice cream, sweetened milk, or hard sauce.

Bars

Bars are neither a cake, pudding, or cookie, but are somewhat in-between. They often have a filling, usually fruit or nut, and are commonly served, cut from a 13x9x2-inch cake pan, into squares or rectangles, to be eaten with the fingers.

Pumpkin bars

    4 eggs (may use reconstituted whole powdered eggs)
    1⅔ cups sugar
    1 cup vegetable oil
    1 can (16 oz.) pumpkin puree or 1½ pints canned pumpkin chunks, drained and mashed
    2 cups flour
    2 tsp. ground cinnamon
    ½ tsp. ground cloves
    2 tsp. baking powder
    1 tsp. baking soda
    1 tsp. salt

In a mixing bowl, beat eggs, sugar, oil, and pumpkin together well. Combine flour, cinnamon, cloves, baking powder, baking soda, and salt. Gradually add to pumpkin mixture and beat until smooth and light. Pour into an ungreased 13x9x2-inch pan. Bake at 350° F for 25-30 minutes. Cool completely. These bars are especially good iced with Cream cheese frosting.

Minnesota harvest bars

½ CUP SHORTENING

1½ CUPS FLOUR

1⅓ CUPS PUMPKIN PUREE

2 CUPS BROWN SUGAR

4 EGGS, BEATEN (MAY USE RECONSTITUTED WHOLE POWDERED EGG)

1 CUP CHOPPED NUTS

1 CUP CHOPPED DATES

1 TSP. BAKING POWDER

1 TSP. SALT

½ TSP. BAKING SODA

1 TSP. CINNAMON

1 TSP. NUTMEG

1 TSP. GINGER

1 TSP. VANILLA

Combine all ingredients and beat well. Pour into a greased and floured 13x9x2-inch pan. Bake at 350° F for 25-30 minutes. When cooled, sprinkle powdered sugar over paper doilies to make a pretty design if you wish. Otherwise, just sprinkle on powdered sugar or ice with your favorite frosting.

Best date bars

2½ CUPS PITTED DATES, CUT UP

¼ CUP SUGAR

1½ CUPS WATER

⅓ CUP COARSELY CHOPPED WALNUTS

1¼ CUPS FLOUR

1 TSP. SALT

½ TSP. BAKING SODA

1½ CUPS ROLLED OATS

1 CUP BROWN SUGAR, FIRMLY PACKED

½ CUP BUTTER OR MARGARINE, SOFTENED

1 TBSP. WATER

In a medium saucepan, combine dates, sugar, and water. Cook, stirring often, until very thick. Stir in walnuts; cool. Meanwhile, sift flour, salt, and baking soda together in a mixing bowl. Add rolled oats and brown sugar. Cut in butter until mixture makes a rough crumb. Sprinkle 1 Tbsp. water over it and stir gently. Place half into greased 13x9x2-inch baking pan. Pat down evenly with fingers. Spread with date mixture. Cover with remaining rolled oat mixture and pat down evenly. Bake at 350° F for 35-40 minutes or until top is lightly browned. Cool completely and cut into bars.

Walnut slice

½ cup shortening
1 Tbsp. sugar
1 egg, beaten (may use reconstituted whole powdered egg)
3 Tbsp. milk (may use reconstituted powdered milk)
1 tsp. vanilla
1 cup flour
2 tsp. baking powder
¼ tsp. salt

Cream shortening and sugar together until fluffy. Add egg, milk, and vanilla. Add sifted dry ingredients and mix well. Pour out into a greased 13x9x2-inch pan. Pat entire bottom crust ingredients down with fingers to cover bottom evenly. Bake at 325° F for 15 minutes or until golden brown on edges. Remove from oven and let cool.

Topping:

1¼ cups brown sugar, firmly packed
2 eggs, beaten
2 Tbsp. flour
½ cup coconut
1 cup chopped walnuts
1 tsp. baking powder

Mix sugar, eggs, coconut, nuts, and baking powder well. Pour onto crust evenly. Bake at 350° F until lightly browned on top. When cool, ice thinly with Buttercream frosting. Cut into squares.

Chocolate walnut bars

1 cup butter or margarine, softened
2 cups sugar
4 eggs, beaten
1 Tbsp. vanilla (yes, 1 Tbsp.!)
2 cups flour
½ tsp. salt
2 cups chopped walnuts
2 squares (1 oz. each) unsweetened chocolate, melted

In a mixing bowl, cream butter, and sugar together. Beat in eggs and vanilla. Add flour and salt; mix well. Fold in walnuts. Spread half of batter into greased 13x9x2-inch pan. Add melted chocolate to the remaining batter and mix well. Spread the chocolate batter on top of the first batter, being careful not to stir them together; you want separate-colored layers. Bake at 350° F for 30-35 minutes. Cool completely. Frost with Buttercream frosting.

Hawaiian bars

1 pkg. yellow cake mix

3 pkgs. (3 oz. each) instant vanilla pudding mix (or double the pudding recipe used in Floating Island on page 221.)

4 cups cold milk (may use reconstituted powdered milk) omit if using homemade pudding!

1½ tsp. coconut extract

1 pkg. (8 oz.) cream cheese, softened or 1 heaping cup fresh cream cheese

1 can (20 oz.) crushed pineapple, well drained

2 cups heavy cream, whipped and sweetened

2 cups flaked coconut, toasted

Mix cake batter according to package directions. Pour into two greased 13x9x2-inch cake pans. Bake at 350° F for 15 minutes or until cake tests done. Cool completely. In a large mixing bowl, combine pudding mixes and milk or just put pudding in bowl if using homemade pudding. Add coconut extract. Beat well. Add the cream cheese and beat again well. Stir in pineapple. Spread over the cooled cakes. Top with whipped cream and sprinkle with toasted, flaked coconut. Chill very well and cut into squares to serve.

Reese's bars

1 cup peanut butter

½ cup butter, melted

1¾ cups powdered sugar

½ tsp. vanilla

¼ tsp. salt

1½ cups chocolate chips

2 Tbsp. vegetable oil

Combine peanut butter, butter, powdered sugar, vanilla, and salt in a large bowl. Mix well until mixture forms a ball. Pat into a greased 8x8-inch square pan. Melt chocolate chips and oil together. Pour smoothly on peanut butter mixture in pan. Cool and cut into bars.

Lemon lush

1st layer (crust):
- 1½ cups flour
- 3 Tbsp. sugar
- 1½ sticks butter or margarine (¾ cup), softened
- 1 cup walnuts or pecans, ground

Mix flour, sugar, softened butter, and ground nuts together well. Pat down in greased 13x9x2-inch pan, evenly with fingers. Bake at 350° F for 20 minutes. Allow to cool down completely on wire rack, in pan, before adding fillings.

2nd layer:
- 1 pkg. (8 oz.) cream cheese (or 1 heaping cup fresh cream cheese) softened
- 1 cup whipped cream or Cool Whip
- 1 cup powdered sugar

Mix softened cream cheese, whipped cream (or Cool Whip), and powdered sugar until smooth and light. Spread evenly over first layer.

3rd layer:
- 2 pkgs. (3 oz. each) instant lemon pudding OR homemade lemon pudding on page 222.
- 3½ cups milk (can use reconstituted powdered milk)

Beat pudding and cold milk together; spread evenly over second layer.

Topping:
- 2 cups or more whipped cream or Cool Whip

Add remaining whipped cream on top and cut into squares to serve.

Tip: I make this in a 9x9-inch square pan, which gives me a thicker crust and layers. It doesn't go as far, but oh-how-good it is!

Rhubarb delight

Filling:
- ¼ cup water
- 4 cups rhubarb
- 3 Tbsp. cornstarch
- ½ cup sugar
- splash lemon juice

Mix water with rhubarb and lemon juice and cook in saucepan until rhubarb is tender. Add cornstarch with sugar and slowly add to rhubarb, stirring and heating until thickened. Set aside to cool.

Crust:
- 1 cup butter or margarine, softened
- 1½ cups flour
- ¼ cup powdered sugar

¾ CUP GROUND WALNUTS OR PECANS

Mix together butter, flour, powdered sugar, and ground nuts. Press into a greased 9x12-inch baking pan and bake at 350° F for 15 minutes. Let cool completely.

1st layer:

1½ CUPS POWDERED SUGAR

2 PKGS. (8 OZ. EACH) CREAM CHEESE, SOFTENED OR 2½ CUPS FRESH CREAM CHEESE

When cool, mix powdered sugar and cream cheese until fluffy. Spread on crust. Pour on cooled filling. Top with whipped cream and a sprinkle of nuts.

Rhubarb bars

Crust:

1 CUP BUTTER OR MARGARINE

2 CUPS FLOUR

2 TBSP. SUGAR

Blend butter, flour, and sugar (like pie crust pastry). Press into bottom and sides of a 13x9x2-inch pan and bake for 10 minutes at 350° F. Remove from heat and cool.

Filling:

4 CUPS RHUBARB, SLICED

3 EGG YOLKS, RESERVE WHITES

1¼ CUPS SUGAR

2 TBSP. FLOUR

1½ CUP CREAM (OR USE CANNED MILK)

⅛ TSP. SALT

In a mixing bowl, blend rhubarb, egg yolks, sugar, flour, cream or canned milk, and salt. Pour over crust and bake at 350° F for 40-45 minutes.

Topping:

3 EGG WHITES

½ CUP SUGAR

½ TSP. VANILLA

1 CUP COCONUT

1 CUP CHOPPED WALNUTS

With a clean beater, beat egg whites until soft peaks form, then gradually blend in sugar. Continue beating until stiff peaks form. Gently fold in vanilla, coconut, and nuts. Pour over top of bars and bake 10 minutes at 375° F; watch closely so it doesn't overbake! Cut into squares and serve warm or cool.

Cherry bars

- 1 cup butter or margarine, softened
- 2 cups sugar
- 4 eggs
- 1 tsp. vanilla
- ¼ tsp. almond extract
- 3 cups flour
- 1 tsp. salt
- 2 cans (21 oz. each) cherry pie filling or 3 pints home-canned cherry pie filling

Glaze:
- 1 cup powdered sugar
- ½ tsp. vanilla
- ½ tsp. almond extract
- 2-3 Tbsp. milk

Topping:
- slivered toasted almonds (optional but nice!)

Cream butter and sugar until light and fluffy. Add eggs, beating well after each egg is added. Mix in the extracts. Mix flour and salt in small mixing bowl. Add to the creamed mixture and mix until well combined.

Spread 3 cups of batter onto a greased 13x9x2-inch cake pan. Spread with pie filling evenly. Drop the remaining batter by spoonfuls over the filling. Bake at 350° F for 30-35 minutes or until a toothpick inserted in the middle comes out clean. Cool on a wire rack, in pan.

Combine the glaze ingredients and drizzle over bars. While glaze is still moist, sprinkle on slivered toasted almonds. Cut into squares and serve.

Almond poppy seed bars

- 3 eggs (may use reconstituted whole powdered eggs)
- 2¼ cups sugar
- 1½ cups milk (may use reconstituted powdered milk)
- 1 cup vegetable oil
- 1½ tsp. almond extract
- 1 Tbsp. vanilla
- 3 cups flour
- 4 tsp. poppy seeds
- 1½ tsp. baking powder
- 1 tsp. salt

In a mixing bowl, beat eggs, sugar, milk, oil, and flavorings. Mix flour, poppy seeds, baking powder, and salt. Add to the egg mixture and stir until well combined. Spread evenly onto greased 13x9x2-inch baking pan. Bake at 350° F for 20 minutes or until golden brown. Cool on a wire rack. Ice bars with the glaze for Cherry bars (see previous recipe). Cut into squares and serve.

Butterscotch meringue squares

¾ CUP BUTTER OR MARGARINE

2 CUPS BROWN SUGAR, FIRMLY PACKED, DIVIDED

½ CUP SUGAR

3 EGG YOLKS, RESERVE WHITES

1 TSP. VANILLA

2 CUPS FLOUR

¼ TSP. BAKING SODA

¼ TSP. SALT

1 PKG. (6 OZ.) BUTTERSCOTCH CHIPS

1 CUP COCONUT

¾ CUP NUTS

3 EGG WHITES

Cream butter, 1 cup brown sugar, sugar, and egg yolks together. Beat until fluffy. Add vanilla, mix in. Sift in flour, baking soda, and salt. Mix well. Press into bottom of a greased 13x9x2-inch pan. Sprinkle butterscotch chips, coconut, and nuts over first mixture. With a clean mixer, beat egg whites until soft peaks form, then beat in 1 cup brown sugar gradually. Continue beating until stiff peaks form. Spread on top. Bake at 350° F for 35-40 minutes. Do not let meringue get too brown.

Brownies

2 CUPS SUGAR

¾ CUP BUTTER OR SHORTENING

4 EGGS, BEATEN (MAY USE RECONSTITUTED WHOLE POWDERED EGG)

1 TSP. VANILLA

½ CUP CHOPPED WALNUTS

1 CUP FLOUR

1 TSP. BAKING POWDER

½ TSP. SALT

½ CUP COCOA

Cream sugar and butter well. Add eggs, vanilla, and nuts. Mix well. Sift together flour, baking powder, salt, and cocoa. Add to sugar mix and stir well. Pour into a greased and floured 13x9x2-inch baking pan. Bake at 350° F until it shrinks from edges of pan. Center will still seem soft. Let cool completely, then cut into squares.

Butter pecan bars

¾ cup butter or margarine, melted
1 cup brown sugar, firmly packed
1 cup sugar
2 eggs, beaten (may use reconstituted whole powdered egg)
1¼ cup flour
½ tsp. baking soda
1 cup pecans, chopped
1 tsp. vanilla

Cream butter with sugars. Add eggs and beat well. Add sifted flour and baking soda. Then add nuts and vanilla. Mix well. Pour into a lightly-greased 8x8x2-inch pan and bake at 350° F for 30-40 minutes. Do not overbake. Cut into bars while still slightly warm.

Apple bars

Crust:

2¾ cups flour
1 cup plus 2 Tbsp. shortening
1 tsp. salt
milk
1 egg yolk, beaten

Mix flour, shortening, and salt, as for pie dough. Add enough milk to egg yolk to make ⅔ cup. Stir into flour mixture to make dough. Divide into 2 equal portions. Roll 1 part into rectangle. Place on lightly-greased cookie sheet.

Filling:

7-8 cups thinly sliced, peeled apples
⅔ cup sugar
½ tsp. cinnamon
¼ tsp. allspice

Mix apples, sugar, cinnamon, and allspice in a bowl. Spread on dough. Roll out remaining dough and spread over apples. Bake until crust is golden brown. Let cool.

Icing:

1 cup powdered sugar
½ tsp. vanilla
1-2 Tbsp. water
3 Tbsp. finely ground nuts

To ice, mix powdered sugar, vanilla, and water until smooth. Spread over warm top. Sprinkle with ground nuts. Cut into squares when cool.

Raspberry bars

½ CUP BUTTER OR MARGARINE
½ CUP SUGAR
1 CUP FLOUR
RASPBERRY JAM

Cream butter and sugar together in bowl, then mix in flour. Spread in a 8x8x2-inch lightly-greased baking pan. Top with raspberry jam. (Heating the jam a little helps it to spread better.)

Topping:
1 CUP BROWN SUGAR
2 CUPS COCONUT
3 TBSP. BUTTER OR MARGARINE
1 TSP. VANILLA
1 EGG, BEATEN (MAY USE RECONSTITUTED WHOLE POWDERED EGG)

Mix brown sugar, coconut, butter, vanilla, and egg until well blended and spread on top of jam. Bake at 350° F for 30 minutes. Cut into squares while still hot.

Down south pecan bars

¼ CUP BUTTER OR MARGARINE
⅓ CUP BROWN SUGAR, FIRMLY PACKED
1 CUP FLOUR
¼ TSP. BAKING POWDER
¼ CUP CHOPPED PECANS

Cream butter and brown sugar together until smooth. Slowly add flour and baking powder. Mix until resembles a coarse meal. Add chopped pecans. Press into a greased 8x8-inch pan and bake at 350° F for 10 minutes.

Pecan topping:
2 EGGS
¾ CUP CORN SYRUP
¼ CUP BROWN SUGAR, FIRMLY PACKED
½ TSP. SALT
1 TSP. VANILLA
¾ CUP PECANS

Beat eggs until foamy. Add corn syrup, brown sugar, salt, vanilla, and pecans. Mix well and pour over first layer. Bake at 350° F for 25-30 minutes. Serve with whipped cream.

Lemon cheese bars

Crust:
>1 box yellow cake mix
>
>1 egg (may use reconstituted whole powdered eggs)
>
>⅓ cup vegetable oil

Mix dry cake mix, egg, and oil until crumbly. Reserve one cup. Press remaining mixture in an ungreased 13x9x2-inch cake pan. Bake at 350° F for 15 minutes.

Filling:
>1 pkg. (8 oz.) cream cheese, softened or 1 heaping cup fresh cream cheese
>
>⅓ cup sugar
>
>1 Tbsp. lemon juice
>
>1 egg

Meanwhile, beat softened cream cheese, sugar, lemon juice, and 1 egg until light and smooth. Spread over baked layer. Sprinkle with reserved crumb mixture. Bake at 350° F for 15 minutes longer. Cool and cut into bars.

Chocolate diamond bars

>1 box German chocolate cake mix
>
>1 cup coconut
>
>½ cup butter
>
>1 cup pecans, chopped
>
>2 eggs, beaten (may use reconstituted whole powdered eggs)

Mix ingredients for crust together in mixing bowl and pour into a 13x9x2-inch greased cake pan.

Topping:
>1 pkg. (8 oz.) cream cheese, softened
>
>½ cup butter or margarine
>
>1 lb. powdered sugar

Beat cream cheese, butter, and powdered sugar together and spread carefully over other mixture and bake at 350° F for 30-35 minutes. Cool and cut into bars.

Pineapple bars

>2 cups flour
>
>2 cups sugar
>
>2 eggs, beaten (may use reconstituted whole powdered eggs)
>
>1 large can crushed pineapple, drained
>
>½ tsp. salt

Mix ingredients together well and bake in greased 13x9x2-inch cake pan at 350° F for 30 minutes. Let cool.

Topping:

- ½ cup butter or margarine
- 1 pkg. (8 oz.) cream cheese, softened
- 1 tsp. vanilla
- 2 cups powdered sugar

Cream butter, cream cheese, vanilla, and powdered sugar together. Beat until fluffy and smooth. Spread over bars and cut.

Strawberry bars

- 1 cup butter or margarine, softened
- 1½ cups sugar
- 2 eggs
- 1 tsp. grated lemon peel
- 3¼ cups flour, divided
- ¾ cup slivered almonds, chopped
- 1 tsp. baking powder
- ½ tsp. salt
- 1 jar (12 oz.) strawberry preserves or 1 pint, less 4 Tbsp., homemade preserves

In a large mixing bowl, cream the butter and sugar. Add eggs, one at a time, beating well after each addition. Beat in lemon peel. Combine 3 cups flour, almonds, baking powder, and salt; gradually add to creamed mixture until mixture resembles coarse crumbs (do not overmix).

Set aside 1 cup of dough. Press the remaining dough into a greased 15x10x1-inch baking pan. Spread preserves to within ¼ inch of edges. Combine the reserved dough with the remaining flour; sprinkle over preserves. Bake at 350° F for 25-30 minutes or until lightly browned. Cool on wire rack. Cut into bars.

Apple butter bars (You'd swear they were date bars!)

- 1½ cups flour
- 1 tsp. baking soda
- 1 tsp. salt
- 2½ cups rolled oats
- 1½ cups sugar
- 1 cup butter or margarine, melted
- 1½ cup apple butter

Sift flour, baking soda, and salt; mix in rolled oats and sugar. Add melted butter. Press half of mixture down into greased 13x9x2-inch cake pan. Spread with apple butter. Cover with remaining oat mixture and pat down lightly. Bake at 350° F for about 45-50 minutes or until lightly brown. Cut into squares.

Apricot bars

¾ CUP BUTTER OR MARGARINE

1 CUP SUGAR

1 EGG, BEATEN (YOU MAY USE RECONSTITUTED, WHOLE POWDERED EGG)

2 CUPS FLOUR

¼ TSP. BAKING POWDER

1⅓ CUPS SHREDDED COCONUT

½ CUP CHOPPED WALNUTS

½ TSP. VANILLA

1 JAR (12 OZ.) APRICOT PRESERVES OR 1 PINT, LESS 4 TBSP., HOMEMADE APRICOT PRESERVES OR JAM

Cream butter and sugar together in mixing bowl. Add egg, beat well until light and fluffy. In another bowl, sift together flour and baking powder. Gradually add to butter/sugar mixture, mixing well. Add coconut, walnuts, and vanilla extract. Mix well. Spread ⅔ of dough into a greased 13x9x2-inch baking pan. Press down evenly with finger tips. Spread evenly with preserves (warming preserves helps it spread easier). Crumble on the rest of the dough. Top with walnut halves, if you wish. Bake at 350° F for 30 minutes or until top is golden brown. Cool in pan and cut into squares.

Chocolate brownies

½ CUP BUTTER

1 CUP WHITE SUGAR

2 EGGS (MAY USE RECONSTITUTED WHOLE POWDERED EGG)

1 TSP. VANILLA EXTRACT

⅓ CUP UNSWEETENED COCOA POWDER

½ CUP FLOUR

¼ TSP. SALT

¼ TSP. BAKING POWDER

½ CUP CHOPPED NUTS (OPTIONAL)

Lightly grease and flour an 8x8x2-inch square pan. In a large saucepan, melt butter. Remove from heat, and stir in sugar, eggs, and vanilla. Beat in cocoa, flour, salt, and baking powder. Add nuts. Spread batter into prepared pan. Bake in 350° F for 25 to 30 minutes. Do not overcook. Cool in pan on wire rack. Frost with chocolate frosting, if you wish.

Lemon almond bars

Crust:

½ CUP BUTTER OR MARGARINE

¼ CUP POWDERED SUGAR

1 CUP FLOUR

Combine butter with powdered sugar until smooth. Slowly mix in flour. Spread evenly in bottom of an 8x8x2-inch square baking pan. Bake at 350° F for 10 minutes.

Filling:
- 2 EGGS (MAY USE RECONSTITUTED WHOLE POWDERED EGG)
- 1 CUP SUGAR
- ¼ CUP FLOUR
- 1 TSP. GRATED LEMON PEEL
- 2 TBSP. LEMON JUICE
- ½ CUP GROUND, TOASTED ALMONDS

Combine filling ingredients and pour over the crust. Bake an additional 20 minutes. Cool completely in the pan on a wire rack. Sprinkle top with powdered sugar, sprinkled through a paper doily for a pretty pattern or just sprinkle it on. Cut into squares.

Scotch shortbread

Shortbread is kind of a cross between a bar and a cookie. It tastes like a rich, butter cookie, but is *so* very easy to make because you just press it into a pan — no shaping, rolling, cutting, or dropping! It only takes a few minutes to make and it's one of my favorite recipes.

- 1⅓ CUPS BUTTER OR MARGARINE (BUTTER MAKES THE BEST SHORTBREAD)
- 1 TSP. VANILLA
- 1 CUP POWDERED SUGAR
- 3 CUPS FLOUR
- 1 TSP. SALT

Cream butter, vanilla, and powdered sugar together until light and fluffy. Slowly mix in flour and salt. Mix well. Press dough evenly with finger tips into an 8x8-inch lightly-greased baking pan. Prick in several places with a fork. Bake at 375° F for 15 minutes or until top is just golden brown on the edges. Cut while warm into squares. Cool in pan on wire rack completely before taking out of pan.

Cookies

Like bars, cookies come in all flavors imaginable, from drop cookies to cookies cut with elaborate cutters into a myriad of different shapes. Luckily, most cookies are very easy to make. So much so that they are often the very first baking children do on their own. And they are so much fun, too! What would a holiday season be without a cookie-baking session? Mom used to bake Christmas cookies for a week before Christmas, to fill large boxes with different shapes and flavors of wonderful cookies: iced, cut-out Christmas cookies, turtle cookies, thumbprint cookies, gingersnaps, shortbread, date-filled cookies, and many more.

I can remember my first attempts, as a child, at cutting out fancy shapes. I was covered with flour and sugar, but loved every second of it. What adult or child doesn't love making cookies? All of the following cookies have simple ingredients, right from your pantry, and can be made very easily. And I guarantee that all of them taste great, too!

Peanut butter cookies

2½ CUPS FLOUR

½ TSP. SALT

1 TSP. BAKING POWDER

½ TSP. BAKING SODA

1 CUP PEANUT BUTTER (CRUNCHY OR SMOOTH)

1 CUP SHORTENING

1 CUP SUGAR

1 CUP BROWN SUGAR, FIRMLY PACKED

2 EGGS (MAY USE RECONSTITUTED WHOLE POWDERED EGG)

Sift dry ingredients together. Cream peanut butter and shortening together, then beat in sugars until light and fluffy. Add eggs and beat well. Slowly add dry ingredients and mix well. Roll balls the size of a walnut in your fingers, then press down on a lightly-greased cookie sheet, about 2 inches apart. Flatten tops with fork dipped in flour, then make a crisscross mark the other way. Sprinkle with sugar. Bake at 350° F about 10-12 minutes or until just barely browning on edges of bottom. Don't overbake or they get hard.

Chocolate chip cookies

1¼ CUPS BROWN SUGAR, FIRMLY PACKED

1 TBSP. VANILLA (YES, TBSP.)

2 TBSP. MILK (MAY USE RECONSTITUTED POWDERED MILK)

1 EGG, BEATEN (MAY USE RECONSTITUTED WHOLE POWDERED EGG)

¾ CUP SHORTENING

1¾ CUPS FLOUR

1 TSP. SALT

1 TSP. BAKING SODA

½ - 1 BAG CHOCOLATE CHIPS

1 CUP CHOPPED WALNUTS (OPTIONAL)

Cream brown sugar, vanilla, milk, egg, and shortening together until light and fluffy. Sift dry ingredients together, then slowly add to other mix. Mix well. Mix in chocolate chips and walnuts. Drop in spoonfuls onto lightly-greased cookie sheet, allowing 2 inches between cookies for spreading out on baking. Do not press down. Bake at 375° F for about 8 minutes. Do not brown cookies; they should just be browning on edges of bottom so they are still soft. Remove from oven and let set on cookie sheet for 5 minutes, then gently remove onto wire cooling rack with spatula.

New Mexico cowboy cookies

When we lived in New Mexico, I baked dozens of Cowboy cookies to sell at our little general store in Gladstone (population 3!), way out in the middle of the high plains along the Santa Fe Trail. Tourists and cowboys alike flocked to the store to eat these cookies and stuff a few away for a snack later on.

1 CUP BROWN SUGAR, FIRMLY PACKED
1 CUP SUGAR
1 CUP BUTTER OR MARGARINE
2 EGGS, BEATEN (MAY USE RECONSTITUTED WHOLE POWDERED EGG)
2 CUPS FLOUR
1½ TSP. BAKING POWDER
½ TSP. SALT
2 CUPS OATMEAL
½ CUP CHOPPED WALNUTS
1½ CUPS CHOCOLATE CHIPS

Cream brown sugar, sugar, and butter together until smooth. Add eggs, then beat until fluffy and light. Sift flour, baking powder, and salt together, then slowly mix into sugar/butter mixture. Mix until smooth. Add oatmeal, walnuts, and chocolate chips. Mix well, then spoon out onto lightly-greased cookie sheet about 2 inches apart. Bake at 350° F for about 10 minutes or until the edges of the bottoms are just lightly brown. Let stand on the cookie sheet for a few minutes, then gently lift off onto a wire rack to cool.

Oatmeal cookies

1½ CUPS BUTTER, MARGARINE, OR SHORTENING
2½ CUPS BROWN SUGAR, FIRMLY PACKED
4 EGGS, BEATEN
2 TSP. VANILLA
2 CUPS FLOUR
2 TSP. CINNAMON
1½ TSP. BAKING SODA
1 TSP. SALT
4 CUPS ROLLED OATS

Cream butter and sugar together well. Add eggs and vanilla, then beat until fluffy and light. Sift flour, cinnamon, baking soda, and salt together. Slowly mix into butter/sugar/egg mix. Beat well. Add rolled oats and mix well. Spoon onto lightly-greased cookie sheet, allowing 2 inches space between cookies. Bake at 375° F for about 10 minutes or until edges of bottoms are just starting to get golden. Remove from pan gently and cool on a wire rack.

Cleon's rolled oat cookies

These rolled oat cookies are different; they are cake-like, tender, and light. Cleon was Mom's cousin, who developed this recipe. It's a family favorite!

⅔ CUP SHORTENING
3 EGGS, BEATEN (MAY USE RECONSTITUTED WHOLE POWDERED EGG)
1 CUP SUGAR
1 CUP BROWN SUGAR, FIRMLY PACKED
3 CUPS FLOUR
1 TSP. SALT
1 TSP. CINNAMON
1 TSP. BAKING SODA (ADDED TO WATER)
1 CUP WATER
3 CUPS ROLLED OATS
1 CUP RAISINS
1 CUP CHOPPED NUTMEATS

Cream first 4 ingredients together until light and fluffy. Sift flour, salt, and cinnamon together and slowly add to mixture. Mix well. Add baking soda to water and slowly add to the mix. Blend in rolled oats, raisins, and nutmeats. Mix well. Spoon out onto lightly-greased cookie sheets, leaving 2 inches between cookies. Do not press down. Bake at 350° F for about 10 minutes or until edges of bottom are just starting to brown. Remove from pan and cool on wire racks.

Oatmeal lace cookies

These are delicate cookies that spread out, like lace, on the cookie sheet — beautiful and tender, yet chewy.

1 CUP QUICK OATS
1 CUP SUGAR
3 TBSP. FLOUR
¼ TSP. BAKING POWDER
1 TSP. SALT
¼ LB. MELTED BUTTER (ONE STICK)
1 TSP. VANILLA
1 BEATEN EGG

Mix first 5 ingredients together. Add next 3 ingredients. Refrigerate overnight. Drop small amounts about 3 inches apart on a cookie sheet lined with aluminum foil. Bake at 325° F for 10-12 minutes. Let cool and peel off of foil.

Lottie's crumb cookies

1 CUP SHORTENING
2 CUPS SUGAR
3 EGGS, BEATEN

- 1 cup molasses
- 5 cups flour
- 2 tsp. cinnamon
- 1 tsp. cloves
- 2 tsp. baking soda
- 5 cups stale cake or cookie crumbs (break cookies up with rolling pin in cake pan)

Cream shortening and sugar together until smooth. Add eggs and molasses, then beat until light and fluffy. Sift flour, cinnamon, cloves, and baking soda together and add to mix. Beat well. Stir in cake or cookie crumbs. Drop by spoonfuls onto lightly-greased cookie sheet leaving 2 inches between cookies. Sprinkle with sugar and put a small bit of jelly in the center of each. Bake at 375° F for 8-10 minutes or until just barely golden brown around edges of bottom. Cool on wire rack.

Molasses crinkles

- ¾ cup shortening
- 1 cup brown sugar, firmly packed
- 1 egg, beaten (may use reconstituted whole powdered egg)
- ¼ cup dark molasses
- 2¼ cups flour
- 2 tsp. baking soda
- ¼ tsp. salt
- ½ tsp. cloves
- 1 tsp. ginger
- 1 tsp. cinnamon

Cream shortening and sugar together until smooth. Add egg and molasses. Beat until light and fluffy. Sift dry ingredients together and add to mix. Mix well. Chill, covered for 1 hour. Form into small balls. Dip in sugar and place on a lightly-greased cookie sheet. Indent the center with your finger and fill with jam or jelly of your choice. Bake at 375° F for about 10 minutes. Do not overbake.

Pecan sandies

- 2 cups butter or margarine
- 1 cup powdered sugar
- 2 Tbsp. water
- 4 tsp. vanilla
- 4 cups flour
- 2 cups chopped pecans

Cream butter and powdered sugar together until smooth. Add water and vanilla. Mix well. Gradually mix in flour. Fold in pecans. Roll in small balls and place on an ungreased cookie sheet, about 2 inches apart. Press down with fingers. Bake at 300° F for about 20 minutes. Cool on a wire rack. When cool, dust with additional powdered sugar.

Ice box cookies

When I was a child, these were my very favorite cookies, and today they are right up at the top, as well. When I was real little, Grandma really DID have an ice box and thus they were called "ice box cookies." Today they are called refrigerator cookies because hardly anyone remembers having ice boxes. But I still remember saving bits of brown sugar to feed the ice man's white horse out in front of our house…along with the milk man and junk man's horses, as well. Mom said I'd outgrow my love of horses. Hmmm. Right now I have five, plus a mule and two donkeys. I didn't outgrow my love of horses…or ice box cookies. I even love them unbaked. I remember getting my fingers slapped after stealing cookie after cookie off the cookie sheet. It was worth it. And I didn't get slapped very hard. I think Mom knew how good unbaked ice box cookie dough was!

1 CUP BUTTER

1 CUP SHORTENING

1 CUP SUGAR

1 CUP BROWN SUGAR, FIRMLY PACKED

3 EGGS, BEATEN

½ TSP. SALT

1 TSP. CINNAMON

6 CUPS FLOUR

1 CUPS CHOPPED NUTS

Cream butter, shortening, and sugars together until fluffy. Add eggs and beat until light. Sift dry ingredients together and slowly add to mix. Add chopped nuts. Mix well then form into a roll on waxed paper about 2 inches in diameter. Chill overnight, still in waxed paper, to prevent odors from absorbing and to prevent drying out. You may also want to seal in plastic wrap, as well. The next day, slice with a sharp knife about ½-inch thick and bake on a lightly-greased cookie sheet at 375° F for about 10 minutes or until edges of bottom are just starting to get golden. Do not overbake.

Almond butter cookies

½ CUP BUTTER OR MARGARINE, SOFTENED

¼ CUP SUGAR

½ CUP FINELY CHOPPED BLANCHED ALMONDS

1 TSP. ALMOND EXTRACT

1 CUP FLOUR

ADDITIONAL BLANCHED ALMONDS

Cream butter and sugar together until smooth. Stir in almonds and almond extract. Mix in flour and stir until dough is soft and well blended. Form into balls and place on an ungreased baking sheet about 2 inches apart. Flatten with greased bottom of a glass, dipped in sugar. Press whole almond in center of each cookie. Bake at 350° F for 9-10 minutes or until slightly browned.

Sour cream cookies (a very old family recipe)

- 1 CUP SHORTENING
- 2 CUPS SUGAR
- 2 EGGS, BEATEN (MAY USE RECONSTITUTED POWDERED WHOLE EGG)
- 4 CUPS FLOUR
- 1 TSP. BAKING SODA
- 1 TSP. SALT
- 1 TSP. NUTMEG
- 1 CUP SOUR CREAM (MAY USE RECONSTITUTED POWDERED SOUR CREAM)

Cream shortening with sugar until smooth. Add beaten eggs and beat until light and fluffy. Sift dry ingredients and add alternately with sour cream. (This makes a very soft dough.) Gently roll out about ½-inch thick and cut with a 3-inch round cookie cutter (I use a wide mouth canning jar ring). Sprinkle liberally with sugar and bake on a lightly-greased cookie sheet at 375° F for 8-10 minutes or until edges are just lightly golden brown.

Filled cookies (from Jackie's great-grandmother Eliza Lilly)

- 1 CUP SHORTENING
- 1 CUP SUGAR
- 1 EGG, BEATEN
- ½ CUP MILK
- 1 TSP. VANILLA
- 3½ CUPS FLOUR
- 2 TSP. BAKING POWDER
- 1 TSP. SALT

Cream shortening and sugar until well blended. Add egg, milk, and vanilla and beat until light and fluffy. Sift flour, baking powder, and salt and add to mixture. Mix well and roll out dough on lightly-floured surface ½-inch thick. Cut cookies into rounds with cookie cutter or glass. Put rounds on lightly-greased cookie sheet and place a spoonful of filling on center of bottom round.

Filling:
- ¾ CUP SUGAR
- 2 TBSP. FLOUR
- ½ CUP GROUND RAISINS
- 1 CUP BOILING WATER

Mix all ingredients together in saucepan and slowly cook into a thick paste, stirring to avoid scorching. Cool. Then fill cookies.

Dip a finger in water and moisten edge of cookie around edges after filling. Place another round on top and seal by pressing the edges with the tines of a fork dipped in flour. Bake at 350° F until edges are very lightly browned. Remove from pan and cool on a wire rack.

Jelly thumbprint cookies

    1 CUP BUTTER
    ¼ CUP SUGAR
    2 EGG YOLKS
    2⅓ CUPS FLOUR
    ½ TSP. SALT
    JAM

Cream butter and sugar until smooth. Add egg yolks and beat until light and fluffy. Sift flour and salt into sugar/egg/butter mix a little at a time until smooth. Shape tablespoonfuls into balls. Place on an ungreased cookie sheet. Press each with finger, making an indentation in the center. Place a drop of jam of your choice in the center. (It is nice to use several different colors of jam.) Bake at 350° F for 15-18 minutes or until lightly browned on edges of bottom. Remove and cool on wire rack.

Soft molasses drops

    1 CUP SHORTENING
    1 CUP SUGAR
    1 EGG, BEATEN (MAY USE RECONSTITUTED WHOLE POWDERED EGG)
    ½ CUP MOLASSES
    3 CUPS FLOUR
    2 TSP. BAKING SODA
    1 TSP. SALT
    1 TSP. GINGER
    1 TSP. CINNAMON
    ¾ CUP BUTTERMILK, SOUR CREAM, OR HOME CANNED MILK MIXED WITH ¾ TBSP. VINEGAR

Cream shortening and sugar until light, then add egg and molasses. Beat well until light and fluffy. Sift dry ingredients together. Combine milk and vinegar, if necessary. Add buttermilk, sour cream, or milk/vinegar (whichever you choose), alternately with dry ingredients. Mix well. Drop by spoonfuls onto a greased cookie sheet, leaving 2 inches between cookies. Bake at 375° F for about 10 minutes. Remove from cookie sheet and cool on wire rack.

Vanilla drop cookies

    ¾ CUP SHORTENING
    1¼ CUPS SUGAR
    2 EGGS, BEATEN (MAY USE RECONSTITUTED WHOLE POWDERED EGG)
    3 CUPS FLOUR
    1 TBSP. BAKING POWDER
    1 TSP. SALT
    ⅔ CUP MILK (MAY USE RECONSTITUTED POWDERED MILK)
    1 TSP. VANILLA

Cream shortening and sugar until blended. Add eggs and beat until light and fluffy. Sift dry ingredients together and add alternately with milk and vanilla. Mix well. Chill. Drop by spoonfuls onto lightly-greased cookie sheet, 2 inches apart. Bake at 400° F for about 10 minutes. You may also add raisins or chopped nuts if you wish.

Best-ever spritz cookies

1 CUP BUTTER, SOFTENED
⅔ CUP SUGAR
2 TSP. VANILLA
1 EGG, BEATEN
2¼ CUP FLOUR
½ TSP. SALT

Cream butter with sugar and vanilla until smooth. Add egg and beat until light and fluffy. Sift dry ingredients in slowly, mixing well. Beat until smooth and light. If dough is too soft to shape, cover and chill about 45 minutes. Place dough in cookie press and form shapes about 1 inch apart on ungreased cookie sheet. Bake at 400° F for about 6-8 minutes only until edges are slightly golden brown. Cool on wire rack. If you wish, you may also divide dough into separate bowls and add a bit of different colored food coloring to each.

Date surprise cookies

½ CUP SHORTENING
½ CUP SUGAR
2 EGGS, BEATEN
1 TSP. VANILLA
1½ CUPS FLOUR
½ TSP. BAKING SODA
¼ CUP CREAM

Mix all of the above ingredients very well and set aside.

36 PITTED DATES
WALNUT MEATS

Stuff whole pitted dates with a walnut meat and drop dates into cookie batter. Coat well. Place on a lightly-greased cookie sheet and bake at 375° F for about 10 minutes or until just lightly golden brown.

Bird's nest cookies

½ CUP BUTTER OR MARGARINE
¼ CUP BROWN SUGAR
1 EGG YOLK
1 CUP FLOUR
1 EGG WHITE, BEATEN
CHOPPED NUT MEATS
JAM

Cream butter and sugar until smooth. Add egg yolk and beat until light and fluffy. Add flour slowly. Beat well. Form into balls. Dip in slightly beaten egg white, then roll in chopped nuts. Place on lightly-greased cookie sheet and press centers with your finger tip. Bake at 350° F for 8 minutes. Remove from oven. Press centers down again and bake 10 minutes more. Remove from oven and fill centers with a dab of jam.

Turtle cookies

They look like chocolate turtles! These are cake-like "humps" with chocolate glaze and pecan pieces arranged to resemble a head, tail, and four legs. They are really cute and good to eat, too!

½ CUP BUTTER OR MARGARINE
½ CUP BROWN SUGAR, FIRMLY PACKED
1 EGG + 1 EGG YOLK, WHITE RESERVED
¼ TSP. VANILLA
1½ CUPS FLOUR
¼ TSP. BAKING SODA
¼ TSP. SALT
PECAN PIECES CUT TO RESEMBLE LEGS, HEAD, AND TAIL

Assembly:
Cream butter and brown sugar together until smooth. Add egg and egg yolk, reserving egg white. Beat until fluffy and light. Add vanilla. Sift flour, baking soda, and salt together and slowly add to above mix. Stir well. Chill.

Arrange pecan pieces in groups of five or six (head, legs, and tail if you wish) on greased baking sheets. Beat egg white until frothy. Remove cookie dough from refrigerator and shape dough into balls the size of a large walnut. Dip bottom into egg white and press lightly down onto pecan head and legs. Repeat for the rest of the cookies. Bake at 350° F for 10-15 minutes. Cool completely on a wire rack. Be careful not to knock off the heads and legs!

Glaze:

⅓ CUP CHOCOLATE CHIPS
¼ CUP MILK
1 TBSP. BUTTER OR MARGARINE
1 CUP OR MORE POWDERED SUGAR

Melt chocolate chips in milk and butter. Blend until smooth and take off heat. Add 1 cup or more of powdered sugar to make a medium thick glaze. Spoon glaze over "turtles" to cover the shell. I glaze mine on a wire rack so the excess can drip through onto waxed paper or newspaper. These cookies store well, covered, so you can make them ahead of time.

Sugar cookies

½ CUP BUTTER
½ CUP SHORTENING
1 CUP SUGAR
1 EGG (MAY USE RECONSTITUTED WHOLE POWDERED EGG)
1 TSP. VANILLA
2¼ CUPS FLOUR
½ TSP. BAKING POWDER
½ TSP. BAKING SODA
ADDITIONAL SUGAR

Cream butter, shortening, and sugar together. Add egg and vanilla. Beat well until light and fluffy. Sift flour, baking powder, and baking soda together. Slowly add to creamed mixture. Mix well. Shape into 1-inch balls. Roll balls in sugar. Place on a lightly-greased cookie sheet and flatten with a glass. Bake at 350° F for 10-12 minutes until bottom edges are just starting to become golden.

Billy goat cookies

1 CUP BUTTER OR MARGARINE
2 CUPS SUGAR
½ CUP SOUR CREAM (MAY USE RECONSTITUTED POWDERED SOUR CREAM)
3 EGGS (MAY USE RECONSTITUTED WHOLE POWDERED EGG)
1 TSP. VANILLA
4 CUPS FLOUR
4 TSP. BAKING POWDER
½ TSP. BAKING SODA
2 CUPS CHOPPED DATES

Cream butter and sugar together until light and fluffy. Add sour cream, eggs, and vanilla. Mix well. Sift flour, baking powder, and baking soda together and slowly add to creamed mix. Mix again. Fold in chopped dates. Drop by spoonfuls onto an ungreased cookie sheet. Bake at 350° F for 12-15 minutes; until edges are just golden brown.

Christmas cutout cookies

- 1 cup shortening
- 1½ cups sugar
- 2 eggs (may use reconstituted whole powdered egg)
- 2 tsp. baking powder
- 2 tsp. baking soda
- 4 cups flour
- 2 tsp. cream of tartar
- ½ tsp. salt
- 1 cup milk
- 1 tsp. vanilla

Cream shortening well. Add sugar and eggs and blend together. Sift baking powder, baking soda, flour, cream of tartar, and salt together and add to creamed mixture alternately with the milk. Stir in vanilla. Check dough consistency; if dough is too dry, add a tablespoon more of milk at a time; if dough is too sticky, add a tablespoon more of flour at a time, until the dough is of a workable consistency. Try to use as little flour as possible to avoid tough cookies.

Refrigerate for several hours or overnight. Roll out to a 1/16-inch thickness on a lightly-floured surface or parchment paper. Cut into desired shapes. Carefully lay on lightly-greased cookie sheet and bake at 350° F for 10-12 minutes or just until the bottom edges are golden brown. Cool 5 minutes on pan, then carefully remove from pan to cool on a wire rack. Meanwhile, make frosting:

Frosting:
- ¼ cup butter or margarine
- 1 tsp. vanilla
- 1¾ cups powdered sugar

Cream butter, vanilla, and powdered sugar together until smooth. Add enough powdered sugar to make a fairly thick frosting. Divide into small bowls and add different colored food coloring if you wish. Frost as you wish using an icing bag with tips, sugar sprinkles, or other decorations. These cookies keep well, so you can make them in advance.

Christmas cutout cookies II

- ½ cup shortening
- 1 cup sugar
- 1 egg (may use reconstituted whole powdered egg)
- 2 tsp. baking powder
- 2½ cups flour
- ½ tsp. salt
- ½ cup milk (may use reconstituted powdered milk)
- 1 tsp. vanilla

Cream shortening well. Add sugar and egg and blend together. Sift baking powder, flour, and salt together and add to creamed mixture alternately with the milk. Stir in vanilla. Check dough consistency; if dough is too dry, add a tablespoon more of milk at a time; if dough is too sticky, add a tablespoon more of flour at a time, until the dough is of a workable consistency. Try to use as little flour as possible to avoid tough cookies.

Refrigerate for several hours or overnight. Roll out to a 1/16-inch thickness on a lightly-floured surface or parchment paper. Cut into desired shapes. Bake at 350° F for 10-12 minutes; only until bottom edges are golden. Cool on pan for 5 minutes, then gently remove to wire racks to cool. Frost and decorate, as desired.

Do-it-yourself "Little Debbie" cookies

1 CUP BUTTER OR MARGARINE
3 CUPS BROWN SUGAR, FIRMLY PACKED
4 EGGS
2 TSP. VANILLA
3 CUPS FLOUR
2 TSP. CINNAMON
½ TSP. NUTMEG
1 TSP. SALT
1½ TSP. BAKING SODA
3 CUPS ROLLED OATS

Cream butter, sugar, and eggs together until light and fluffy. Add vanilla and mix. Sift flour, spices, salt, and baking soda together and slowly mix in with creamed mixture. When smooth, add rolled oats. Drop on a lightly-greased cookie sheet about 3 inches apart, in large spoonfuls. Flatten with a glass dipped lightly in water. Bake at 350° F until bottom edges are just starting to become golden; do not overbake. Cool on a wire rack.

Filling:
2 EGG WHITES, BEATEN
3 CUPS POWDERED SUGAR
1 TBSP. VANILLA
1¼ CUPS SHORTENING

When cool, make filling: Beat egg whites until stiff. Set aside. Mix powdered sugar, vanilla, and shortening together until smooth, then gently fold in egg whites. Spread onto flat surface of each cookie, then top with the flat surface of another, making a sandwich.

Sparkly lemon sugar cookies

½ CUP BUTTER OR MARGARINE

½ CUP SHORTENING

1 CUP SUGAR

1 EGG

1 TSP. VANILLA

2¼ CUPS FLOUR

½ TSP. BAKING POWDER

½ TSP. BAKING SODA

LEMON JUICE

ADDITIONAL SUGAR

Cream butter, shortening, and sugar together until smooth. Add egg and vanilla; mix well until light and fluffy. Sift flour, baking powder, and baking soda together. Slowly add to creamed mixture. Shape into 1-inch balls and place on a lightly-greased cookie sheet. Press down with a glass dipped in sugar. Bake at 350° F for 10-12 minutes or until bottom edges are just turning golden. Lightly drizzle lemon juice on tops of cookies, then quickly sprinkle sugar over it. Do one cookie at a time or have a helper. The lemon and sugar dries to a crunchy, sparkly lemon crust that is absolutely delicious!

Caramel cookies

1 CUP BUTTER OR MARGARINE

1 CUP SHORTENING

½ CUP BROWN SUGAR

1 CUP SUGAR

2 EGGS, BEATEN (YOU MAY USE RECONSTITUTED WHOLE POWDERED EGG)

2 TSP. VANILLA

3¾ CUPS FLOUR

1 TSP. SALT

½ TSP. BAKING SODA

Cream shortening, butter, and sugars. Beat well until light and fluffy. Add beaten eggs and vanilla. Beat again. Sift flour, salt, and baking soda to creamed mixture. Place dough in cookie press and form into shapes onto an ungreased cookie sheet. Bake at 350° F for 10-12 minutes or until bottom edges are just starting to become golden brown.

Gingersnaps

1 CUP SUGAR

¾ CUP SHORTENING

¼ CUP LIGHT MOLASSES

1 EGG, BEATEN (MAY USE RECONSTITUTED WHOLE POWDERED EGG)

2 CUPS FLOUR

2 TSP. BAKING SODA

½ TSP. SALT

½ TSP. CINNAMON

½ TSP. GINGER

½ TSP. CLOVES

EXTRA SUGAR

Cream sugar and shortening together very well. Add molasses and egg. Sift flour, baking soda, salt, and spices together into creamed mixture and mix well. Chill dough for 1 hour. It makes handling it much easier. Roll into balls the size of a large walnut and roll in a bowl of sugar. Bake on a lightly-greased cookie sheet at 375° F for 9-10 minutes.

Oatmeal peanut butter chocolate chip scotchies

½ CUP BUTTER OR MARGARINE

½ CUP PEANUT BUTTER (CRUNCHY IS BEST)

1½ CUPS BROWN SUGAR, FIRMLY PACKED

2 EGGS, BEATEN (MAY USE RECONSTITUTED WHOLE POWDERED EGG)

1 TSP. VANILLA

2 CUPS FLOUR

1 TSP. BAKING SODA

2 TSP. BAKING POWDER

1 TSP. SALT

1½ CUPS ROLLED OATS

½ BAG SEMISWEET CHOCOLATE CHIPS

½ CUP WALNUTS CHOPPED (OPTIONAL)

Cream butter, peanut butter, and sugar together until blended. Add eggs and mix until light and fluffy. Add vanilla; mix again. Sift flour, baking soda, baking powder, and salt into creamed mixture. Mix well. Add rolled oats, chocolate chips, and walnuts. Mix thoroughly. Drop rounded tablespoonfuls of dough onto lightly-greased cookie sheet and bake at 350° F for 12 minutes or until bottom edges are just turning golden brown.

Pineapple cookies

- 1 cup shortening
- 2 cups brown sugar, firmly packed
- 2 eggs, beaten (may use reconstituted whole powdered egg)
- 1 cup crushed pineapple, drained
- 1 tsp. vanilla
- 4 cups flour
- 1 tsp. salt
- 2 tsp. baking soda

Cream shortening and brown sugar until smooth. Add beaten eggs, pineapple, and vanilla. Mix again. Sift dry ingredients into creamed mixture and blend well. Drop onto lightly-greased cookie sheet and bake at 350° F for 10-12 minutes or until bottom edges are just golden brown. These are especially good frosted with a cream cheese frosting.

Pumpkin cookies

- 1 cup shortening
- 1 cup brown sugar, firmly packed
- 1 egg (may use reconstituted whole powdered egg)
- 1 cup pumpkin or squash, cooked or canned and pureed
- 2 cups flour
- 1 tsp. baking powder
- 1 tsp. baking soda
- ½ tsp. salt
- 1 tsp. cinnamon
- ¼ tsp. cloves

Cream shortening and brown sugar together until smooth. Add egg and mix again. Add pumpkin and blend until smooth. Sift flour, baking powder, baking soda, salt, and spices together into creamed mixture. Mix well. Drop onto lightly-greased cookie sheet and bake at 350° F for 10-12 minutes. These cookies are good as they are, but you may also frost or glaze them, as you wish.

Raisin cookies

- ½ cup butter or margarine
- 1 cup brown sugar, firmly packed
- 1 egg, beaten (may use reconstituted whole powdered egg)
- ½ cup sour cream (may use reconstituted powdered sour cream)
- 1⅔ cups flour
- ¼ tsp baking soda
- 1 tsp. baking powder
- ½ tsp. salt
- ¼ tsp cinnamon
- ½ cup raisins

½ CUP PECAN PIECES (OPTIONAL)

POWDERED SUGAR FOR DUSTING

Cream butter and brown sugar together until smooth. Add egg and beat until light and fluffy. Fold in sour cream. Mix well. Sift dry ingredients into creamed mix and blend thoroughly. Add raisins and pecan pieces and mix well. Drop onto lightly-greased, floured cookie sheet and bake at 350° F for 12-15 minutes. Cool on wire rack. Sift powdered sugar over cookies when cool.

Fancy chocolate logs

Mom used to make these for special occasions. They look and taste like you've fussed and fussed over them, but they are really very fast to put together and are buttery chocolate tender! The extra chocolate shot on the ends makes them even better. I look forward to holidays now, so I can make them too.

½ CUP SHORTENING

½ CUP SUGAR

1 EGG, BEATEN

1 SQUARE (1 OZ.) UNSWEETENED CHOCOLATE

1 TBSP. CREAM (OR MILK)

1 TSP. VANILLA

¼ TSP. SALT

2 CUPS FLOUR

JAM OR MELTED CHOCOLATE CHIPS

CHOCOLATE SPRINKLES

Cream shortening and sugar together until smooth. Add egg and beat well until light and fluffy. Gently melt chocolate square and mix with cream and vanilla; pour into creamed mixture. Stir well. Sift dry ingredients together into creamed ingredients. Mix well. Use a cookie press with a corrugated ribbon tip. Form 2-inch cookie strips on ungreased cookie pans. Bake at 400° F for 8-10 minutes. When cool, dip ends of ribbons in melted raspberry jam or chocolate chips and dip in chocolate sprinkles.

Candies

Unfortunately, in modern times, candy has gotten a reputation for being difficult to make. As a result, very few homestead cooks even attempt it. But as candy gets more and more expensive, it's certainly tempting to give it a try. Luckily, candy is *not* hard to make. Like home canning, if you just follow good directions, you can turn out batch after batch of excellent candy in very little time, using ingredients usually found in well-stocked home pantries.

Holidays and other special occasions simply beg for homemade candies. Imagine giving a box full of fudges, toffees, caramels, and chocolate creams, hand-dipped by *you*! You can make your candies as plain and delectable or as fancy and exquisite as you wish.

A candy thermometer is very nearly indispensable. You want a candy thermometer that fastens to the side of the pan, which holds the bulb up off of the bottom of the pan (where it might either break or read incorrectly), yet lets the bulb remain in the boiling candy. With it, you'll be able to accurately tell what temperature your candy is without determining whether it is at "soft ball," as for fudge, "firm ball," as for caramels, "hard ball," as for taffies and divinity, "brittle" or "medium crack," as for hard candies, or even "very brittle," as for some hard candies. It eliminates making a cold water test, which is dropping a teaspoon of syrup into a dish of cold water to see what stage of cooking the syrup has reached. A thermometer takes the guesswork out of candy making, which makes it much easier.

Some candies require sweetened condensed milk. If you do not have this, you can easily make your own. Here's how:

Sweetened condensed milk

¾ CUP GRANULATED SUGAR

⅓ CUP WATER

¼ CUP BUTTER

1 CUP NONFAT DRY MILK POWDER

Heat sugar and water in a saucepan until sugar dissolves. Add butter. Stir until butter is melted. Heat to a boil. Place milk powder in the work bowl of a food processor or blender. Process, while slowly adding butter mixture, until smooth. Cool and cover.

Old-time chocolate fudge

2½ SQUARES UNSWEETENED CHOCOLATE

2½ CUPS SUGAR

¼ TSP. SALT

1 CUP LIGHT CREAM (OR MILK)

2 TBSP. CORN SYRUP

2½ TBSP. BUTTER

1 TSP. VANILLA

Break chocolate into small pieces and place in a large, heavy-bottomed saucepan with sugar, salt, cream or milk, and corn syrup. Place over low heat and stir until the mixture begins to boil. Cook to 236° F (soft ball), stirring frequently to prevent scorching. Remove from heat; add butter, wipe pouring edge of pan with butter. Let syrup cool undisturbed to 110° F (lukewarm); beat it with a heavy spoon. Beat until a small amount of fudge dropped from the spoon will hold its shape or until the fudge loses its gloss. Pour fudge onto a cool marble slab. Knead until creamy. Do not knead too long or the fudge will become too soft. Put ball into a buttered 8x8-inch pan and press or roll out to the thickness desired. You can also skip the kneading and just pour out into a buttered pan. This is less creamy and coarser than kneaded fudge, but it is still very good.

Chocolate fudge II

2 CUPS SUGAR

¾ CUP LIGHT CREAM

2 OZ. SWEET BAKER'S CHOCOLATE, CHOPPED

1 tsp. corn syrup
⅛ tsp. salt
2 Tbsp. butter plus extra for buttering pans
1½ tsp. vanilla
½ cup chopped walnuts or pecans

Cut a square of waxed paper to line a 9x5x5-inch loaf pan with enough to extend over the edges by 2 inches. Spray inside with Pam or brush with butter or oil.

Butter the sides of a heavy medium saucepan. Mix sugar, cream, chocolate, corn syrup, and salt, stirring over high heat until boiling. Reduce heat to a slow boil (medium-low). Cook, uncovered, stirring occasionally for 10-15 minutes until candy thermometer reads 236° F (soft ball), adjusting burner as needed to regulate temperature.

Remove from heat; add butter and vanilla without stirring. Do not stir; set aside to cool for an hour or until mixture is 110° F. Beat with a wooden spoon or electric mixer until fudge becomes dull and is no longer glossy. Fudge will become thick when ready. Stir in nuts. Spread in pan evenly. Mark squares using a fork (do not cut) while still warm. If desired, extra chopped nuts may be sprinkled over and pressed lightly into the top. Refrigerate.

After the fudge sets up, lift it from the pan and cut into squares using a knife dipped into hot water.

Grandma's chewy chocolate fudge

2 cups sugar
6 Tbsp. cocoa
2 Tbsp. vegetable oil
1 cup milk or light cream
1 Tbsp. light corn syrup
2 Tbsp. butter
1 tsp. vanilla

Mix all ingredients except vanilla together and cook in a saucepan over medium low heat, stirring often. Watch the candy thermometer carefully and as soon as the fudge reaches 230° F, remove from heat. Add vanilla, stir in, and immediately pour into a buttered pan. Cool quickly in refrigerator or freezer (or set outdoors in the winter).

Too-easy chocolate fudge

3 CUPS SEMISWEET CHOCOLATE CHIPS
1 CAN (14 OZ.) SWEETENED CONDENSED MILK
¼ CUP BUTTER OR MARGARINE
1 CUP CHOPPED WALNUTS (OPTIONAL)

Place chocolate chips, sweetened condensed milk, and butter or margarine in large saucepan. Cook over low heat, stirring frequently until melted and blended. Stir in nuts, if desired. Pour into well-greased 8x8-inch glass baking dish. Refrigerate until set. May double recipe and use a 13x9x2-inch buttered baking pan.

Peanut butter fudge

2 CUPS BROWN SUGAR, FIRMLY PACKED
1 TBSP. BUTTER
½ CUP MILK
1 TSP. CORNSTARCH
1 TBSP WATER
1 TSP. VANILLA
1 CUP CREAMY PEANUT BUTTER

Grease an 8x8-inch square pan. In a saucepan over medium heat, combine the brown sugar, butter, and milk. Cook until the mixture reaches the soft ball stage (234-240° F). Combine the cornstarch and water, add to the saucepan and mix well. Remove from heat and beat for 2 minutes. Stir in the vanilla and peanut butter until thoroughly blended. Spread batter evenly into the prepared pan. Let cool, then cut into squares and enjoy.

Orange chocolate nut fudge

2½ CUPS SEMISWEET CHOCOLATE CHIPS
1 CAN (14 OZ.) SWEETENED CONDENSED MILK
½ CUP CHOPPED PECANS
2 TSP. GRATED ORANGE PEEL

Butter an 8x8-inch square pan. Melt chocolate chips with sweetened condensed milk in the top of a double boiler or in saucepan. Stir until smooth. Remove from heat and stir in pecans and grated orange peel. Pour chocolate mixture into prepared pan. Chill 2 hours, or until firm, and cut into squares.

Easy black walnut fudge

3¾ CUPS CONFECTIONERS' SUGAR
6 TBSP. BUTTER
3 TBSP. MILK (MAY USE RECONSTITUTED POWDERED MILK)
1 PINCH SALT
1 TBSP. VANILLA
¼ CUP BLACK WALNUT PIECES

Grease a 9x5-inch pan. Set aside. In a 3-quart saucepan, over very low heat, mix together confectioners' sugar, butter, milk, and salt until mixture is creamy. Add vanilla and black walnuts. Stir. Pour quickly into greased 9x5-inch pan. Refrigerate until firm, then cut into squares. Store in an airtight container in the refrigerator.

Maple fudge

> 1 CUP WHITE SUGAR
> 1 CUP BROWN SUGAR
> 1 CUP HEAVY CREAM
> 1 TSP. MAPLE-FLAVORED EXTRACT
> 1 TSP. BUTTER

In a large glass bowl, stir together the white sugar, brown sugar, cream, and maple extract. Place in saucepan and cook over medium heat, stirring often, until a candy thermometer registers 234-240° F. While the fudge is cooking, fill the sink with 2 to 3 inches of cold water. When the fudge has cooked, place the bowl into the cold water, being careful not to get any water into the mix. Stir in the butter, and continue stirring until the mixture is thick enough to form. Pour into a buttered 8-inch square dish, and let stand at room temperature for 30 minutes. Cut into small squares, and store in the refrigerator.

Vanilla fudge

> 2 CUPS SUGAR
> ⅛ TSP SALT
> ¾ CUP HEAVY CREAM
> ½ CUP MILK (CAN USE RECONSTITUTED POWDERED MILK)
> 1 TBSP. CORN SYRUP
> 1 TSP. VANILLA

Combine sugar, salt, cream, milk, and corn syrup in heavy saucepan. Cook over medium heat, stirring frequently, until syrup reaches 234-240° F (soft ball). Remove from heat, add vanilla, and wipe pouring edge of pan with a little butter. Cool to lukewarm, then beat with a heavy spoon until the fudge is no longer glossy. Turn out onto a marble slab and knead until smooth, then turn into a buttered pan and roll or press out to an even thickness or turn into a buttered 8x8x2-inch pan without kneading (resulting fudge won't be as smooth and creamy).

Dipped candies

You can make your own chocolate-dipped candy, just like the professional (expensive!) kind, in only a few minutes. You can dip just about anything in chocolate and instantly have a "fancy" dessert. The basic dip can be a simple chocolate chips/paraffin mix (*Yes*, paraffin! It's in your expensive candy, many candy bars, and it is edible...in reasonable amounts!). The paraffin is to keep the chocolate from slipping off of the candy (or fruit) that is dipped and to help keep it from melting easily while at room temperature or in your fingers.

Tip: It helps to refrigerate or even freeze soft candies before they are dipped to keep them from melting when in contact with the warm chocolate.

Basic dipping chocolate

    2 CUPS SEMISWEET CHOCOLATE CHIPS
    ⅓ STICK BUTTER
    ¼ BAR (16 OZ.) FOOD-GRADE PARAFFIN

Melt in double boiler over low heat. Dip candy with toothpick. Place on waxed paper.
OR:
Instead of the above mix, you can just use Chocolate Almond Bark, which is already mixed and just needs to be melted gently and proceed with dipping.

Here are some recipes for you to dip in chocolate:

Peanut butter balls

    1½ CUPS CRUNCHY PEANUT BUTTER
    1 STICK BUTTER
    ½ CUP CHOPPED ROASTED, SALTED PEANUTS
    3 CUPS POWDERED SUGAR

Mix ingredients together well and roll into small balls. Dip in chocolate mixture. Refrigerating overnight helps keep the balls stiff while dipping. Fill toothpick holes after dipping with small swirl of chocolate.

Coconut nut balls

    ¼ LBS. BUTTER
    1 CAN (14 OZ.) SWEETENED CONDENSED MILK
    ½ TSP. VANILLA
    2 LBS. POWDERED SUGAR
    2 CUPS CHOPPED NUTS
    4 CUPS FLAKED COCONUT

Melt butter until soft, add milk and vanilla. Mix the sugar, nuts, and coconut well, then add the butter, milk, and vanilla. The mixture will be stiff. Refrigerate for a few minutes. Roll by hand into small balls and place on waxed paper, in large cake pan. The next day melt your dipping chocolate mixture in a double boiler or saucepan. Stick the candy balls on a toothpick and dip in the hot chocolate mix. Place on waxed paper. When done, go back and fill each toothpick hole with a little swirl of chocolate.

Chocolate-covered cherries

    ⅓ CUP LIGHT CORN SYRUP
    ½ TSP. SALT
    1 TSP. VANILLA
    1 LB. POWDERED SUGAR

1-3 TBSP. SWEETENED CONDENSED MILK

1 JAR MARASCHINO CHERRIES

Mix first 5 ingredients and knead until like dough. Take a small amount and cover a maraschino cherry. Put in freezer for a few minutes. Then dip in chocolate dip. When dry, fill toothpick hole with a little swirl of chocolate. Let these ripen for 3-4 weeks in a cool place (not refrigerator).

Pecan caramel turtles

½ LB. SOFT CARAMELS

2 TBSP. HEAVY CREAM

1¼ CUPS SALTED, TOASTED PECAN HALVES

4 OZ. DIPPING CHOCOLATE

Melt caramels with cream over hot water in a double boiler. Let cool a few minutes. Arrange pecan halves, three together, on a waxed paper covered cookie sheet that has been chilled. Spoon caramel over pecan nutmeats. When spooning caramel over these, let the tops of pecans show. Cool (until firm). Spoon melted chocolate over this. Refrigerate or chill in freezer. You may then turn candies over and spoon a small amount of chocolate over bottoms to cover.

Maple cream chocolates

4 CUPS POWDERED SUGAR

½ CUP BUTTER

4 TBSP. CREAM OR EVAPORATED MILK

1 TBSP. MAPLE FLAVORING

Mix all together; chill and form into balls. Chill balls, then dip into chocolate with toothpick. Cool. When dry, fill toothpick holes with a small swirl of chocolate.

Chocolate-dipped jellies

SEVERAL JARS OF FIRM JELLY — DIFFERENT FLAVORS

CHOCOLATE TO DIP

Slice several kinds of jelly into ¼-inch cubes. Place on waxed paper-lined cookie sheet, sprinkled with cornstarch. Place cubes so they are in a single layer, not touching. Let cubes air dry until tacky and partially dried. Place in freezer and freeze. Remove from freezer and dip in chocolate. When chocolate is set, fill toothpick holes with swirl of chocolate. Keep covered and chilled.

Chocolate-dipped dried fruit

SEVERAL VARIETIES OF DEHYDRATED FRUIT (SUGAR-COATED DRY PINEAPPLE PIECES WORK NICELY, AS WELL AS DEHYDRATED SWEET CHERRIES, PIECES OF APRICOT, STRAWBERRY SLICES, ETC.)

DIPPING CHOCOLATE

Dip dried fruit in chocolate and place on a waxed paper-lined cookie sheet to cool. Fill toothpick hole in chocolate with a swirl of chocolate.

Peppermint patties

1 CAN (14 OZ.) SWEETENED CONDENSED MILK

1 TBSP. PEPPERMINT EXTRACT

RED OR GREEN FOOD COLORING

6 CUPS POWDERED SUGAR

ADDITIONAL POWDERED SUGAR

1½ LBS. CHOCOLATE ALMOND BARK, MELTED, OR DIPPING CHOCOLATE

In a large mixer bowl, combine sweetened condensed milk, extract, and food coloring. Add 6 cups sugar; beat on low speed until smooth and well blended.

Turn mixture onto surface well sprinkled with powdered sugar. Knead until pliable then roll into ¾-inch balls. Place 2 inches apart on waxed paper-lined cookie sheets. Flatten each ball into an 1½-inch patty with a glass dipped in powdered sugar. Let dry one hour or longer.

Turn over and let dry at least one hour. With fork, dip each patty into warm candy coating (draw fork lightly across rim of pan to remove excess coating). Invert onto waxed paper-lined baking sheets. Let stand until firm. Store covered at room temperature or in refrigerator.

Dipping other foods

You can also dip large nuts, such as Brazil nuts or filberts, in chocolate, using a fork to hold the nut during dipping. Peanuts, cashews, and pecans can also be coated with chocolate, although it's generally best to arrange several together on a piece of waxed paper on a cookie sheet and spoon the melted chocolate over them, making cluster candies.

Fruit-flavored small gumdrops are great dipped in chocolate; you can even use pieces of orange slice candy.

Other items, such as various shaped pretzels, cookies, (such as smaller shortbreads or spritzes) or even fudge (cool very cold first) may also be dipped in chocolate.

Haystacks (Chow mein noodles covered in chocolate)

This is a very easy "candy" to make, and it only takes a few minutes to make a bunch. Just mix a package of chow mein noodles into 1 bag of melted semisweet chocolate chips and spoon out onto a waxed paper-lined cookie sheet and let dry. You can vary this recipe by adding your choice of nutmeats and/or raisins.

Cream cheese mints

- 2½ CUPS POWDERED SUGAR
- 4 OZ. CREAM CHEESE OR 1 CUP FRESH CREAM CHEESE
- 1-2 DROPS OF MINT EXTRACT

Mix all of the above well, then shape into balls the size of marbles. Roll in sugar and press into molds or flatten slightly. Keep covered and cool until served.

Taffy

- 1 CUP SUGAR
- ½ TBSP. CORNSTARCH
- ⅔ CUP CORN SYRUP
- 1 TBSP. BUTTER
- ½ CUP WATER
- ½ TSP. SALT
- FLAVORINGS (LEMON, ORANGE, PEPPERMINT, CHERRY, PINEAPPLE, ETC.)

Combine sugar and cornstarch into a saucepan, and add corn syrup, butter, and water. Stir until boiling point is reached, and boil until mixture reaches 256° F or until a small portion forms a ball when tested in cold water. Add salt, pour onto a greased slab and allow to cool slightly until the mixture can be handled. Divide into separate portions, and color and flavor each portion as desired, while it is being pulled. Coat hands with butter or cornstarch to prevent sticking. Pull out and fold over. Repeat until light in color.

Lemon, orange, peppermint, lime, strawberry, or pineapple flavors may be used, and pink, green, yellow, or orange color pastes. (Don't use too much color — the candies are usually quite pale and pastel in tint.)

Roll into cylinders, then cut into pieces with buttered kitchen scissors. If you plan on keeping the taffy a while before eating, wrap each piece in waxed paper or plastic wrap to keep it from getting sticky.

Old-fashioned molasses taffy

 2 CUPS MOLASSES
 1 CUP SUGAR
 2 TBSP. BUTTER
 1 TBSP. VINEGAR
 ¼ TSP. SALT

Combine ingredients in a 3-quart heavy saucepan. Stir with a wooden spoon until sugar is dissolved; bring to a boil over medium heat, stirring frequently. Continue to cook to the hard ball stage (260° F).

Pour taffy into a large (about 13x9x2-inch) buttered and chilled shallow pan or platter (do not scrape cooking pan). Turn edges to center with heavy spatula.

When candy is cool enough to handle, pull taffy with buttered hands until taffy is light in color and hard to pull. Roll into cylinders. Cut in bite-size pieces with buttered scissors. Cool, then wrap pieces individually in waxed paper; store in airtight containers.

Divinity

 2 CUPS SUGAR
 ½ CUP LIGHT CORN SYRUP
 ½ CUP WATER
 PINCH SALT
 2 EGG WHITES
 1 TSP. VANILLA
 ½ CUP CHOPPED WALNUTS (MAY ALSO USE BRAZIL NUTS, BLACK WALNUTS, PISTACHIOS, OR CANDIED RED CHERRIES INSTEAD OF WALNUTS)

Combine sugar, syrup, water, and salt in a heavy, large saucepan over low heat. Stir until sugar is dissolved. Then cook without stirring to 252° F (very firm ball). Just before syrup reaches 252° F, beat egg whites until stiff but not dry. Wipe crystals from the pouring edge of the pan with a damp cloth. Pour syrup in a very fine stream over the egg whites, beating constantly while pouring. Do not scrape bottom of pan. Continue beating until the mixture holds its shape. Add vanilla and nuts. Drop quickly from the tip of a spoon onto waxed paper in individual peaks. Cool. Divinity does not last well, so make and serve fresh.

Nougat

 1 CUP SUGAR
 ½ CUP WATER
 3 TBSP. LIGHT CORN SYRUP
 ½ CUP HONEY
 2 EGG WHITES
 ¼ TSP. SALT
 1 CUP ALMONDS, BLANCHED AND TOASTED OR WALNUTS, CHOPPED
 ¾ CUP PISTACHIO NUTS, CHOPPED

    ½ CUP CANDIED CHERRIES, CHOPPED
    1 TSP. VANILLA

    Combine sugar, water, corn syrup, and honey in top of double boiler, placing it directly over low heat; stir until sugar is dissolved. Cook without stirring to 290° F (brittle). Just before the syrup reaches 290° F, beat the egg whites with the salt until stiff but not dry. Remove syrup from heat. In a very fine stream, pour syrup over egg whites, beating constantly with beater. Beat 2 minutes after all the syrup has been added. Fold in nuts, cherries, and vanilla. Return to top of double boiler; place over water and cook, stirring constantly, until mixture dries, about 20-30 minutes. The candy is done when a small amount, taken out on a spoon and allowed to cool, holds its shape nicely and is not sticky to the touch.

    Pack into buttered square pan and allow to stand 24 hours. Remove from pan and cut into square pieces with a sharp knife. Wrap the pieces in waxed paper or dip in chocolate.

Vanilla caramels

    1 CUP SUGAR
    1 CUP LIGHT CORN SYRUP
    1 CUP LIGHT CREAM
    ¼ TSP. SALT
    2 TBSP. BUTTER
    6 TBSP. EVAPORATED MILK (MAY USE HOME CANNED MILK)
    2 TSP. VANILLA

    Combine sugar, corn syrup, cream, and salt in a heavy saucepan. Place over low heat and stir until sugar is dissolved. Cook to 232° F (very soft ball), stirring occasionally. Add butter and evaporated milk alternately. Continue cooking, stirring constantly to prevent scorching. Cook to 242 to 244° F. Test frequently by dropping bits in cold water to determine the consistency desired in finished caramels. Remove from heat and add vanilla, stirring only enough to blend. Pour in one end of a buttered 8x8-inch square pan and tip pan to let caramel syrup flow evenly across pan to an even depth. Do *not* scrape bottom of saucepan, as it will cause caramels to become lumpy and grainy. (Just eat it!)

    When caramels are firm, cut with a sharp knife into 1-inch squares and wrap in waxed paper or plastic wrap. You may also dip caramels in chocolate, if desired.

    For nut caramels, just add ½ cup chopped walnuts or other nuts before pouring into pan. Black walnuts make especially good caramels.

Caramel nut roll

    With buttered hands, shape cooled caramels into a long roll about 1½-inches thick. Roll in chopped nuts. Cool. Cut into ½-inch slices, if you wish.

Maple pecan pralines

    1½ CUPS BROWN SUGAR, FIRMLY PACKED
    ¾ CUP MAPLE SYRUP
    1 CUP MILK (MAY USE RECONSTITUTED POWDERED MILK)
    2 TBSP. BUTTER OR MARGARINE
    1 CUP PECANS

Combine sugar, syrup, and milk in a heavy saucepan. Place over low heat and stir until sugar is dissolved. Cook to 230° F (very soft ball). Add butter and cook to 236° F (soft ball), stirring occasionally to prevent scorching.

Remove from heat and let stand five minutes without stirring. Add nuts and stir until slightly thick and syrup begins to look cloudy. Drop from a tablespoon in patties on a waxed paper-lined cookie sheet. Let stand until cold.

For hickory nut pralines, decrease maple syrup to ¼ cup and substitute chopped hickory nuts for pecans.

Peanut butter cups

    2 CUPS POWDERED SUGAR, SIFTED
    1 CUP PEANUT BUTTER
    ¾ CUP GRAHAM CRACKER CRUMBS, FINE
    ½ CUP BUTTER OR MARGARINE, SOFTENED
    CHOCOLATE ALMOND BARK

Combine powdered sugar, peanut butter, graham cracker crumbs, and butter. Mix well. Chill for 1 hour. Roll into ¾-inch balls. Melt chocolate almond bark. Dip balls into chocolate and place on waxed paper to set. Or place a small amount of chocolate (1 tsp.) in bottom of a paper candy cup. Add peanut butter ball, flattened, and coat top with chocolate spooned on.

Easy peanut butter candy

    1 CUP PEANUT BUTTER
    1 CUP CORN SYRUP
    1¼ CUPS POWDERED MILK
    1¼ CUPS POWDERED SUGAR

Mix all of the above ingredients very well. Roll into 1-inch balls, chill, and eat. Very easy, quick, and tasty, too!

Peanut brittle

    3 CUPS SUGAR
    1½ CUPS LIGHT CORN SYRUP
    1 CUP PLUS 2 TBSP. WATER
    ¼ CUP BUTTER
    1 LB. (3 CUPS) PEANUTS
    1½ TSP. BAKING SODA

Mix sugar, syrup, and water together in a heavy, large saucepan. Bring to a boil over medium heat. Cook to 230° F; add butter. Cook to 280° F, stirring occasionally. Add peanuts at 280° F. Stir constantly until mixture reaches 305° F (hard crack). Remove from heat. Quickly stir in baking soda and pour on 2 well-buttered cookie sheets. Using 2 forks or your buttered hands, begin stretching the brittle as it cools, working from the edges to center. This makes a very thin candy that is easy to chew, instead of a thick very hard candy. Cool and break into medium-sized pieces.

Apricot yum-yums

½ CUP DRIED APRICOTS
½ CUP GROUND NUTS (BRAZIL NUTS, HAZELNUTS, FILBERTS, ETC.)
½ CUP SHREDDED COCONUT
2 TBSP. CANDIED ORANGE PEEL, CHOPPED FINELY OR GROUND
ORANGE JUICE

Mix above ingredients well and moisten with a little orange juice. Shape into small balls and roll in powdered sugar. You may also dip these in chocolate for an extra treat.

Old-fashioned popcorn balls

5 QUARTS POPPED CORN
2 CUPS WHITE SUGAR
1 CUP LIGHT CORN SYRUP
½ CUP BUTTER
¼ CUP WATER
SALT TO TASTE
1 TSP. VANILLA EXTRACT
1 TSP. DISTILLED WHITE VINEGAR (OPTIONAL)

Make popcorn; shake to dip out fluffiest popcorn. In a saucepan over medium heat, combine the sugar, corn syrup, butter, and water. Stir and heat to hard-crack stage or 300° F. Remove from heat, add vanilla, salt, and vinegar; mix well.

Pour slowly over popped popcorn while stirring. Wait 5 minutes and shape into 3-inch round balls.

Caramel corn

    2 CUPS BROWN SUGAR, FIRMLY PACKED
    1 CUP BUTTER OR MARGARINE
    ½ CUP LIGHT CORN SYRUP
    1 TSP. SALT
    ½ TSP. BAKING SODA
    1 TSP. VANILLA
    7 QUARTS POPPED CORN
    ½ CUP SALTED PEANUTS (IF DESIRED)

Combine sugar, butter, corn syrup, and salt together in a heavy saucepan and bring to a boil. Boil 5 minutes, stirring occasionally to prevent scorching. Remove from heat and add baking soda and vanilla. Pour over popped corn in large, shallow container. If adding peanuts, add while you first stir the syrup and popcorn together so they are evenly distributed. Stir well. Put on pans and bake at 250° F for 1 hour, stirring every 30 minutes. Cool and break apart.

Spiced nuts

    1 EGG WHITE
    1 TBSP. WATER
    ¼ TSP. SALT
    ½ TSP. CINNAMON
    ½ CUP SUGAR
    1 QUART PECANS OR WALNUTS

Beat egg white until frothy, then add water, salt, cinnamon, and sugar. Mix well, then stir in nuts. Pour out onto a cookie sheet and bake at 250° F for 1 hour, stirring several times during baking.

Basic pantry mixes

There are many more homemade mixes that you can mix and use, but these are the ones that I find most useful in my day-to-day cooking, especially when I am very busy and need to slap together a tasty, filling meal.

Biscuit mix (also used for cobblers, dumplings, etc.)

8½ CUPS FLOUR
1½ CUPS DEHYDRATED SHORTENING
¾ CUP POWDERED MILK
¼ CUP BAKING POWDER
1 TBSP. SALT
2 TSP. CREAM OF TARTAR (DON'T OMIT)
1 TSP. BAKING SODA

Mix all ingredients very well and store in an airtight container. To make biscuits, mix ½ cup water (or a little more, if needed) to 2 cups biscuit mix. Stir well and turn out on lightly-floured surface. Roll ball out to ½-inch thick and cut biscuits with biscuit cutter (I use a regular canning jar ring). Place on lightly-greased cookie sheet, about 1 inch apart. Bake at 375° F until golden; about 10-15 minutes.

Biscuit mix (using regular shortening)

10 CUPS FLOUR
2 CUPS POWDERED MILK
10 TBSP. BAKING POWDER
2 TSP. SALT
2 CUPS VEGETABLE SHORTENING

Only use this if you make biscuits frequently, since the shortening can turn the mix rancid after a few weeks of storage at room temperature.

Mix ingredients until shortening is very well cut into dry ingredients. To use, mix 2 cups biscuit mix with about 1 cup water and knead into a smooth ball. Stir well and turn out on lightly-floured surface. Roll ball out to ½-inch thick and cut biscuits with biscuit cutter (I use a regular canning jar ring). Place on lightly-greased cookie sheet, about 1 inch apart. Bake at 375° F until golden; about 10-15 minutes.

Cornbread mix (complete)

- 5 cups flour
- 5 cups cornmeal
- 1 cup sugar
- 1⅓ cups dehydrated margarine or butter
- ¼ cup powdered milk
- ½ cup dehydrated egg
- ⅓ cup baking powder
- 2½ tsp. salt

To use this mix, add 1 cup of water, or a bit more, to 3 cups mix. Pour into a lightly-greased 8x8-inch pan and bake at 350° F for about 20 minutes or until top is just browning. Let cool a few minutes before taking out of pan.

Cornbread mix

- 4 cups flour
- 4½ cups cornmeal
- ⅔ cup sugar
- ¼ cup baking powder
- 2 cups powdered milk
- 1 Tbsp. salt

To use, combine 2½ cups mix with 1 egg, 1 cup water, and 2 Tbsp. vegetable oil. Pour into a lightly-greased 8x8-inch pan and bake at 350° F for about 20 minutes or until top is just browning. Let cool a few minutes before taking out of pan.

Muffin mix

- 8 cups flour
- 2½ cups sugar
- 1¼ cups dehydrated shortening*
- ½ cup powdered milk
- ⅓ cup baking powder
- 1½ tsp. salt

*If you don't have dehydrated shortening, omit and add ½ cup shortening, cut into 2½ cups dry ingredients when you want to make muffins.

To make muffins, combine 3⅛ cup muffin mix with 1 egg and enough water to make 2 cups of liquid. Spoon into lightly-greased muffin tins, filling about half full. Bake at 400° F until tops are just golden. Let stand a few minutes before removing from pans.

Pancake and waffle mix (complete)

- 8 cups flour
- ¾ cup dehydrated shortening

¾ cup powdered milk

¾ cup sugar

⅔ cup dehydrated whole eggs

⅓ cup baking powder

1 Tbsp. salt

To use, combine 1 cup mix with 1 cup water. Let rest a minute, then heat the griddle and lightly grease. Heat the griddle enough to make a drop of water skitter when it hits the pan. Pour mix out onto griddle; I use a smaller ladle and all of my pancakes are just about the right size. Bake until many bubbles form on pancakes and edges show golden brown. Turn pancakes and bake the other side. Remove from griddle onto a plate and keep warm while the rest of the pancakes are baked. Wipe the griddle with a lightly-greased piece of cloth and repeat baking until all pancakes are finished.

Pancake mix

12 cups flour

4 cups powdered milk

1 cup baking powder

1 cup sugar

1 Tbsp. salt

To use, mix 1 egg, 3 Tbsp. vegetable oil, and 1 cup water in with 2 cups mix. Mix well and let rest a minute and use.

To make pancakes, heat the griddle and lightly grease. Heat the griddle enough to make a drop of water skitter when dropped on it. Pour mix out onto griddle; I use a smaller ladle and all of my pancakes are just about the right size. Bake until many bubbles form on pancakes and edges show golden brown. Turn pancakes and bake the other side. Remove from griddle onto a plate and keep warm while the rest of the pancakes are baked. Wipe the griddle with a lightly-greased piece of cloth and repeat baking until all pancakes are finished.

Fruit crisp topping mix

5 cups rolled oats

5 cups packed brown sugar

5 cups flour

2 tsp. cinnamon

1½ tsp. baking powder

1½ tsp. baking soda

½ tsp. salt

Combine and store in an airtight container. To make fruit crisp, place fruit (pie filling) in bottom of 8x8-inch baking pan. Cut ¼ cup butter into 1 cup mix and sprinkle on top of fruit. Bake at 350° F for 30 minutes. Or sprinkle over muffin tops or pies.

Country gravy mix

- 6 cups flour
- 4 cups powdered milk
- 1½ cups dehydrated butter or margarine
- ¾ cup beef soup base (powdered)
- ½ cup dehydrated onions (chopped or powdered)
- 1½ tsp. ground sage
- 1½ tsp. ground thyme
- 1 tsp. black pepper

To use, combine 3 cups hot water with 1 cup of mix, stirring constantly, bring to a boil until thickened. You may also substitute chicken soup base for the beef for a quick gravy to use with leftover chicken or turkey chunks.

Cheese sauce mix

- 4½ cups cheese powder
- 2⅔ cups powdered milk
- 2⅔ cups dehydrated butter or margarine
- 2⅔ cups flour
- 2 tsp. onion powder

Mix 1 cup hot water with ½ cup mix, bring to a boil, stirring constantly. You can use this with pasta for macaroni and cheese, over nachos, as a sauce over asparagus, broccoli, or cauliflower, or as a baked potato topping.

White sauce mix

- 4 cups powdered milk
- 4 cups flour
- 4 cups dehydrated margarine or butter
- 2 tsp. salt

Mix ½ cup mix with 1 cup hot water, add salt and/or pepper (if desired), bring to a boil in a sauce pan, stirring constantly, until thickened.

Casserole sauce mix

- 4 cups powdered milk
- 1½ cups cornstarch
- ½ cup chicken or beef bouillon powder
- 1 tsp. dried, crushed thyme
- 1 tsp. dried, crushed basil
- ½ tsp. pepper

Mix all ingredients very well. To use, combine ⅓ cup dry mix and 1 cup water in saucepan and cook, stirring constantly, until thickened. Use in casserole or "cream of" soups.

Mom's homemade Shake 'n Bake twin

    1 CUP FLOUR
    1 CUP CORNMEAL
    2 TSP. SALT
    1 TSP. GARLIC POWDER
    ¼ TSP. BLACK PEPPER
    ¼ TSP. RED PEPPER

Mix well. Dampen meat (pork, chicken, fish) with water. Place mix in a large plastic bag or in a large bowl. Place meat in mix and thoroughly coat with dry mix. Place in a shallow pan and bake at 350° F until meat is tender.

El's homemade Shake 'n Bake

    4 CUPS FLOUR
    4 CUPS GROUND INEXPENSIVE CRACKERS
    4 TBSP. SALT
    2 TBSP. SUGAR
    2 TSP. GARLIC POWDER
    2 TSP. ONION POWDER
    3 TBSP. PAPRIKA
    ¼ CUP VEGETABLE OIL

Mix all of the above together well and store in an airtight container until needed. Use only what you need; this makes several "batches."

Hot chocolate mix (large batch)

    12 CUPS POWDERED MILK
    3 CUPS NON-DAIRY COFFEE CREAMER
    4 CUPS POWDERED SUGAR
    2½ CUPS UNSWEETENED COCOA POWDER

To use, mix 3 Tbsp. in 1 cup very hot water; stir well and add mini-marshmallows, if you wish.

Hot chocolate mix (small batch)

    4 CUPS POWDERED MILK
    1 CUP UNSWEETENED COCOA POWDER
    2½ CUPS POWDERED SUGAR
    ½ TSP. SALT

Mix ¼ cup mix with 1 cup boiling water and add mini-marshmallows and whipped cream.

Miscellaneous handy recipes

Eggnog

    4 eggs, beaten
    ⅓ cup sugar
    ⅛ tsp. nutmeg
    2 tsp. vanilla
    ⅛ tsp. salt
    ½ cup very cold cream
    4 cups milk

Add all of these to a mixing bowl and beat until smooth. Serve cold.

Marshmallow cream

    2 cups sugar
    2½ cups light corn syrup, divided
    1 cup water
    ⅞ cup egg whites
    1 tsp. vanilla

In a heavy saucepan, cook sugar, 2 cups corn syrup, and water to 240° F.
In a large mixing bowl, beat egg whites and ½ cup corn syrup until light and fluffy.
Slowly add hot syrup while beating. When mixed beat hard for 3 minutes. Add vanilla. Use in any recipe you wish.

Cream cheese ball

    2 pkgs. (8 oz. each) cream cheese
    1 cup bacon bits (TVPs)
    1 Tbsp. dehydrated onion powder
    2 tsp. seasoning salt
    ½ cup chopped walnuts or pecans, salted

Soften cream cheese. Mix with bacon bits, onion powder, and seasoning salt. Blend well. Form into a ball with buttered hands and roll in chopped nuts. Chill and serve with crackers.

Sweet fruit dip

    1 cup mayonnaise
    ½ cup sugar
    2 Tbsp. lemon juice
    ½ cup softened cream cheese

Mix all ingredients together until smooth. Put in covered bowl and refrigerate until use.

Hot and spicy seasoning (no salt)

    2 Tbsp. savory, crushed
    1 Tbsp. dry mustard
    1 Tbsp. onion powder
    1 Tbsp. curry powder
    1 Tbsp. chile powder (as hot as you like)
    1 Tbsp. garlic powder

Combine all ingredients and mix well. Pour into a large shaker for table use.

Kelly's to-die-for fresh salsa

    2½ cups tomatoes, chopped
    ½ cup onions, chopped
    ½ cup finely chopped green pepper
    3 jalapeño peppers, seeded and chopped
    2 Tbsp. sugar
    1 can (15 oz.) diced tomatoes or 1 pint home canned diced tomatoes
    1 clove garlic, minced
    1 Tbsp. vinegar
    1 Tbsp. lemon juice
    1 can (8 oz.) tomato sauce or ½-pint home canned tomato sauce
    2 Tbsp. vegetable oil
    ½ tsp. oregano
    1 tsp. fresh cilantro

Mix together and refrigerate, covered, until serving.

Whipped topping from powdered milk

    ½ cup powdered milk
    ½ cup cold water
    2 Tbsp. lemon juice
    ½ cup sugar
    1 tsp. vanilla

Beat milk and cold water together in a mixing bowl and beat until peaks form. Add lemon juice and beat 3-4 minutes. Add sugar gradually, while beating, then add vanilla. Beat well and serve.

Salad dressings — ready made

Homemade Miracle Whip twin

    1 EGG
    ⅔ CUP SUGAR
    ¾ CUP VEGETABLE OIL
    1 TBSP. LEMON JUICE
    2 TSP. SALT
    ½ TSP. DRY MUSTARD
    ⅓ CUP CORNSTARCH
    ½ CUP VINEGAR
    1¼ CUPS HOT WATER

Mix first 6 ingredients very well. In a heavy saucepan, cook cornstarch and vinegar until thickened. Add hot water. Bring to a boil. Boil until thick and clear, then blend into other ingredients. Beat hard until smooth. Refrigerate in a sealed jar until use.

Homemade mayonnaise

    ¼ TSP. PAPRIKA
    ½ TSP. DRY MUSTARD
    1 TSP. SALT
    2 EGG YOLKS
    1 TBSP. VINEGAR
    2 CUPS VEGETABLE OIL
    2 TBSP. LEMON JUICE

Combine dry ingredients in a small mixing bowl. Add egg yolks and vinegar; beat until smooth. Add oil slowly, alternating with lemon juice. Beat constantly during next 3 additions. Refrigerate in a sealed jar. Will keep for several weeks.

Mrs. Troxler's salad dressing

    2 HEAPING TBSP. FLOUR
    2 TSP. SALT
    2 TSP. DRY MUSTARD
    1 CUP SUGAR
    2 CUPS WATER
    1 CUP VINEGAR
    2 EGGS

Mix dry ingredients together in a small bowl. In a larger bowl mix liquid ingredients, including beaten eggs, together in heavy saucepan and bring to near boiling. Slowly mix in dry ingredients with wire whisk until smooth and thickened. Cool and store in a sealed jar in the refrigerator until use.

No-cook mayonnaise

    1 egg
    1 cup vegetable oil
    2 Tbsp. vinegar
    ½ tsp. dry mustard
    1 tsp. salt

Beat egg and salt together. Slowly add vegetable oil, a little at a time, beating constantly. Then add vinegar, mustard, and salt, beating well. Refrigerate in a sealed jar until use.

French dressing

    1 cup sugar
    ½ cup vegetable oil
    ½ cup salad dressing or mayonnaise
    ½ cup catsup
    ¼ cup vinegar
    1 Tbsp. onion, chopped very finely
    ½ tsp. paprika
    Worcestershire sauce
    1 tsp. salt

Beat all ingredients together thoroughly and store in a refrigerated, covered jar until use. Shake well before use.

Creamy Italian dressing

    1 cup mayonnaise
    ½ tsp. onion powder
    1 tsp. garlic powder
    ½ tsp. oregano
    ½ tsp. basil
    1 Tbsp. sugar
    2 Tbsp. vinegar

Mix well and refrigerate several hours in a sealed jar before serving. Shake well before serving.

Sweet Italian dressing

    ½ cup vinegar
    ½ cup salad oil
    ¼ cup sugar
    1 clove garlic, crushed
    1 tsp. dry oregano
    1 tsp. crushed basil

Mix well and allow to blend, then shake before serving.

Chunky blue cheese dressing

- ½ cup sour cream (may use reconstituted powdered sour cream)
- ½ cup mayonnaise
- 1 Tbsp. lemon juice
- 1 Tbsp. vinegar
- 2 oz. crumbled blue cheese

Mix sour cream, mayonnaise, lemon juice, and vinegar very well until smooth and creamy. Crumble blue cheese into dressing and stir in. Refrigerate several hours or longer in sealed jar.

Ranch salad dressing

- ¼ cup milk or buttermilk (may use reconstituted powdered milk or buttermilk)
- ½ cup sour cream
- 1 cup mayonnaise
- 1 tsp. garlic powder
- 1 tsp. dill weed
- 1 Tbsp. parsley
- 1 tsp. onion powder

Mix milk and sour cream together until smooth and creamy. Add other ingredients and mix well. Refrigerate in a sealed jar for several hours before use.

Creamy garlic dressing

- ½ cup light cream
- 1 quart mayonnaise or salad dressing
- 3 finely chopped garlic cloves
- ½ tsp. salt

Mix cream and mayonnaise or salad dressing together until light and smooth. Add garlic cloves and salt. Mix well. Store in a sealed jar in the refrigerator for several hours (or days) until use.

Coleslaw dressing

- 1 cup mayonnaise
- ⅓ cup vinegar
- ½ cup sugar
- 1 Tbsp. celery seed
- ½ tsp. onion powder

Mix well and pour over shredded cabbage in mixing bowl. Mix well, cover, and refrigerate until use. Overnight is best.

Citrus salad dressing

　　2 eggs, beaten
　　1 cup orange juice
　　½ cup heavy cream, whipped
　　2 Tbsp. cornstarch
　　1 cup sugar
　　juice of 2 lemons or 2-3 Tbsp. bottled lemon juice

Combine first five ingredients in a heavy saucepan. Bring to a boil, stirring as it thickens. Cool. This is a nice dressing for fruit pieces and sweetened whipped cream.

Salad dressing — dry mixes

You can also make several salad dressing mixes, like you buy at the store, right from your pantry, to use as you need. They are so convenient to have handy! And they require no refrigeration.

Basic salad dressing mix

　　3 cups sugar
　　1½ cups powdered milk or powdered buttermilk
　　¼ cup onion powder
　　2 Tbsp. dry mustard
　　2 Tbsp. salt
　　2 Tbsp. garlic powder
　　2 Tbsp. celery salt

Mix well and keep in a sealed jar on your pantry shelf. To use, simply mix ½ cup of the mix with ½ cup water and ⅓ cup vinegar. While beating, gradually add ¾ cup of vegetable oil.

To make this into Thousand Island dressing, simply add ½ cup barbecue sauce and 1 Tbsp. chopped sweet pickle relish, thinning with relish juice to reach desired consistency. You may also add chopped hard-boiled egg if you wish.

Ranch dressing mix

　　1 cup powdered milk or powdered buttermilk
　　6 Tbsp. onion powder
　　3 Tbsp. garlic powder
　　3 Tbsp. parsley (rubbed)

To use this mix in a salad dressing, combine 3 Tbsp. of the mix with ½ cup mayonnaise and ½ cup buttermilk (may use reconstituted powdered buttermilk). Add just enough buttermilk, in addition, to thin as you wish. To use as a ranch dip, mix 3 Tbsp. mix with ¾ cup sour cream and ¼ cup buttermilk (may use reconstituted powdered buttermilk).

French dressing mix

    1½ cups sugar
    ½ cup cheese powder
    2 Tbsp. dry mustard
    1 Tbsp. onion powder
    1 tsp. garlic powder
    ½ tsp. salt
    1 Tbsp. paprika
    1 Tbsp. celery salt
    ½ tsp. black pepper

To use, mix ¾ cup mix with ¾ cup vinegar, ¼ cup water, and 1½ cups vegetable oil while mixing constantly. Add 1 cup tomato sauce or catsup. Blend well and store in a sealed jar in the refrigerator until use. Stores several weeks.

Sauces

Nacho sauce

    1 cup powdered cheese
    2 Tbsp. chopped, sliced jalapeños
    1 cup milk (or powdered milk, reconstituted) or enough to make a thick cheese sauce
    1 tsp. onion powder
    1 Tbsp. butter or margarine

Mix powdered cheese with enough milk to make a thick, but pourable, cheese sauce. In a heavy saucepan, slowly heat, adding more milk to keep proper consistency. When very warm, not boiling, add onion powder and butter. Stir while heating a little more. When hot, remove from heat and add chopped jalapeños (more or less to suit your taste). Serve with deep-fried corn tortillas or tortilla chips.

Horseradish sauce

    1 cup mayonnaise
    ½ cup sour cream
    ¾ Tbsp. horseradish (best if not fresh but refrigerated in vinegar)

Combine all until well mixed. Store in a sealed jar, in the refrigerator.

Prepared mustard

    ½ cup dry mustard
    ½ cup vinegar
    3 tsp. turmeric

Mix together until smooth and put in in a small, sealed jar until use.

Horseradish vinegar

>SEVERAL FRESH, LARGE HORSERADISH ROOTS
>
>VINEGAR
>
>SALT (OPTIONAL)

Scrub and trim the horseradish roots. Peel them, then grate finely. (Do it outside, as it *is* powerful stuff! It's good for the sinuses!) A blender is best, covered, of course. Put in mixing bowl, add salt if you wish, and add just enough vinegar to cover. Pack into half-pint, wide mouth jars and keep sealed, in refrigerator, until use. This keeps for months.

Tartar sauce

>½ CUP MAYONNAISE
>
>2 TBSP. DILL PICKLE, FINELY CHOPPED
>
>2 TBSP. GREEN ONION, FINELY CHOPPED
>
>2 TSP. LEMON JUICE

Mix all ingredients together until well blended. Store in a sealed jar in the refrigerator until use.

Seafood cocktail sauce

>½ CUP CATSUP
>
>2 TBSP. HORSERADISH IN VINEGAR
>
>1 TSP. WORCESTERSHIRE SAUCE

Mix all of the above until well blended. Store in a sealed jar, in the refrigerator, until needed.

Honey mustard sauce

>¼ CUP MAYONNAISE
>
>¼ CUP PREPARED MUSTARD
>
>3 TBSP. HONEY
>
>2 TSP. BROWN SUGAR

Mix all ingredients well and store in a sealed jar in the refrigerator until used.

Whole berry cranberry sauce

>4 CUPS FRESH CRANBERRIES
>
>2 CUPS WATER
>
>2 CUPS SUGAR

Wash and sort berries, removing any stems. In a large pot, mix sugar and water and bring to a boil. Boil until sugar is dissolved. Add cranberries. Boil until skins pop. Ladle hot sauce into hot, sterilized jars, leaving ¼-inch headroom. Wipe top of jars and place hot, previously simmered lid on jar and screw down ring firmly tight. Process in a boiling water bath canner for 10 minutes. If you live at an altitude above 1,000 feet, consult your canning book for directions on increasing your processing time to suit your altitude, if necessary.

Jellied cranberry sauce

4½ CUPS FRESH CRANBERRIES
2 CUPS WATER
2½ CUPS SUGAR

Wash and sort berries, removing any stems. Place in a large pot with water and boil until skins pop. Press through a sieve. Add sugar to pulp and juice. Place back in kettle and slowly bring to a boil. Stir frequently. Bring almost to the jelling point (when a small amount of sauce slides from the spoon in a sheet instead of drops. Ladle hot sauce into hot, sterilized jars, leaving ¼-inch headroom. Wipe top of jars and place hot, previously-simmered lid on jar and screw down ring firmly tight. Process in a boiling water bath canner for 10 minutes. If you live at an altitude above 1,000 feet, consult your canning book for directions on increasing your processing time to suit your altitude, if necessary.

Index

A

Ada's finger rolls 111
Almond butter cookies 238
Almond poppy seed bars 226
Anna's favorite applesauce cake 193
Apple bars 228
Apple blackberry pie 166
Apple bread 132
Apple butter bars 231
Apple cake with lemon sauce 196
Apple cake with warm sauce 198
Apple cobbler 209
Apple dumplings 165
Apple pancakes 145
Apple pecan pie 166
Apple snow 214
Apricot baked squash 80
Apricot bars 232
Apricot yum-yums 261
Asparagus popovers 82
Asparagus quiche 154
Asparagus with sesame seeds 81
Aunt Hannah's gingerbread 211

B

Bagels 131
Baked cauliflower 86
Baked ham 34
Baked Indian pudding 220
Baked lemon pudding 213
Baked lima beans and ham 75
Baked mashed potatoes 68
Baked peach pancake 143
Baked pork chops or steak 31
Baked spaghetti squash 80
Baked Spanish rice 57
Baked squash with brown sugar 80
Baked stuffed fish 46
Baked sweet potatoes with apples and raisins 88
Baking powder biscuits 104
Banana cream pie 168
Banana nut bread 115
Barbecue beef on a bun 17
Barbecued pork 32
Basic buttercream frosting 199
Basic dipping chocolate 254
Basic salad dressing mix 273
Basic two-crust pie pastry 163
Basmati rice 101
Bean bake 72
Bean soup 65
Beef enchiladas 56
Beef stew 20
Beef stroganoff 21
Best baked cheesecake 183
Best buttermilk pancakes 144
Best date bars 221
Best ever lemon pie (and it is!) 172
Best ever spritz cookies 241
Billy goat cookies 243
Bird's nest cookies 242
Biscuit mix 263
Biscuit mix (using regular shortening) 263
Black walnut cake 195
Black walnut pie 180
Blueberry cheesecake glaze 184
Blueberry muffins 138
Boston baked beans 71
Bread pudding 217
Brown betty 217
Brownies 227
Brown rice 100
Brunswick stew 60
Buckwheat griddle cakes 144
Buffalo Bill's chili 59
Burritos 28
Butter braid 126
Buttercream frosting II 200
Buttered noodle ring 48
Butter horns (crescent rolls) 108
Buttermilk biscuits 104
Butter pecan bars 228
Butterscotch meringue squares 227

C

California fruit filling 204
Campfire-roasted corn on the cob 76
Candied carrots 70
Cantaloupe salad 92
Caramel cookies 246
Caramel corn 262
Caramel custard 214
Caramel nut roll 259
Carrot mushroom stir-fry 72
Carrot pudding 217
Casserole sauce mix 266
Cauliflower au gratin 86
Chapatis (Indian flatbread) 110
Cheddar cheese crackers 159

Cheese biscuits 105
Cheese cornmeal crackers 158
Cheese sauce mix 266
Cheesy potatoes 69
Cherry bars 226
Cherry cheesecake glaze 184
Cherry cobbler 206
Cherry filling 205
Cherry pie 167
Chicken and dumplings 42
Chicken cacciatore 42
Chicken cordon bleu 41
Chicken fried steak 22
Chicken noodle soup 66
Chicken (or turkey) and biscuits 52
Chicken or turkey pot pie 50
Chiffon cake (like an angel food cake) 187
Chile relleno bake 54
Chiles rellenos 88
Chimichangas 29
Chocolate brownies 232
Chocolate chip cookies 234
Chocolate-covered cherries 254
Chocolate cream cheese frosting 200
Chocolate custard filling 204
Chocolate diamond bars 230
Chocolate-dipped dried fruit 256
Chocolate-dipped jellies 255
Chocolate fudge II 250
Chocolate pie 170
Chocolate walnut bars 222
Christmas cutout cookies 244
Christmas cutout cookies II 244
Chunky blue cheese dressing 272
Cinnamon bread 122
Cinnamon caramel pecan rolls 136
Citrus frosting 201
Citrus salad dressing 273
Cleon's rolled oat cookies 236
Coconut frosting 202
Coconut nut balls 254
Cold cabbage salad 93
Coleslaw dressing 272
Color vision cake 191
Cornbread 106
Cornbread mix 264
Cornbread mix (complete) 264
Cornbread stuffing 37
Corn chips 160
Corn fritters 112
Cornmeal corn fritters 112
Cornmeal loaves 122

Cornmeal waffles 146
Corn pudding 76
Corn salsa 75
Corn tortillas 110
Cottage pudding 216
Country cauliflower 87
Country gravy mix 266
Country meatloaf 28
Cousin Jack's pasties 24
Crackers 158
Cranberry bread 115
Cranberry cream cheese pie 169
Cranberry muffins 139
Cranberry raisin pie 170
Cranberry salad 98
Cream cheese ball 268
Cream cheese frosting 200
Cream cheese mints 257
Creamed asparagus on toast 82
Creamed beans and potatoes 79
Creamed new potatoes 67
Creamed peas over tuna sandwiches 84
Creamy coleslaw 93
Creamy garlic dressing 272
Creamy Italian dressing 271
Creamy wild rice soup 62
Cuban-style black beans 74
Cucumber and onion sour cream salad 94
Curried eggs 151
Curried turkey with rice 40
Custard pie 170

D

Daffodil pudding 216
Date surprise cookies 241
Debbie's carrot cake 189
Deep-fried potato boats 70
Dessert waffles 147
Deviled eggs 152
Devil's float 214
Devil's food cake 194
Dilled barbecued turkey breast 40
Dilled corn and peas 75
Dinner rolls 107
Divinity 258
Do-it-yourself "Little Debbie" cookies 245
Double-quick dinner rolls 106
Down south pecan bars 229
Dried apple pie 165

E

Easy black walnut fudge 252
Easy breadsticks 132
Easy caramel frosting 202
Easy peanut butter candy 260
Easy potato rolls 108
Easy rhubarb upside-down cake 196
Egg casserole 153
Egg Fu Yung 156
Eggnog 268
Eggplant Parmigiana 90
Egg salad sandwich filling 152
Eggs a la goldenrod 153
El's homemade Shake 'n Bake 267
English muffins 129
Everyday waffles 146
EZ fudge frosting 202

F

Fancy chocolate logs 249
Farmstead potato salad 94
Filled cookies (from Jackie's great-grandmother Eliza Lilly) 239
Fish chowder 64
Five-fruit salad 97
Flaked fish in cream sauce 47
Flaky pastry for a one-crust pie 164
Flemish carrots 71
Floating island 212
Florence Bates' white cake 189
Flour tortillas 109
Fluffy white frosting 201
Foolproof omelet 152
French dressing 271
French dressing mix 274
French fries 69
French onion soup 63
Fresh blueberry cobbler 207
Fresh fruit salad 98
Fresh orange filling 204
Fresh rhubarb crisp 208
Fried chicken tenders 44
Fried green tomatoes 86
Frijoles con queso 72
Frosty snowberry cake 190
Fruit crisp topping mix 265
Fry-steamed cabbage 87

G

German pot roast 18
German Stollen 137

Gingersnaps 246
Glazed onions 77
Glazed parsnips 91
Glazed raisin bread 126
Glazed sweet potatoes 87
Graham cracker pie crust 164
Graham crackers 159
Graham gems (whole wheat muffins) 140
Graham pudding 218
Gram Richards' sweet potato salad 100
Grandma Eddy's butterscotch pie 168
Grandma Eddy's rhubarb pie 176
Grandma Eddy's sourdough starter 127
Grandma Rhead's spice layer cake 188
Grandma's chewy chocolate fudge 251
Grandma's light biscuits 105
Grandma's oatmeal bread 121
Great-Grandma Jones' layer cake 186
Great-Grandma Jones' lemon raisin pie 173
Green bean casserole 78
Green beans with tomatoes 80
Green tomato pie/mock apple pie 180
Griddle cakes 142
Grilled chicken salad 99
Grilled turkey breasts 38

H

Half-time spoon rolls 107
Ham loaf 35
Hard sauce (without alcohol) 216
Harvard beets 89
Hash brown potatoes 70
Hawaiian bars 223
Haystacks (Chow mein noodles covered in chocolate) 256
Hearty farm soup 60
Hearty potato soup 60
Herbed beef stew 20
Hickory nut cake 195
Hoe cakes 147
Homemade bread 119
Homemade "cream of" soups 63
Homemade mayonnaise 270
Homemade Miracle Whip twin 270
Homemade pizza 55
Homemade Rice-A-Roni 102
Honey almond filling 205
Honey graham crackers 160
Honey mustard sauce 275
Honey whole wheat bread 120
Horseradish sauce 274
Horseradish vinegar 275

Hot and spicy seasoning (no salt) 269
Hot Cha 58
Hot chocolate mix (large batch) 267
Hot chocolate mix (small batch) 267
Hot milk cake 187
Hummingbird cake 194
Hush puppies 111

I

Ice box cookies 238
Igloo cake 191
Indian fry bread 112
Iowa cornmeal pancakes 145
Italian vegetable soup 62

J

Jackie's baked beef stew 19
Jackie's famous apple pie 164
Jambalaya 52
Jam cheesecake glaze 183
Jasmine rice 101
Jellied cranberry sauce 276
Jelly thumbprint cookies 240
Jeri's no-knead bread 125
Just-right baked custard 212

K

Kelly's to-die-for fresh salsa 269
Key lime pie 171

L

Lane cake 198
Laredo pinto beans 73
Lasagna 51
Layered lettuce salad 94
Lemon almond bars 232
Lemon bread 116
Lemon cheese bars 230
Lemon custard pudding cake 210
Lemon filling 204
Lemon lush 224
Lemon meringue pie 172
Lemon pudding 213
Lottie's crumb cookies 236

M

Mandarin chicken salad 96
Maple cream chocolates 255
Maple fudge 253
Maple pecan pralines 260

Marinated fresh tomatoes 85
Marshmallow cream 268
Mashed potatoes 68
Meringue cradle cake (self-iced) 190
Midwest corn and bacon casserole 53
Mincemeat pie 174
Minestrone 65
Minnesota harvest bars 221
Molasses crinkles 237
Mom's best ever fruitcake 136
Mom's best-ever white bread 119
Mom's brown bread 117
Mom's butter tarts 181
Mom's chocolate nut donuts 149
Mom's glazed meatballs 25
Mom's homemade Shake 'n Bake twin 267
Mom's lemon/lime cottage cheese salad 97
Mom's muffins 138
Mom's orange glory rolls 135
Mom's pickled beets 90
Mrs. Lucas' buttercream frosting 200
Mrs. Troxler's cake 192
Mrs. Troxler's salad dressing 270
Muffin mix 264
Multigrain bread 124
Mushrooms over toast 83
Mustard pork medallions 30
My favorite bran muffins 140
My Grandma Eddy's pancakes 142

N

Nacho chips 160
Nacho sauce 274
New England clam chowder 64
New Mexico cowboy cookies 234
New Mexico peach pie 174
No-cook mayonnaise 271
No-fuss coconut cake 185
Noodle and ham casserole 49
Northwoods blueberry pie 168
Nougat 258
Nutty rhubarb muffins 139
Nutty white frosting 201

O

Oatmeal cookies 235
Oatmeal lace cookies 236
Oatmeal peanut butter chocolate chip scotchies 247
Oatmeal pie 174
Old English plum pudding 219
Old-fashioned baked macaroni and cheese 48

Old-fashioned berry shortcake (for raspberries, blackberries, etc.) 211
Old-fashioned cream of tomato soup 61
Old-fashioned molasses taffy 258
Old-fashioned peach pie 173
Old-fashioned popcorn balls 261
Old-fashioned pot roast 16
Old-fashioned rice pudding 215
Old-time chocolate fudge 250
Old-time Italian bread 125
Old-time succotash 76
Old Virginia pecan pie 174
Onion patties 77
Onion rings 76
Onions au gratin 78
Orange chocolate nut fudge 252
Orange date bread 116
Orange kiss-me cake 192
Oriental beef stir-fry 22
Oriental chicken salad 96
Oven-roasted canned turkey dinner 36
Oven-roasted potato wedges 67
Oven-roasted stuffed turkey 36
Oyster stew 64

P

Pancake and waffle mix (complete) 264
Pancake mix 265
Pan-fried fish 46
Pan-fried potatoes 68
Parmesan chicken 44
Parmesan peas 85
Pasta salad 103
Peach cobbler 207
Peach crumb 208
Peach-oat breakfast cake 133
Peach pound cake 193
Peanut brittle 260
Peanut butter balls 254
Peanut butter cookies 234
Peanut butter cups 260
Peanut butter fudge 252
Pea patties 84
Pecan caramel turtles 255
Pecan sandies 237
Peppered steaks 18
Peppermint patties 256
Pepper steak 19
Perfect white bread 118
Pineapple bars 230
Pineapple cookies 248
Pineapple filling 206

Pineapple upside-down cake 196
Pioneer's elderberry pie 171
Plain muffins 138
Plum pie 175
Popovers 113
Popovers with cheese-topped Sloppy Joe mix 26
Poppyseed lemon scones 141
Porcupine meatballs 25
Pork ribs in plum sauce 30
Potato bread 121
Potato cakes 69
Potato chips 161
Potato donuts 148
Potato pancakes 146
Prepared mustard 274
Pumpernickel rye bread 130
Pumpkin bars 220
Pumpkin bread 114
Pumpkin cookies 248
Pumpkin pie 175

Q

Quiche 153
Quick fudge frosting 202
Quick strawberry cheesecake 182

R

Raised donuts 148
Raisin cookies 248
Ranch dressing mix 273
Ranch salad dressing 272
Raspberry bars 229
Red beans and rice 74
Reese's bars 223
Refried beans 73
Rhubarb bars 225
Rhubarb delight 224
Rich vanilla cream filling 203
Roast beef hash 22
Roast chicken 41
Roast pork 31
Rustic country chicken 39
Rye sourdough starter 130

S

Sally Lunn 134
Salmon loaf 47
Salmon patties 47
Salted, baked pumpkin seeds (pepitas) 161
Saltines 157
Salt-rising bread 124

Sausage and egg breakfast 155
Sausage stuffing 38
Scalloped cabbage 87
Scalloped potatoes and pork chops 30
Scotch scones 140
Scotch shortbread 233
Seafood cocktail sauce 275
Sesame green beans 79
Shepherd's pie 48
Shoofly pie 176
Skillet fruit cobbler 209
Skillet scrambled eggs and bacon 154
Skillet strata 154
Sloppy Joes 28
Soft molasses drops 240
Sopapillas (Mexican fry bread) 114
Sour cream apple pie 166
Sour cream cookies (a very old family recipe) 239
Sourdough biscuits 128
Sourdough bread 128
Sourdough pancakes 128
Sourdough starter II (without yeast) 127
Southern fried chicken 44
Spaghetti with meat sauce 49
Sparkling citrus cake 186
Sparkly lemon sugar cookies 246
Spiced carrots 70
Spiced nuts 262
Spinach crunch salad 96
Split pea soup 62
Spoonbread 106
Steak pie 50
Steamed apple pudding 218
Stir-fried chicken and vegetables 43
Strawberry bars 231
Strawberry chiffon pie 177
Strawberry rhubarb pie 177
Strawberry shortcake (with biscuit) 210
Stuffed cabbage rolls 27
Stuffed eggplant 90
Stuffed mushrooms 84
Stuffed onions 78
Stuffed peppers 26
Sugar cookies 243
Sugar pie 178
Summer and winter squash stir-fry 81
Sunray salad 98
Super good fresh strawberry pie 178
Swedish meatballs 23
Swedish pancakes 144
Swedish rye bread 123
Swedish tea ring 134

Sweet and sour chicken 45
Sweet and sour garlic mushrooms 83
Sweet and sour pork 32
Sweet and sour pork, quick method 33
Sweetened condensed milk 250
Sweet fruit dip 269
Sweet Italian dressing 271
Sweet Italian roasted pork loin 29
Sweet potato casserole 88
Sweet potato pie 179

T

Tacos 29
Taco salad 95
Taffy 257
Tamale pie 50
Tamales 34
Tapioca pudding 215
Tartar sauce 275
Texas sheet cake 185
Three-bean salad 93
Tomato corn chowder 61
Too-easy chocolate fudge 252
Tropical bread 113
Tuna salad 94
Tuna-stuffed tomatoes 85
Tuna surprise 56
Turkey a la king 39
Turkey rice casserole 53
Turkey salad 99
Turtle cookies 242
Twice-baked potatoes 68

U

Unscrambled eggs 151

V

Vanilla caramels 259
Vanilla drop cookies 240
Vanilla fudge 253
Vegetable casserole 57
Vegetable pasta salad 92
Vegetables in beet cups 89
Vinegar pie 179
Virginia barbecued chicken 41

W

Wacky cake 188
Waldorf salad 91
Walnut slice 222
Wedding cake filling 203

Wedding frosting 203
Whipped topping from powdered milk 269
White rice 100
White sauce mix 266
Whole berry cranberry sauce 275
Whole wheat bread 120
Whole wheat rolls 109
Whole wheat thin crackers 158
Wild rice 102
Wild rice stuffing 38
Wild rice supreme 54
Will's blackberry cheesecake 182

Y

Yeast-leavened flapjacks 143

Z

Zella's Goo 58

Other titles available from *Backwoods Home Magazine*

Best of the First Two Years of Backwoods Home Magazine
A Backwoods Home Anthology—The Third Year
A Backwoods Home Anthology—The Fourth Year
A Backwoods Home Anthology—The Fifth Year
A Backwoods Home Anthology—The Sixth Year
A Backwoods Home Anthology—The Seventh Year
A Backwoods Home Anthology—The Eighth Year
A Backwoods Home Anthology—The Ninth Year
A Backwoods Home Anthology—The Tenth Year
A Backwoods Home Anthology—The Eleventh Year
A Backwoods Home Anthology—The Twelfth Year
A Backwoods Home Anthology—The Thirteenth Year
A Backwoods Home Anthology—The Fourteenth Year
A Backwoods Home Anthology—The Fifteenth Year
A Backwoods Home Anthology—The Sixteenth Year
Emergency Preparedness and Survival Guide
Backwoods Home Cooking
Can America Be Saved From Stupid People
Chickens—a beginner's handbook
Dairy Goats—a beginner's handbook
Starting Over—Chronicles of a Self-Reliant Woman
Self-reliance—Recession-proof your family
Making a Living—creating your own job
Harvesting the Wild—gathering & using food from nature
The Coming American Dictatorship, Parts I-XI
Hardyville Tales
Growing and Canning Your Own Food

About the author

Jackie Clay is a longtime homesteading columnist for *Backwoods Home Magazine*. She has been writing feature articles for the magazine since 1995 and has answered questions about canning and other self-reliant topics in the "Ask Jackie" column since 1999. She also maintains an online "Ask Jackie" blog at the magazine's website, www.backwooodshome.com/blogs/JackieClay.

Jackie has more than 45 years of experience in growing and canning her own food on homesteads in Michigan, the remote mountains of Montana, New Mexico's high plains, and currently on her family's 80-acre wilderness homestead in northern Minnesota. She also gathers wild food, and raises goats, chickens, and other animals. She has written several books on animal care and enjoys training her horses.